GRIEF IN CROSS-CULTURAL PERSPECTIVE

GARLAND REFERENCE LIBRARY
OF SOCIAL SCIENCE
(VOL. 557)

GRIEF IN
CROSS-CULTURAL
PERSPECTIVE
A Casebook

Larry A. Platt
V. Richard Persico, Jr.

GARLAND PUBLISHING, INC. • NEW YORK & LONDON
1992

Library of Congress Cataloging-in-Publication Data

Grief in cross-cultural perspective : a casebook / Larry A. Platt, co-
editor, V. Richard Persico, co-editor.
    p.   cm. — (Garland reference library of social science ; vol.
557)
    Includes bibliographical references and index.
    ISBN 0-8240-4565-3 (alk. paper)
    1. Death—Social aspects—Cross-cultural studies. 2. Grief—Cross-
cultural studies. 3. Bereavement—Cross-cultural studies.
4. Funeral rites and ceremonies—Cross-cultural studies. I. Platt,
Larry A. II. Persico, V. Richard. III. Series.
HQ1073.G75   1992
306.9—dc20
                                      91-25907
                                          CIP

Printed on acid-free, 250-year-life paper
Manufactured in the United States of America

TO

Karen, my wife and best friend, who has stayed by my side through the worst and best of times and has given a joyful meaning to them both.

Larry A. Platt

TO

My parents, Victor and Rebecca Persico, who have always encouraged and helped me in my every endeavor.

V. Richard Persico

CONTENTS

PREFACE

Death as a significant social event has been a consistent area of inquiry in the field of anthropology for some time. The focus of much of this anthropological research has tended to concentrate on the forms of death rituals enacted by societies in various cultural settings. More recently however, the attention of the discipline has shifted to the examination of the social and cultural meanings of such rituals. Concurrently, there has been a broadening of the scope of these studies to include the patterns of social behaviors and cultural beliefs that comprise the grief responses of the bereaved.

As more anthropological research has been undertaken into the social meaning of death, grief and mourning there has developed a greater need to establish cross-cultural comparisons of such data. Such comparative analyses could obviously point to specific forces influencing grief behaviors that might be commonly shared throughout the rich cultural diversity of societies in today's world. While the need for such expanded inquiry has been called for from a variety of sources including Palgi and Abramovitch (1984) and Counts and Counts (1985), relatively few comparative studies have been undertaken.

One of the most notable efforts to address this specific type of research has been a cross-cultural investigation of grief by Rosenblatt et al. (1976). Her study analyzed ethnographies from seventy-eight different cultural settings for commonalities in the social and psychological aspects of grief. She concluded that some generalizations could be made that are applicable to most of the seventy-

eight societies. These generalizations include:
(a) that grief is a basic human phenomenon
occurring in societies; (b) that the outward
expression of grief and the extended duration of
such expressions are commonplace; and (c) that
recurrences of memories of the deceased as part of
the grieving process is a frequent manifestation.
Unfortunately, the database for this research was
limited only to those sources included in the Human
Relations Area Files. Rosenblatt herself
acknowledged the limitations of her data and called
for more studies on this topic using a broader
database. Nonetheless her initial work points to
the potential fruitfulness of comparative efforts
in the field of thanatology.

Huntington and Metcalf (1979) have also
researched the cross-cultural meanings of death
from samples drawn from various societies.
However, their analysis focused entirely on
mortuary rituals and not on the interactive
phenomenon of grief itself. Even within this
restricted frame of reference however, the authors
note the presence of possible universal beliefs
that might explain patterns of mortuary rituals.

In a more recent work, Humphreys and King
(1981) demonstrate the extreme cultural diversity
of beliefs and behaviors related to the general
phenomenon of death. The data utilized in their
comparative inquiry were derived from the
disciplines of social and physical anthropology,
archeology and history. The findings contained in
the editorial collection provide evidence of a
number of shared cultural similarities among
various Western and non-Western societies. The
most common conceptual linkage among the seventeen
societies surveyed in the volume was "...that death
confronts human beings with an awareness of their
own transience, to which they react with attempts

to salvage out of this disturbing experience some residue to which permanence can be attributed" (p. 5).

Berger and his associates have offered still another compilation of comparative essays focusing on death-related beliefs and practices in India, China, Africa, Japan, Islam and the West (1989). This volume seeks to offer comparative insights into contemporary beliefs and values regarding death. The papers presented in this edition are far more theoretical than empirically based. However, the authors share in the growing insistence of other scholars for more cross-cultural examination of beliefs and behaviors surrounding the phenomenon of death.

Paralleling these various trends in the anthropologic study of death has been a vast array of multi-disciplined studies on human grief responses. For over a half-century the disciplines of sociology, psychology, medicine, nursing and social work have examined grief responses to loss (Parkes 1972; Bowlby 1980; and Raphael 1983). Such investigations have sought to understand the social, cultural, psychological and physical nature of grief, and the major factors that influence the pattern of grief responses among the bereaved.

From this diverse analysis of the phenomenon of grief there has emerged a consistent pattern of findings regarding the significant variables that influence the pattern of human grief response. Although varying labels have been utilized to refer to these factors, the primary variables can be best organized under four broad headings:

1. the social meaning of death;

2. the relationship between the deceased and

the survivors;

3. the significance of mode of death; and

4. the nature of the social support network
available to the bereaved.

The definitional nature of each of these
catagories is important to the goals of this volume
and thus needs to be detailed:

1. The social meaning of death entails the
   various definitions that members of a
   society may attach to the nature of death,
   the origin of death as a cultural concept
   and the survivors' prior death experiences.

2. The relationship between the deceased and
   survivors encompasses the nature of the
   social positions of both the deceased and
   the survivors, the centrality of these relationships and the social significance of
   such ties.

3. The significance of the mode of death refers
   to the manner of death experienced by the
   deceased and the social meaning attached to
   that form of death.

4. The nature of the social support network
   available to the survivors includes the
   social definitions associated with the role
   of the bereaved and the expectations for
   family and societal members to share in
   supportive behavior to aid the grieving
   individuals.

While the role of these elements in shaping
grief response has been well documented, one

consistent weakness has been inherent in most of
these findings. The cultural contexts in which
these investigations have been undertaken have
predominantly been within Western cultural
settings. Very little systematic, comparative
examination of the determinants of grief responses
in non-Western societies has been undertaken to
date. To better understand the significant role
these four major variables play in shaping grief
behavior in other societies, more cross-cultural
investigations into death-related phenomena are
needed.

Such comparative inquiries could well hold the
key for validating the significance of these four
categories of factors in cultural settings markedly
different from Western social environments.
Additionally, cross-cultural analysis could reveal
the unique manner in which such influencing forces
are enacted within various cultural milieus.

This collection of essays seeks to address the
growing need for comparative cultural analysis of
grief and mourning. Twelve studies from diverse
cultural settings have been selected. These papers
focus on the four general categories of factors
that have been widely reported as shaping the grief
responses of the bereaved in highly industrialized
Western societies. While each article may
illustrate several of the four major variables,
they are organized into four sections based on
which factors they best exemplify.

Clearly, the twelve research essays cannot by
themselves validate the significance of the four
general categories of elements affecting human
grief responses. Other reports of research in
markedly different cultural settings and at other
points in time are essential to any attempt to
fully evaluate the nature of human responses to

death. This volume is but an initial effort to
pursue a potentially fruitful area of
thanatological inquiry. I hope that other
researchers will join in the search for a better
understanding of the role of death in the social
fabric of our lives.

References

Berger, A., Rev. P. Badham, A.K. Kutscher, J.
Berger, Ven. M. Perry and J. Beloff, eds. 1989.
Perspectives on Death and Dying: Cross-
Cultural   and   Multi-Disciplinary   Views.
Philadelphia, Pennsylvania: The Charles Press.

Bowlby, John. 1980. Attachment and Loss, Volume
III: Loss. New York: Basic Books Inc.

Counts, Dorothy Ayers, and David R. Counts. 1985.
"'I'm Not Dead Yet!' Aging and Death: Process
and Experience in Kaliai." In Aging and Its
Transformations: Moving   Toward   Death   in
Pacific Societies, edited by Dorothy Ayers
Counts and David R. Counts, 132-155. New York:
University Press of America.

Humphreys, S.C.,   and Helen King, eds. 1981.
Mortality and Immortality: The Anthropology
and Archeology of Death. London: Academic
Press, 1981.

Huntington, R., and P. Metcalf. 1979.
Celebrations of Death: The Anthropology of
Mortuary Ritual. Cambridge: Cambridge
University Press.

Palgi, P., and H. Abramovitch. 1984. "Death: A
Cross-cultural Perspective. Annual Review of
Anthropology.

Parkes, Colin Murray. 1986. <u>Bereavement: Studies of Grief in Adult Life</u>. Connecticut: International Universities Press, Inc.

Raphael, Beverly. 1983. <u>The Anatomy of Bereavement</u>. New York: Basic Books, Inc.

Rosenblatt, P.C. 1981. "Grief in Cross-Cultural and Historical Perspective." In <u>Death and Dying, A Quality of Life</u>, edited by Patricia Pegg and Enroe Metze, 11-18. London: Pitman Books.

ACKNOWLEDGMENTS

No book is without its cadre of faithful supporters who give of their time and talents to make the publication a reality. This collection of essays is no exception. For their tireless efforts at every step down the long road to publication, we would like to thank Sabrina Stephens and Karen Platt. For the abundant technical advice and unwavering moral support we extend our appreciation to Eileen Sconyers. Finally, for the patient and steadfast encouragement of this project from its conception through the final publication of this volume we express our gratitude to Phyllis Korper and Roger Branch.

LAP

VRP

I. SOCIAL MEANING OF DEATH

MEANING AND MATERIALISM:
THE RITUAL ECONOMY OF DEATH

Peter Metcalf

Abstract

Among the Berawan of central northern Borneo, expensive rites of secondary treatment of the dead have been declining in frequency in recent decades. The obvious explanation is 'acculturation'—weakening of traditional belief and re-allocation of resources to new material needs—in effect, the explanation for exceptions to the 'rule' of secondary burial adopted by Robert Hertz (1907). But this catch-all explanation leads us false. The ritual significance of initial funerals remains the same, and expenditure on them continues high. The real source of the change involves newly available credit arrangements made possible by the activities of traders. Despite the impact of such economic factors in conditioning the form of death rites, however, it remains necessary to look to symbolic interpretations in order to understand the meaning of the rituals.

Many rituals, probably the great majority, are not expensive in terms of the energy or finances required to perform them. Some, such as gestures of greeting or respect, may come so close to being conditioned reflexes that it would cost more effort to hold them back than unthinkingly to execute them. At the other end of the spectrum there are grand rites and ceremonies that occupy the

Reprinted from <u>Man</u> 16, no. 4, (1981): 563-578, by permission of the Royal Anthropology Institute of Great Britain and Ireland.

attentions of many people over an extended period. Such complex affairs may demand the commitment of significant material resources. When this occurs, we can be sure that the participants take into account interests that go beyond the expressive. Ritual must then come to terms with economics.

This duality of interest is neatly illustrated by the widespread phenomenon of what we may call ritual economy, the ability of a rite to telescope in scale, to expand or contract in the grandness with which it is celebrated, without any essential change in format or rationale. Perhaps the most celebrated example concerns Nuer sacrifice. The proper sacrificial animal is the ox, but oxen are too valuable to be spared in any but the gravest situations.   At   other   times   a   less   costly substitute will be found, a sheep or a goat or, most parsimonious of all, a cucumber of a certain species. The cucumber is treated as though it were an animal victim; it is presented and consecrated, an invocation is said over it, and it is 'slain' with a spear (Evans-Pritchard 1956: 202-3).

The economy of ritual often serves to explain how it is that a variety of religious observances are described by the participants as being 'the same thing', while appearing very different to the outside observer. Some slight sophistication in Nuer ways is necessary to perceive that the cutting of a cucumber is ritually homologous with the much more emotionally charged sacrifice of an ox. Yet what is varying in the two cases is contingent: the seriousness that the participants attach to the circumstances prompting the rite, their available resources at that moment and their personal whims. What remains constant is the meaning of sacrifice.[1]

These   thoughts   are   prompted   by   the   puzzling variability   of   mortuary   rituals   in   Borneo, especially where we find secondary treatment of the dead, or secondary burial as it is more commonly known. Two minimal features define secondary burial. First, the death rites fall into two parts: an initial and by the nature of things unscheduled funeral; and later, sometimes years later, a prearranged and frequently sumptuous secondary rite. Second, during the latter ritual the bones of the deceased are moved from a place of temporary storage to a final resting place, with or without other processing, such as cleaning or putting in a new container. Within this general framework there is considerable variation in ritual detail from place to place, as one might expect in so ethnically diverse a place as Borneo (Stohr 1959). But in addition, we frequently find variations in the death rites as they are observed within a single community. It may be that even the majority of people are not accorded the full rites of secondary treatment. For them an abridged ritual suffices. These alternative sequences complicate our attempts to explain what the secondary treatment rituals are all about: Why are some individuals selected for special treatment? Are the remainder incompletely processed, in some sense? What is the relationship between the different ritual sequences?

I have already explored some of these issues elsewhere, particularly in connection with the ideological content of the death rites of the Berawan of central northern Borneo (Huntington & Metcalf 1979). But I did not there address the important economic aspects of the rites. Meanwhile, there is a longstanding materialist explanation for the practice of secondary burial deriving from Wilkin (1884). Consequently, this article has two objectives: first, to relate the variety of death rites found among the Berawan to economic factors, showing how the availability of

resources influences the choice of ritual sequence;
second, to measure the classic, and largely
symbolic, analysis of secondary treatment made by
Robert Hertz (1907) against the materialist
explanations suggested by the examination of
economic variables.

Hertz's Handling of the Problem of Exceptions

Hertz dealt with the problem of non-standard
rites largely by pushing it aside.

His essay has several interwoven themes, the
most striking and original to do with the
metaphorical relationship of body and soul.[2]   It
was a landmark in the study of ritual. Yet it has
its flaws, reflecting perhaps the limitations of
library research. His handling of exceptions to
the 'norm' of secondary treatment is a case in
point. Hertz was no doubt aware that even in
communities practicing secondary treatment it is
frequently the case that not all corpses are so
processed. But he has little to say about these
exceptions. In this he no doubt reflects the
sources he employed in making his study, accounts
by travellers, missionaries and the like, which
stress the most elaborate obsequies and barely
mention humbler rites. Insofar as he addresses the
issue of exceptions at all, he treats it as
evidence of social change: some unstable mixture of
practices resulting from devolution or
acculturation. The full rites of secondary
treatment are painful and inconvenient, he tells
us, and therefore:

> many tribes, as a result of either
> spontaneous evolution or foreign influence,
> have come to spare themselves the bother
> and the risks of this ceremony. Some, for
> this reason, have advanced the celebration

feast they owe to the deceased so as to
make it coincide with the immediate
funeral, which thus becomes the final one.
Elsewhere the feast has kept its date but
only traces of the original custom of
change of sepulture have survived. Thus
the Alfuru of central Celebes...limit
themselves to pulling out all the weeds
from the grave. (Hertz 1960: 58)

As a general postulate, this appeal to vestiges
weakens the main argument of the essay. The power
of Hertz's statement lies in his relating
particular rites and beliefs to one another. But
if secondary rites can be fused with initial ones,
then we can find secondary burial wherever we
choose to look, and all power is lost. Is a church
sexton weeding a graveyard evidence of previous
extended death rites? There is no need to labor
the point further.

Debilitating as the passage is in implication,
the example that Hertz chose is not in fact
evidence for survivals. The process of
acculturation among the Alfuru can be documented
(Kruyt 1895). Having adopted Islam, they abandoned
secondary burial. Presumably, they also abandoned
the eschatology that went along with it, at least
in formal professions of faith, so that their post-
conversion rites and beliefs are in conformity with
Hertz's main statement. They simply provide
another negative case; the loss of an interesting
custom is no doubt unfortunate, but the argument is
not impaired. Moreover, what has been happening in
recent decades among the Berawan appears at first
sight similar to what occurred among the Alfuru a
century ago.

Like the Alfuru, the Berawan have been affected
by conversion to a world religion. The Berawan

comprise some sixteen hundred people, distributed among four longhouse communities in the lower Baram River watershed in northwest Borneo (Metcalf 1976). Two of the communities are now Christian; another is divided between Christians and a local revivalist cult. Only one village has continued steadily in the old religion, preserving the institution of secondary disposal of the dead. But even in that longhouse, the full rites of secondary treatment are only rarely carried out these days. Meanwhile, material change is clearly in evidence. Many of the family apartments of the longhouse boast furnishings brought from the coastal towns, and trade store shorts are preferred to the traditional breechcloth. It is easy to assume that the recent decline in frequency of the elaborate and costly rites of secondary treatment are a simple consequence of acculturation--that the acquisition of an outboard motor is now a more attractive way to expend resources than the performance of an arcane ritual.

Two features render this interpretation suspect. First, the full rites have always been reserved for a minority of individuals. Second, expenditure on funerals as such continues high.

Frequency of Secondary Treatment

Berawan rites of secondary treatment, or secondary disposal, of the dead are the noisy climax of a ritual sequence that lasts for a year or more.[3] The Berawan name for them is _nulang_, and I use it to avoid the cumbrous English phrases. The etymology of the term is significant. It is a cognate of the word for bone (_tulang_), the initial /n/ indicating a verbal form, so that _nulang_ means 'to bone'. Nulang are the grandest and most ritually complex of Berawan festivals.

However in recent years <u>nulang</u> have become exceptional events, even in the longhouse that retains the old ways. One occurred in 1973 and another in 1975.[4] Prior to these two occasions, no <u>nulang</u> had been carried out for over eight years. There had been splendid funerals during that time, but none had been extended to complete the full ritual sequence. The usual reasons cited by outsiders for this decreasing frequency concern a weakened belief in the traditional religion and prohibitive cost. But the 'withering away' of 'superstition' that the missionary looks for is not at the root of these changes, and traditional concepts of death and the soul have remained basically unmodified. Meanwhile, economic factors have indeed had an impact, but not in the expected fashion.

Certainly <u>nulang</u> were more common in the past. In addition to the accounts of the Berawan themselves, a census of graveyards provides material evidence. There is a considerable variety of styles of mortuary edifices (Metcalf 1977a). Some contain only one set of remains, others several. Some are clearly associated with secondary treatment, because they provide sufficient space to accommodate only the collected bones and not a corpse. Moreover, every major edifice of traditional type implies at least one <u>nulang</u>, because an extended period is required to construct and decorate it. Berawan custom does not allow work to begin on a tomb before death occurs, and therefore the corpse for which it was built must have been temporarily stored elsewhere. There are a sufficient number of these mausoleums to indicate that <u>nulang</u> were not infrequent in the half century before 1950, when religious innovation began. It is difficult to make any meaningful estimate of their frequency, but if we aggregate all four Berawan communities together the rate must have exceeded one a year.

However, it is equally certain that during the same period the majority of funerals have not included nulang.   They have instead utilized an abridged ritual sequence, in which the funeral rites that occur immediately after death (patai) are made the final ones.   Berawan say that both options have always been available, and again the contents of the cemeteries bear them out.   Each cemetery contains only a small number of finely carved tombs, and even the oldest, which date back a century or more, contain traces of simple tombs of a type not associated with secondary treatment. It remains possible that in the remote past all deceased persons received nulang.   Ritual schemata indicating this are found in other parts of Borneo. For example, the Ma'anyan of southern Borneo perform rites of secondary disposal on a regular basis, processing at one time all the dead accumulated in the interim (Hudson 1966: 361-98). But Berawan usage contains no precedent for such a mass nulang: all the evidence points to the conclusion that extended and abridged rites have coexisted indefinitely.

The problem of exceptions to the full rites therefore remains.   It is not possible to dismiss them as a mere symptom of change.   Instead, the two sequences must be brought into a coherent relationship with one another, as I have done at length elsewhere.[5]   Berawan themselves insist that the two sequences are alternatives, that they are ritually 'the same thing'.   We are evidently presented with an instance of that kind of ritual economy that we saw in Nuer sacrifice.   In the context of our present concern with economics, this conclusion draws our attention away from the format of the rites, towards a consideration of their varying scale, regardless of format.

Expenditure on Mortuary Rites

The striking fact is that expenditure on funerals (<u>patai</u>) continues high, despite the infrequency of <u>nulang</u>.[6] It follows that costs do not increase in direct proportion to the time taken to complete the rites. Although <u>nulang</u> are usually celebrated on a relatively grand scale, it is often the case that funeral ceremonies conducted immediately after death can grow costly enough to compete with them in splendor.

One might imagine that there is a temptation to divert the relatively large sums involved into some private acquisition such as a shotgun or outboard motor. This cannot happen because no one individual or domestic group contributes or controls all the money. All close relatives of the deceased will be expected to contribute, and they will be spread among several family apartments (<u>ukuk</u>) in the longhouse. Since the co-residents of an apartment share a common farm or farms, and pool

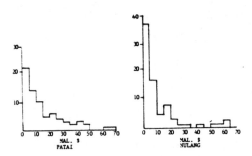

FIGURE 1. Comparison of the costs of an important funeral (patai) and a nulang: numbers of contributors making donations of one hundred dollars or less. All sums are in Malaysian dollars.

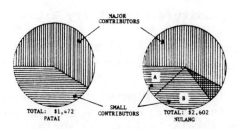

FIGURE 2. Comparison of the costs of an important
funeral (patai) and a nulang: share of
the expenses raised from various sources.
'A' indicates the small contributions
from the natal house of the deceased, 'B'
from the village that he married into.

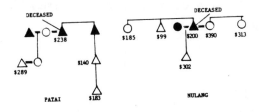

FIGURE 3. Comparison of the costs of an important
funeral   (patai)   and   a   nulang:
relationships of major contributors to
the deceased.

the products of their labor, this means that the
resources of several productive units within the

community are drawn upon immediately. But the load is spread even more widely. Every family, and almost every adult person, will make some contribution, however small, to every funeral that occurs, excluding only the briefest. Funerals have a powerful integrative function for the longhouse. Consistently to fail to contribute or participate is to cut oneself off. In the case of a deceased person who has married in from some other Berawan house, the obligation extends also to members of his or her natal community.

Although the contributions are numerous, most are not large. Figures 1-3 present details of two major death rites (all sums mentioned are in Malaysian dollars). The series on the left hand side of the figures refer to a moderately expensive funeral (patai), and those on the right to the nulang held in 1973. Figure 1 shows how the value of small contributions were distributed, 'small' in this context being less than $100. On both occasions, most contributions were of less than $5, with steadily fewer in each succeeding category, and only a few in the $40 to $70 range. The effect is more marked in the case of the nulang, reflecting the fact that it had been planned over several months. The advance notice thus provided allowed community members to make substantial contribution in kind. Even so, over nine hundred Malaysian dollars in small contributions were raised at the nulang, versus six hundred and thirty at the funeral.[7]

Figure 2 shows how the expenses of the rites were met. The nulang was considerably more expensive, yet the funeral still amounted to nearly three-fifths as much. The commitment of resources can best be understood in terms of local wage rates, then about five dollars per day for casual labor in lumber camps, so that the nulang cost the equivalent of about five hundred man-days of cash labor. Moreover, this contribution does not include the very considerable non-cash contributions which are by their nature difficult to quantify, such as food provided to guests accommodated in almost every family apartment in the house, and labor donated for the innumerable chores that such festivals entail.

This nulang was the most expensive death ritual to occur during 1972 and 1973. The one held in 1975 was on a more modest scale, and the cash expenditure for it did not exceed $1,800. During the period of fieldwork there were funerals (patai) more costly than that analysed in the figures, but none exceeded $2,000, and there were also, of course, cheaper funerals. A stillborn baby is buried at once, so that the funeral, if so it may be called, costs next to nothing. The brief and simple rites performed for a child less than ten years old might cost one to two hundred dollars, those for a teenager or adult of no particular standing perhaps six to nine hundred dollars, and more elaborate affairs for people of substance a thousand dollars or more. Although the most expensive rites of all are invariably nulang, and the least expensive patai, there is thus a considerable range of overlap in costs. If one knew only that a mortuary rite had cost between one and two thousand dollars, it would not be possible to predict with confidence which event it was.

Aside from the difference in total cost, figure 2 shows an overall similarity in the manner in which the money for the two rites was raised. Despite the great number of small contributions, in both the nulang and the funeral more than half the costs were borne by a handful of major contributors (57 per cent and 59 per cent, respectively). Visitors' contributions made up only a thin slice

of the costs of the nulang, and were insignificant
at the funeral.   The small contributions to the
nulang are shown divided between two communities.
The dead man had married into the traditionalist
house at an early age, but had never lost his ties
with his birthplace.   The long preparations
necessary for his final rites had allowed time for
significance support to be mobilised from his natal
house.   His surviving siblings were two of the
major contributors.

The relationships of major contributors to the
deceased are shown in figure 3.   In both cases, the
dead men themselves appear as major contributors,
and this represents their cash savings at death,
augmented perhaps by the sale of some valuable
item.   The most common items sold are groves of
trees.   (Clothes, beads, jewelry, musical instru-
ments, and other property intimately associated
with the dead person cannot be sold nor given
away.)   For instance, tne widow of the recipient of
the nulang was obliged to sell a small plantation
of rubber trees to a local trader in order to pay
her contribution.

At the nulang, the largest contributions came
from affinal kin, and a son by a previous marriage.
Donations from the surviving siblings of the dead
man were significant, but less than those of his
affines, reflecting where the major part of his
life had been spent.   In the case of the funeral,
the deceased had married the elderly widow of a
Penghulu (government appointed chief).   Since the
affinal kin were of high rank, they made a
substantial contribution, much of it coming from
the husband of the daughter of the previous
marriage.   The man had joined his wife upon
marriage, as Berawan custom dictates, and after his
wife's mother's husband's death, he found himself
the senior man of the domestic unit and thus

obliged to contribute substantially. Two major contributors to the funeral were consanguineous kin, a nephew of the dead man and the nephew's son. The poor son worked as a primary school teacher, and was always asked on these occasions since he had a regular cash income. His father had a particular attachment to the dead man, because of a shared enthusiasm for the old religion. These examples hint at the web of responsibilities and motivations that determine who the principal contributors will be. There is always the possibility that no one will choose to commit any substantial amount of money to a funeral, and then it will be held on only a small scale. In contrast to other parts of Borneo, there is no particular individual, whether spouse or sibling or child, who can be held responsible for making sure that rites are conducted on a specific scale. On the other hand, if there is a close kinsman who has been awaiting the opportunity to make a display of organizational ability, then he will set to work squeezing money out of anyone who can conceivably be construed as having an interest in the affair. The flexibility of response is an important feature of Berawan death rituals, making them a crucial locus for status competition.

Cash collected in this fashion is spent on the myriad items required to conduct the ritual, prepare the mausoleum, and feed and entertain the great crowd of guests that defines a 'large' funeral. There is no doubt that the necessity for cash to meet recently created demands has increased the expense of modern mortuary rites. Thus concrete has come to be regarded as a necessity in constructing tombs, and cement is not only expensive to purchase initially, but must also be hauled upriver in longboats pushed by fuel-hungry outboard motors. Again, the modern Berawan would be ashamed not to offer his guests coffee and biscuits, and both are served several times during each night of a funeral or _nulang_. Coffee is drunk sweet in interior Borneo, and refined sugar is expensive. Moreover, the guests think it a fine joke to pelt each other with the costly trade store biscuits, a gesture of improvidence thoroughly appropriate to a funeral.

But if _nulang_ have become more expensive, then so have _patai_ also. _Nulang_ is not simply a costly afterthought to the death rites, but is planned for from the moment of death. If a _nulang_ is decided upon, then the _patai_ is conducted on a very modest scale, brief and without guests. Thus the cost of the extended rites is not double that of the abridged rites, and no one person saves enough by avoiding _nulang_ to buy even the most decrepit of outboard motors. When an important member of the community dies, the only decision is between an expensive _patai_ held immediately, or a marginally more expensive but deferred _nulang_.

Moreover, despite modern demands for cement, sugar and such, the main requirement remains what it has always been: rice. By far the largest item in the budget is the cost of food and drink for the guests and all those engaged in the labor of the funeral. Rice provides the staple food eaten in bulk, where coffee and biscuits are mere luxuries. Rice also provides raw material for the main drink, fermented in the form of rice beer or distilled into a strong spirit. Great quantities of both are drunk during the nights of the festival. Rice flour is the basis of many of the special cakes and delicacies prepared by the womenfolk, and these can be substituted for trade store biscuits. The other essentials require not cash but labor: labor to hunt for game to provide meat for the guests, to fish, to cut the timber for the death edifice, and to erect the mausoleum, to prepare and cook rice, and so on. The ability to persuade people to devote their efforts in this way, to associate the prestige of the kinsmen of the bereaved with the prestige of the whole house, is a mark of high status. Rice and labor are as essential ingredients now as they were in the pre-cash economy.

Social Status and Choice of Ritual Sequence

In terms of scale, the mortuary rites make a statement about the social standing of the deceased and his or her close kin. Where an emphatic claim is to be made, the events are held on a large scale; where there is less at stake, a simpler affair serves the ritual function just as well. This is the phenomenon of ritual economy. We may now return to the question of format. Nulang is certainly not for the poor, but neither is it the preserve of a small elite; it is an option also for people of the middling sort, and consequently how one sequence is chosen over another calls for explanation.

On each occasion that a death occurs, the particular circumstances of the case must be weighed, and decisions made about major features of ritual format. Alternatives are discussed very soon after death occurs, usually within an hour or so. In attendance are the close kin of the deceased, senior people of the community, and anyone else who feels that he or she has an interest in the matter. It will be decided whether to use a jar or coffin for storage of the body, how many days the funeral is to last, who is to be invited, and so on. But the very first decision must be between the extended and abridged sequences. Frequently there is one circumstance that weighs so heavily in that decision that it immediately tips the balance. However, what that

circumstance might be is complicated by the
heterogeneity of potentially relevant factors, and
also by the changing force with which they have
been felt in recent decades. In the interests of
simplicity, I first describe the range of factors
involved, including ritual efficacy, social status,
scheduling and availability of resources, and then
consider the impact of modernity upon them.

In strictly ritual terms, close kin are
unlikely to feel any particular restraint. Nulang
is not necessary in order to transmit the deceased
to the land of the dead, nor does the promise of it
avert the danger from the errant soul in the
interim. As noted above, Berawan insist that the
two sequences are ritually 'the same thing'. It
remains true that only in nulang are Berawan
notions of eschatology expressed in full. But the
need to express those notions is not an important
consideration for the major contributors to the
event. From the point of view of the community,
there are definite benefits to be gained from the
occasional performance of nulang because the
totality of the ancestors, from whom come many
blessings, are brought into communion with the
living. But only if several years go by without
any performance will there develop opinion in favor
of one. For the recipient of the rites, nulang
provides a moment of consummate glory, yet there is
no suggestion that the dead who receive secondary
treatment enjoy any special privilege in the land
of the dead. Only if an august older person has
expressed a sentimental desire to receive nulang
will the close kin feel obliged to favor this
option for ritual reasons.

In terms of social status, there is, as we have
seen, no direct relationship between rank and
ritual sequence. We cannot assume that the 'best'
people receive nulang and the rest only a funeral.

Events may turn out to the contrary. Noble families can afford <u>nulang</u>, but they are also more likely to have on hand the necessary surplus of rice, pigs, and other necessities to enable them to proceed directly with a <u>patai</u> funeral on a grand scale. If they happen also to have a family vault already prepared, and do not wish to make an individual edifice for the dead person, then there is no need of delay. High prestige death rites of the abridged kind have always occurred. In 1972 a Wakil Penghulu (assistant government chief) died after a long illness. His death was not unexpected and plans had been made to accumulate the necessary surplus. He also died at a convenient time, after the harvest, when rice stocks were at their largest and manpower could be readily diverted from other activities. Moreover, his vault lay waiting for him, having been initially constructed some years before for his brother. Under these circumstances there was no reason to delay, and no loss of prestige. This illustrates that, within certain limits, it is not social status per se that determines choice of ritual sequence. Instead it tends to be factors of a practical nature.

A compelling reason for selection of the extended rites is the occurrence of death at an inconvenient moment, for example during harvest. With urgent work to be done at the farms, it is next to impossible to conduct any but the meanest of funerals. Even were the close kin prepared to settle for this, pressure from senior members of the community would be exerted to bring about a <u>nulang</u>, assuming that the deceased was of some importance. Unlike death itself, <u>nulang</u> can be scheduled to fit into the season of greatest ritual activity between the end of one agricultural cycle and the beginning of the next.

When two villages are involved, extended rites

are often indicated.   For instance, if a person
dies while visiting another Berawan community, it
is more convenient to store the corpse temporarily
in the graveyard of that house, and to bring the
remains home later when putrefaction is completed.
Again, if an individual (usually a man) has married
into a longhouse other than his natal one, then
there will be two sets of kin that need to be
mobilized on his death, and consequently the
extended rites are called for.   It is often men of
the more prominent families that marry in this way,
so that nulang becomes associated with high status
through this third variable.

A more important instance of the indirect
association of format and hierarchy concerns the
building of mausoleums.   Traditionally these
monuments stood up to thirty feet tall, were built
with dense hardwoods and elaborately carved.   Since
they took many months to complete, extended rites
were necessary at least for their first occupants.
The construction of such tombs involved greater
commitment of labor than the rituals, and
constituted communal recognition of those
responsible for building them.

Perhaps the weightiest factor of all is the
availability of resources, principally rice.
Traditionally, it was unusual for rice stocks on
hand to be sufficient for a grand funeral, unless
the death occurred right after harvest.   Otherwise
there was no choice but to plant more farms and
plan a nulang.   At one Berawan longhouse, the final
rites for a leader who died in 1940 were postponed
year after year until 1946 because the Japanese
occupation forces kept requisitioning the surplus
rice that the community diligently assembled.   The
circumstances were exceptional, and thirty years
later old people there still complained bitterly
about it.   But had it been a series of bad harvests

that had brought about the shortfall, their response would have been the same: to postpone the death rites until a stock of rice was available.

These are the kinds of circumstances that bring about the selection of an extended mortuary sequence. Where none of them is operative, close kin generally opt for the abridged sequence because of its marginally lower cost and considerably fewer demands on time. However hectic, a funeral is over in a couple of weeks, whereas a nulang can take months to prepare. Meanwhile the ritual equivalence of the two sequences ensures that no one will be accused of impious or unfilial behavior. Nor is this anything new.

What has tipped the balance away from nulang with increasing frequency in recent decades is a side effect of the intrusion of a cash economy, namely, the availability of credit. Many Berawan families, especially those of solid standing in the community, are known on a personal basis to shopkeepers in the bazaars, mainly Chinese with wide-ranging business interests. To these entrepreneurs, or their agents who trade up-river out of small boats, the Berawan sell rubber, fish and jungle produce. From them it is possible to raise cash, sometimes by the sale of rubber gardens or heirloom property such as antique brassware, but more commonly in the form of a loan against future earnings. Some of these shopkeepers are familiar with Berawan ways, and readily understand the need for a loan. Previously, when grand mortuary rites were called for, there was no alternative but for the community to accumulate rice over a period of time. Nowadays a family is able to proceed as if it had a large stock of rice on hand, by simply borrowing it from a trader.

It might seem at first glance that this would

undermine one function of the rites.   It is the exceptional nature of large-scale rites, with their multitude of guests, that makes them important events in the negotiation and confirmation of power relationships.   Nowadays, evidently, lesser men could out of hubris commit themselves beyond what is appropriate.   But this does not happen.   In the first place, it is unlikely that all who would be called upon for a major contribution would be prepared to go into debt in order to make such a gesture; more importantly, the solid backing of the entire community is still essential.   By failing to provide labour, or invite guests and accommodate them in their own rooms, or even themselves participate in the gatherings, the majority can very easily undercut the proceedings regardless of how much money is spent.

Availability of credit is the primary reason for the recent decline in frequency of <u>nulang</u>.   A secondary feature working in the same direction is the move to concrete in the construction of mausoleums.   Since the Second World War, only a handful of the lofty and beautiful wooden tombs have been built.   Increasingly, mausoleums are chunky concrete boxes.   These require a lot of labor to build the boxing and pour the concrete, but if the manpower and materials are available they can be built relatively rapidly. Consequently it is possible to complete a death edifice during the ten-day maximum duration of an elaborate funeral.   By contrast, the construction of a wooden tomb could not be hurried; it required the attention of skilled carpenters and carvers over several months.   It is this feature of wooden tombs that explains the persistence of <u>nulang</u> in the nineteen twenties and thirties, when some Berawan houses became wealthy, by the standards of the times, from the profits of their extensive rubber gardens.   This wealth might have tipped the balance away from nulang at an earlier date, had the new styles of tombs and the materials to build them been available. As it was, some of the most magnificent wooden tombs date from that era.

Credit and concrete are the novel features that have made nulang a rarity. They represent the impact of sociological and technological innovation. But they operate in a very different manner from that envisaged in our original concept of 'acculturation', which masked just how much had not changed about Berawan ritual activity. Berawan continue to invest significant resources in death rites. Now as in the past, they have the option of doing so either within the abridged sequence or with nulang, at least in the traditionalist village. And what is required to bring off the festival remains the same: access to a stock of rice and the cooperation of the community.

The first effect of this economic analysis is to show the inadequacy of 'common sense' assumptions about culture change. The point has been made before, but is worth underlining, that acculturation in and of itself provides no explanation for the way things are. As in the case of its nineteenth-century equivalent, diffusion, specific theories must be called upon to explain what innovations are adopted and how. Perhaps because the process of acculturation seems so prosaic, we constantly talk as if its effects were immediately recognizable and its outcome certain, and they are not.

Hertz fell into this error. By citing the effects of 'foreign influence', he avoided dealing with the implications of exceptions to the rites of secondary treatment. This blind spot distorted his view of the rituals, so that he failed to make a place in his scheme for grand but abridged rites, such as the Berawan have. This flaw is real, because it hampers our ability to apply his symbolic argument to the full range of mortuary rites found in Borneo, but a small one. Meanwhile, some writers have seen a more serious objection.

Materialist versus Symbolic Explanation

A second effect of this analysis is to demonstrate the extent to which economics controls the form that Berawan mortuary rites take, and consequently to throw doubt upon competing ideological explanations. Almost a century ago, the Dutch ethnographer Wilken argued that the lapse of time that occurs between death and secondary burial is simply a function of the necessity to accumulate sufficient wealth (1884: 77). With its own idiosyncrasies and elaborations, the Berawan material bears him out. So what was there left for Hertz to explain?

Miles (1965) has put forward a similar argument. He provides a valuable account, one of the very few based upon modern fieldwork, of socio-economic aspects of secondary burial among the Ngaju of southern Borneo. Berawan and Ngaju are separated by hundreds of miles, and it is not surprising that there are many differences of detail in their death rites. Berawan store corpses awaiting secondary treatment in coffins or jars above the ground; Ngaju simply bury them. Secondary storage is also dissimilar: the Berawan have separate containers for each set of remains within the mausoleum, whereas the Ngaju put them together in a communal bone depository. This might be taken to imply that Jgaju funerals are the occasion for the expression of great community solidarity, but this is evidently not so. In contrast to the Berawan case, the responsibility to carry out secondary rites falls on particular individuals, and is the subject of litigation (Miles 1965: 171-3). This individualization of ritual duty may be a result of the abandonment of the traditional longhouse in favor of dispersed residence.

In the present context, it is the similarities with the Berawan case that are striking. The Ngaju equivalent of Berawan nulang is called tiwah. Tiwah may be celebrated on a very grand scale, or more modestly, or not at all, showing the same range of variation as the Berawan death rites. Moreover, the variation is predominantly a function of wealth, what I have called ritual economy. Miles finds Wilken's explanation validated, and, by implication, Hertz's redundant.

In addition Miles finds a technical fault in Hertz's symbolic analysis. Ngaju informants told him that if sufficient resources were ready to hand tiwah could be performed immediately after death occurred (Miles 1965: 163, 169). This makes no sense in Hertz's plan of things, because the soul cannot be transmitted to the land of the dead until the bones are free of putrescence. Here is a situation where the economic and symbolic explanations predict different outcomes, and the former appears supported. Can we not now dispense with the latter?

I believe not. First, let me deal with the technical point. Tiwah, we are told, may be performed immediately after death, in ideal circumstances.   But what does such a tiwah comprise? If secondary treatment in the NgaJu manner were applied to a corpse only recently buried, it would involve digging up an only partially decomposed body.   Even were this tolerable, how could such a corpse be put into the communal depositaries, which are boxes or jars designed to receive only bone fragments? Miles concedes that _tiwah_ does not necessarily involve secondary treatment of the corpse; sometimes the participants content themselves with planting a pole over the grave as a memorial (Miles 1965: 163). Miles' error is terminological. The Berawan term _nulang_ genuinely refers to ritual format: secondary treatment is implied etymologically and required ritually. This is not true of the Ngaju term _tiwah_, which would be more accurately glossed as 'festival of the dead'. It refers to scale. Hooykaas (1965: 388) notes that the Balinese term _tiwa-tiwa_ is cognate with Ngaju _tiwah_, and glosses both simply as 'mortuary ritual' without any implication of secondary burial. When _tiwah_ is performed immediately after death it is simply the equivalent of Berawan abridged rites celebrated on a grand scale.

As to the charge of redundancy, this impression is also created by collapsing variables of format and scale. Two minimal features define secondary burial, and economics can only provide explanations for one of them. Wilken offers a credible explanation for why large-scale funerary rituals might be delayed, and hence a reason for the two-phase nature of the rites. Death cannot be conveniently scheduled, _nulang_ and _tiwah_ can. But the same argument applies to any of a whole host of memorial ceremonies for the dead, some individual, some collective, some calendrical, some not, found in different parts of the world. For example, the festival of the dead (_gawai hantu_) of the Iban of western Borneo shares these features with _tiwah_: it is expensive, irregular and planned over a considerable period. But it is not a rite of secondary treatment. What most distinguishes _nulang_ and similar rites is that they involve manipulation of the remains of the deceased, including moving them from a place of temporary storage to some final resting place. There is nothing in the economics of the rites that explains this feature. Innumerable ritual formats could be devised that would allow the expenditure of resources on a grand scale. The question is: why this one?

This is, in the end, the most interesting question about the secondary burial rites of Borneo, and it is the one that Hertz answers. Even if he failed to take account of grand but abridged rites, Hertz was aware of the variability of scale in the mortuary rituals of Borneo, and what underlay that variability. He points out that the death of a chief calls forth a much greater response from the community than that of a person of lesser status. This is explicitly a socioeconomic argument, its conclusion relatively unexciting. The more stimulating aspect of Hertz's discussion is the symbolic one, because it preserves and illuminates the peculiarity of Bornean practices. Moreover, it does not merely explain the gross features of the death rites (the double funeral, the manipulation of the bones) but also the details of a long ritual cycle. In the Berawan case, for instance, the mourning usages visited upon a widow, the practice of offering food to the corpse, the songs sung at the nulang, and much else besides, can all be clearly understood by grasping the symbolic identifications that underlie the whole cycle and give it coherence (Metcalf & Huntington 1979: 68-81). None of this would be accessible to explanation in terms of economic variables. Hertz's contribution is that he shows us how the essential values of a culture may be thrown into particular relief by its use of the corpse as symbol.

One final point. I have allowed that certain

aspects of Berawan and Ngaju death rites are best explained in terms of economics, while others can only be understood by a symbolic analysis. I am consequently open to charges of eclecticism, which in the view of some anthropologists (Harris 1968: 284) implies theoretical woolly-headedness. I hope that it is clear why I think that different explanatory frameworks are necessary in order fully to understand the nature of ritual behavior. If this is eclecticism, so be it. It seems to me merely the realization that different questions have different answers.

Notes

1. As Levi-Strauss has pointed out (1862: 224), substitution is specifically a feature of sacrifice. The feature that I am pointing to is a more general one, and can be observed in other domains of ritual. To cite a trivial example: a Berawan shamanistic performance requires the preparation of a food offering including eight boiled eggs, eight being a ritually significant number. But Berawan allow their chickens to range freely around the house, and finding that many eggs may be laborious. If the hour is late, or the circumstances not serious, a single egg will do.

2. Hertz's essay concerns those societies that do not see death as instantaneous but rather as a process. The secondary burial rites of Borneo provide his key material. Hertz argues that during the 'intermediate period' between initial and final mortuary rites the individual is conceived of as neither alive nor finally dead. During this time the soul undergoes a metamorphosis similar to that

of the corpse; the latter provides a model for the former. As the corpse is formless and repulsive during the process of decomposition, so the soul is homeless and malicious. Unable to enter the land of the dead, it lurks miserably on the fringes of human habitation.   In its discomfort, it may inflict illness and further death upon the living. Mourning observances are designed to deflect this hostility. The 'great feast' terminates this ugly period by honouring the now dry bones of the deceased, and celebrating the admission of the soul to the company of the ancestors. Hertz allows that the secondary rites may be delayed by the need to accumulate a surplus, but he argues that the irreducible period that must elapse is the time required for the bones to become free of decaying flesh (Huntington & Metcalf 1979: 61-7).

3. Shorn of its many small familial observances, the sequence consists basically of two extended public rituals that require the co-operation of the entire longhouse community, separated by a period when the corpse is allowed to complete the process of decomposition. Immediately after death, the corpse is subjected to ritual processing, culminating in its insertion in a coffin or large jar. A funeral is held, lasting up to ten days, during which a vigil is kept over the corpse and non-kin are enjoined to make merry. After the funeral (patai), the coffin or jar is stored for many months, perhaps years, usually on a rough platform in the graveyard,   When this period terminates, the now dry bones of the deceased are brought back to the longhouse for the rites of secondary treatment. Sometimes the bones are cleaned and rehoused in a finer container, and songs are sung to mark the transit of the departed soul to the radiant land of the dead. But more obviously the occasion is one of great public exuberance.   Large crowds gather to feast and

drink, day and night, for up to ten days. Finally, the bones of the person so honored are taken to their place of final storage, a finely decorated mausoleum in the graveyard.

4. Luckily I was present on both occasions. Fieldwork was conducted in Borneo between December 1971 and January 1974, supported by the Foreign Area Fellowship Program, the National Science Foundation, and the Wenner-Gren Foundation. I was also able to make a brief return visit in May 1975, in order to see the second nulang, under the auspices of the Committee on Research and Exploration, National Geographic Society. I thank all these organizations, and the Sarawak Museum which sponsored the work.

5. (Metcalf 1977b; Metcalf & Huntington 1979: 68-80). Briefly, I argue that an identical set of symbolic representation, revolving around the metaphorical relationship of body and soul, is expressed in both the abridged and full sequence. But they are not expressed with equal fullness, and that is why the rites of secondary treatment are an honor. However, the fate of the soul is similar in either case. Even in the abridged rites, the soul does finally enter the land of the dead, although that event goes unmarked by ceremony. Nulang is confirmatory in nature and not instrumental.

6. My remarks mainly concern the longhouse that has continued in the traditional religion. But I have some evidence to show that even in the Christian communities, funerals (without nulang) are still occasionally celebrated in grand style.

7. A further category of contributions is not included in fig. 1, those from 'visitors', non-Berawan who attended simply as sightseers. Many came to the nulang, mostly Iban from nearby houses.

Their contributions were numerous but very small-
in many cases only 25 cents.   Their main interest
was in gambling, cockfighting and card games.
Partly to discourage these activities, cockfighting
winnings were 'taxed' 10 per cent, and cash raised
in this way is included in the visitors'
contribution.

References

Evans-Pritchard, E.E.   1956.   Nuer   Religion.
London: Oxford Univ. Press.

Harris, M.   1968.   The Rise of Anthropological
Theory. New York: T.Y. Crowell.

Hertz, R.   1907.   Contribution à une étude sur la
représentation collective de la mort.
Ann. Sociol. 10, 48-137.

_____.   1960.   Death and the Right Hand,
Trans. R. & C. Needham. New York:
Free Press.

Hooykaas, C.   1965.   Sivaism in Bali: Two
Hypotheses. J. Orient. Inst. 15, 381-90.

Hudson, A.B.   1966.   Death Ceremonies of the Padju
EpatMa'anyan Dayaks. Sarawak Mus. J. 13, 341-
416.

Huntington, R., & P.   Metcalf. 1979.
Celebrations of Death: The Anthropology of
Mortuary Ritual. Cambridge: Univ. Press.

Kruyt, A.C.   1895.   Een en ander aangaande
het geestelijk en maatschappelijk van den Poso
Alfoer. Med. Ned. Zend-Gen. 39, 2-36.

Levi-Strauss, C.   1966.   The Savage Mind.
Chicago: Univ. Press.

Metcalf, P.   1976.   Who are the Berawan?
Ethnic Classification and the Distribution of
Secondary Treatment of the Dead in Central
North Borneo. Oceania 40: 7, 85-105.

_____. 1977a.   Berawan Mausoleums.
Sarawak Mus. J. 24, 121-36.

_____. 1977b.   The Berawan Afterlife: A
Critique of Hertz.   In Studies in Borneo
Societies, ed.   G. Appell. Dekalb: Northern
Illinois Univ. Press.

Miles, D.   1965.   Socio-economic Aspects of
Secondary Burial.   Oceania 35, 161-74.

Stohr, W. 1959.   Das Todesritual der Dayak.
Ethnologica.

Wilken, G. A. 1884-5.   Het animisme bij de volken
van den Indischen Archipel.   Reprinted from
Indische Gids 6:   2, 925-1001; 6:   2, 19-101;
7:   1, 13-59, 191-243.

SYMBOLISM AND SOCIAL CHANGE:

MATTERS OF LIFE AND DEATH

IN WHALSAY, SHETLAND

Anthony P. Cohen

In industrialised society, symbolism, although it may have lost some of its earlier explicitness, is expressed implicitly in the routine behaviour of everyday life. Indeed, it becomes the most important element constituting the social boundaries of self-consciously distinctive communities--boundaries which, empirically, are being increasingly threatened by the forces of infrastructural and social change. This argument, and the methodological and theoretical issues it raises, is illustrated through the ethnography of the spree and the funeral in Whalsay, Shetland. It is suggested that these forms of behaviour, although reminiscent of the past, are now constituted in new ways and symbolically imply new meanings. Focusing upon the boundary, they express the self-image of the community in its changing relationship with the outside world.

Some anthropologists have argued that the importance of symbolism in social behaviour diminishes as societies become technologically

Reprinted from <u>Man</u> (N.S.) 20 (1985): 307-324, by permission of the Royal Anthropological Institute of Great Britain and Ireland.

modern.   But the contrary case, that modernisation may even enhance the salience of symbolism, has also been widely observed.   In this article, I shall argue for the latter view, attempting to illustrate the efficacy of symbolism in boundary marking and maintenance in circumstances of social change which may have undermined the former structural bases of boundary.

It might be more appropriate to see this as a disagreement about what should be regarded as symbolism.   It may be, for example, that Needham, in associating himself with Peacock's denial of symbolism to modern societies (1975), is referring less to symbolism itself than to the explicit expression of symbolism and symbolic classification (Needham 1979:   20).   But this would merely suggest that, whereas more 'traditional' cultures may reserve distinctive forms (for example, myth and ritual to symbolic statements, the idiomatic behaviour of people in 'modern' societies does not discriminate to the same degree between the symbolic and the practical or pragmatic.   I do not want to raise the ghosts of earlier attempts to distinguish between instrumental and expressive behaviour,   first   because   the   dispute   is irresolvable (since is rests upon definition and paradigm) and secondly because the distinction may well have become redundant in the light of the attention paid more recently by anthropologists to the 'implicit' (Douglas 1975), 'tacit' (Sperber 1975), 'unconscious' [Needham 1980] and 'private' (Firth 1973) meanings in symbols.   These arguments reveal the difficulties of assigning meaning to, or assuming a uniformity of meaning in, any behaviour. Hence,   what   is   instrumental   for   some   may   be expressive for others; and, moreover, the 'etic' categories of instrumentality and pragmatism may be quite different from the categories of the people concerned.

These issues are central to the symbolisation of social boundaries. The ethnography which follows suggests that there is a symbolic dimension implicit in apparently 'instrumental' behaviour; and, moreover, that the meanings thus symbolically expressed may vary substantially among the participants. We shall be looking at a community which is highly charged in symbolic terms and which, in this respect, may typify other peripheral communities experiencing intensive social change. In an atmosphere of such boundary consciousness, almost any behaviour, however pragmatic, can be made grist to the mill of cultural symbolization. I do not suggest that this symbolisation expresses an orthodoxy of meaning; only that it allows all behaviour which can be represented as locally distinctive to be treated as a resource for symbolisation.

We owe to Leach the most persuasive and influential suggestions that pragmatic behaviour has a symbolic dimension; and that this symbolisation may be most salient in the context of boundary marking. But, again, Leach's Kachin material focuses especially on explicit symbolism, whereas my present concern is with sentiments which are often unstated. Babcock argues that the implicit expression of contrast is an inherent characteristic of all symbolism (1978: 13), and Boon (1982) suggests that all symbolic systems-- cultures, ethnicities, identities--are antithetical in nature and rationale. Certainly, the juxtaposition of symbolic systems has been widely noted by observers of social change, some of whom have drawn attention to their explicitly oppositional nature. Schwimmer, for example, writes of 'symbolic competition'--a surrogate for the more material competition from which disadvantaged minorities might be excluded (1972).

This kind of symbolic contestation was exemplified in the extraordinarily powerful proclamation by black militants in the United States that 'Black is beautiful' and in the equally extraordinary demonstration by Norwegian Saami of their ethnic integrity in the face of its perceived denial in Norwegian government development plans (cf. Paine 1982). It is evident also in militant 'aboriginal' claims for territorial and customary rights (e.g. Beckett 1977), and in such nativist manifestations as cargo cults and <u>negritude</u>, and in the religious fundamentalism of the disadvantaged.[1]

But, again, these statements have explicit referents; they are ideologies. What I try to illustrate here is the effectiveness in boundary marking of the unspoken symbolic element of ordinary behaviour. Because of its 'silent' nature this symbolism must be regarded as interpretive rather than indexical. The ethnographer's account of its 'meaning' is thus a matter of interpretive surmise rather than of documentary evidence. But, as Geertz (1975), Boon (1982) and others have pointed out, its communicative competence rests upon the interpretive propensities of the individual participants, rather than, mechanically, upon their common vocabulary. 'Symbols', says Boon, '...make experience shareable but not identical....Cultural meanings are...thus not substantively shared but rather <u>exchanged</u>'(1982: 121). And, 'What a speaker means to say...is only a small part of what his or her saying means...'(1982: 118), the other and major part being the meaning attributed by the listener to the symbols used by the speaker. In this view, individuals and groups view each other across social boundaries through the prisms of their interpretive predispositions. The prisms filter out what is not amenable to those predispositions. People may therefore use the 'same' symbolic structures or forms, but to signify

or express quite different meanings which may be
imperceptible to others.

It is in precisely this sense that I draw
attention to the symbolisation of community
boundaries in the context of social change.
Modernisation often involves the importation of
alien structural forms across boundaries--and,
thus, may threaten to displace the existing
structural bases of the boundary. But it does not
follow that these forms take their meanings with
them: rather, they become resources for the
expression of indigenous symbolism and, often, the
re-statement or re-assertion of the boundary.
Unlike the oppositional ideologies mentioned above,
these are not public statements: those on the
other side of the boundary are not expected to
understand them. Were they to be so intelligible
they would be redundant. They are symbolic
statements designed to perpetuate the boundary, not
to demolish it. Their efficacy depends upon the
outside world being unable either to recognise the
boundary at all or recognise it in the terms in
which it is defined by those 'inside'. The pitch
of this private symbolic discourse often puts it
beyond the discernment of the outsider's ear.

The argument, therefore, is that as the outside
world impinges ever more insistently, so people
become increasingly conscious of their cultural
identity, increasingly aware of their cultural
boundaries. In these circumstances all forms of
behaviour can assume significance as symbolic
expressions of identity and cultural
distinctiveness. People within a bounded group
thus use symbols, meaningless or invisible to those
outside, to which the members can assign their own
meanings. These meanings may or may not coincide;
at the very least we should expect that, if not
exactly coincident, they will be regarded as

roughly congruent. It is this process of deploying
and interpreting symbols, as much as its end-
products, which sustain and embellish the felt
boundaries of community. It is a process in which
the community is symbolically constituted.[2]

Whalsay

Whalsay is a fishing and crofting island
community in the northeast of the Shetland Islands
and has a population of approx. 1100. The ways in
which Whalsay people celebrate the community
boundary--and, thereby, question their
peripherality--are not elaborate ceremonial affairs
but are evident throughout Whalsay's routine social
life, from the 'technical' activities of knitting,
fishing, peat-cutting, sailing, boat building, or
the many tasks associated with crofting, to more
directly sociable events such as 'neighbouring',
festive-drinking and burying the dead. They all
admit change, and much of the change originates
outside the community. Indeed, the change may be
so substantial as to reconfigure the traditional
activity. Yet, the activity does not thereby
become any less 'Whalsa'. Rather, in its
transformed state, it becomes a new and modernised
item in the repertoire of symbolic devices through
which the boundaries of the community are given
meaning and, thereby, preserved, and through which
people signal their determination that imposed or
expedient structural change will not make them
'less like themselves'.

The more technical activities, some of which I
have dealt with elsewhere (e.g. 1979; 1980), may
involve new and imported structural forms which are
used, nevertheless, to express indigenous meanings.
The media of symbolic marking I report here, the
spree and funerary practice, involve behaviour

customary in form but which now expresses new
meanings. Both are set against the context of the
rapid change which has overtaken Whalsay's economic
life, rendering materially redundant the old
collaborative groups based on neighbourhood and
close kinship. Both appear, though, to reinvoke
these groups in order to express the resilience of
distinctive local values in a manner which is
tantamount to a rejection of the new and alien,
seen to originate beyond the boundary. In this
respect, both the spree and the funeral are
symbolic statements of forms of organization and
solidarity which have been undermined empirically
by the exigencies of modern economics and
technology. They should not be regarded merely as
atavistic rites for they reincarnate and exploit
these apparently customary forms in new ways and
for new purposes. Moreover, as is particularly
evident in the case of the funeral, they confront
the threat of the new, the 'outside', and
neutralise it, drawing a renewed vitality from the
confrontation. Both cases thus illustrate ways in
which boundary-conscious members of communities
'manage' culturally insidious incursions of the
outside world, not just by translating them into
indigenous idiom but, rather, by incorporating them
and harnessing them to the task of intra-communal
discourse, thereby continually reconstituting the
symbolic boundary.

During the last thirty years, the economy of
Whalsay has changed from one based upon a domestic
division of labour oriented to the exploitation of
multiple sources of subsistence, particularly
crofting and part-time fishing, to the increasingly
specialised, technologically sophisticated and
highly capitalised near-water fishery. This
transformation has been accompanied by a change in
the significance of the basic solidary and
collaborative groups which mediated people's

membership of the community.   These groups were based on close kinship and on neighbouring which often were inextricably mingled.   Their nexus had structural, cognitive and ideological primacy in local social life (see Cohen 1982).   They provided the framework for economic and occupational collaboration in fishing, crofting, peat-cutting, and so forth.   They were, and remain, the constituent archetypes in the mosaic of local identity (Cohen 1978).   Relationships among the members of these groups were intensively, but informally reciprocal.   They contrast starkly with the highly systematic and formalised co-operation of the modern Whalsay fishing crew.   Although the informal reciprocity of the past is now economically redundant, it continues to be invoked symbolically in the organization of close social association.   Although their crucial salience to economic life has decreased under the impact of recent social change, the boundaries of these old solitary and collaborative groups are still known, recognised and tacitly acknowledged in social cognitive mapping.   They are revealed explicitly only in social events, as in the composition and geographical orientation of a spree, and in the allocation of special roles in funerary rites. Indeed, both funeral and spree may be regarded as paradigmatic expressions of such symbolic marking.

The Spree

The spree is a peripatetic party, moving from house to house, collecting the occupants of one to proceed to the next.   Its membership changes continuously, as people branch off in different directions. Indeed, husband and wife may well (and often do) spree separately, each reverting ultimately to a township with which they had or have close ties.

Until fairly recently, sprees were held on several fixed festive occasions such as Christmas, second night of Christmas, Hogmanay, New Year's Day, 'second night' of New Year, Old Christmas, and Regatta—the last night of the annual three-day sailing competition usually held in August. They would also be held on the second night of a wedding, and when crews settled on one of the three customary accounting days in the fishing year. In 1975, a round-the-isle sailing race was instituted, and this too is now a regular occasion for a spree. So, too, is any major social event open to the whole community—the annual dances held by the Football Club and the local branch of the Scottish Rural Women's Institute, for example, when the spree follows the end of festivities in the Public Hall. These major sprees are island-wide affairs, involving all age groups and all localities. More specialised sprees, which I ignore here, are held throughout the year by young people, generally those still unmarried.

I describe a Christmas spree, not because it is representative in form but because these occasions are almost universal in Whalsay. The Christmas Day spree begins in the late afternoon, when neighbours and kinsmen, gathered for tea, turn to the whisky bottle once the teapot has been emptied. The men will already have spent a sociably alcoholic morning at the Loch, sailing or watching the 'Yule Day' model yacht race. With Christmas dinner eaten, the bonfire is kindled and fireworks lighted for the children. The usual catalyst for the start of the spree is the arrival of a visitor bearing a bottle of whisky. He offers his whisky to the company in the form which will be observed through the rest of the spree, well into the early hours of the following day. He obtains a small tumbler from the hostess, fills it to the brim, and offers it to the first drinker, usually the host or hostess. They exchange a brief toast--'Here's aa' da best', or 'Guid health, boys'--and the drinker takes a sip, then returning the glass to the donor. He again fills to the brim the still nearly full glass and offers it to the next drinker, and so the pattern is repeated until everyone has had a drink. Finally, the donor drinks from the glass, and returns the whisky left in it to his bottle. As the night wears on the sips will become less restrained, but the generosity of the donor is never exploited. There is no pressure on unwilling drinkers to imbibe, though to maintain the ritual they may just 'lay a lip in'. When the glass has circulated around the company, the conversation resumes until the next person produces a bottle and starts all over again. A person must not offer his whisky again until everyone else present with a bottle has had a chance to offer his, and the order of offering is not broken. I have never seen a person prompted by others to offer his whisky.

The company will remain in this initial house for an hour or two, until someone suggests moving on. The core members of a spree usually have some ultimate destination in mind, and the spree visits the houses en route, remaining in each long enough for everyone to offer his or her own drink at least once, for conversation, and, as the evening progresses, for food. The traditional fare is reested mutton--dried salt mutton--usually boiled, and bannock. Any one visiting group is likely to meet up with others, and people may leave one to join the other, or eventually head off independently. When the principal destination of the spree is reached, usually between 11 p.m. and midnight, the company rests from its travels for a couple of hours. Here whisky will now be circulating continuously, there will be dancing (usually to Scottish country music but, more recently, to 'Country and Western') and, if people have already 'got'n a bit dram in', singing as well.   The women are active participants in the spree, offering as well as receiving whisky, though they will carry only half-bottles, whereas the men invariably carry full-size bottles.

As will be evident in Figs. 1 and 2, the company assembled at this central point of the spree will represent important dimensions of the social map which locates the host and/or hostess in the community.   They may be close kin; they may be close neighbours.   Often they will be people with whom the host or hostess was previously closely associated through kinship, neighbourhood or some other means, but now separated in everyday life by the exigencies of work and/or residence.   The spree is almost the only occasion when people cross the everyday boundaries of kinship, neighbourhood and occupational associations, and ways in which they do so often reassert their previous structural connections to the community.   The spree thus revives old relationships, those perhaps of childhood or even those of earlier generations and thereby expresses the fundamental modes of people's belonging to the community.

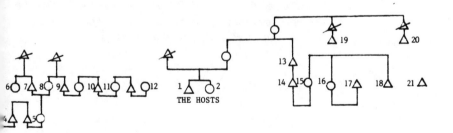

FIGURE 1.   A *spree on Christmas night, 1974.*[3] The spree was held in the house of unmarried siblings 1 and 2. 14 (their

MBS, from whose house the spree
originated earlier in the afternoon),
15, 16, 17 and 18 are all close
neighbors of 1 and 2. 18 is also an
age-mate of 1 (they are in their mid-
fifties) and though not associated by
occupation they trace their association
back to their childhood neighbouring,
friendship at school, and frequent
journeys together to and from leave on
National Service. 19 and 20 are long-
standing friends of the family of 1 and
2; they are sons of their MMBs, and are
regular members of 1's *ccla* fishing
crew (small boat recreational fishing).
The affines 11 and 12 are close
neighbours of 1 and 2, and 12 is one of
their closest friends. 8 and 9 are
children of a now-deceased close
neighbor of 1 and 2 who was also a
crewmate of their father. 6 and 7 are
the children of a now-deceased crewmate
of 1 and 2's father, who was also a
frequent visitor and close friend of
their parents. 5 (7's DH) is a close
neighbor to 1 and 2, and 4 (5's B) is
DH of 3, a neighbour of 1 and 2 and a
close friend of their parents. 21 is
the ethnographer, 1 and 2's closest
neighbour and crewmate of 1.

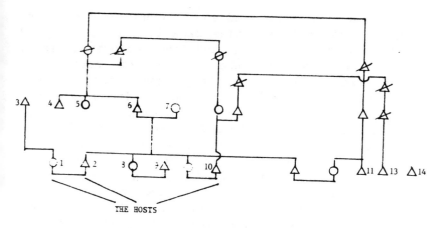

FIGURE 2.   A *Regatta spree, 1980.* The
spree was held in the house of
1 and 2.   1's F is an outsider,
born and resident in Lerwick.
7 (2's M) was born and spent her
childhood on the croft on which
1 and 2, and 10 (2's ZH) now
live.   8 (2's other Z) lives
away from her parents and siblings
with her husband's family.   11 is
2's BWB, and is also his second
cousin.   13 is 10's closest friend
(2 and 10, being co-resident on the
same croft, almost always begin
their sprees together, so that in
this context 10 is a co-host),
although they are not associated in
day-to-day affairs and is, incidentally,
his second cousin.   14 is the
ethnographer, a close neighbour of 1,
2, and 10.

     This 'reversion' to earlier associations is
even more marked at the next stage of the spree.
After leaving the 'central' house, the company
tends to disperse into smaller groups, each going

its own way. A married son or daughter might then walk the couple of miles back to the township in which he or she grew up and lived before marriage. They may call on the cousins or friends of crewmates with whom they had earlier been especially closely associated. These are the people who will be universally recognised as 'their folk', even though their present relationship may be much less intense than those they now have with others. These 'folk' are those who, in former years, would have constituted the co-operative group, a memory now sustained by reciprocal gifting, visiting, the occasional exchange of goods and services and by the spree. They are those who would still be regarded as providing one's social origins. So, lurking beneath the inebriated hilarity of the spree is often a summation of one's social history and an expression of the ethos of belonging.

The successive nights of spreeing on the major festive occasions allow the spreers to revisit numerous landmarks of their social lives so that they are not forced into arbitrary or invidious choices of destination. The recriprocal form of spree drinking is found also at dances, when people continuously exchange bottles for a swig as, indeed, they do on the other rare occasions such as the Christmas and New Year's Day model yacht races, when bottles are legitimately carried.

The importance of the spree used to be recognised by the ready willingness of a host or hostess to rise from their beds and admit late callers. In more recent years, the regular Saturday night spreeing of the younger people has come to be regarded as something of a nuisance, and so a simple signalling device of leaving on the outside light informs callers whether or not they will be admitted. But on the major occasions, most people are anxious to have visitors; and, at the end of a dance, there will be some competition about whose house the company should return to.

The sociable reciprocity of the spree can be seen to evoke the strategic and material reciprocity of social life in the past.   It is significant that as the occasions for such reciprocity have decreased in frequency with the economic changes already described, so the frequency of large-scale sprees has increased. Bonds of reciprocity are thus maintained through symbolic means now that the strategic need for reciprocity has declined.   In this regard, the spree is one item among several in a repertoire of symbolic devices through which Whalsay people are enabled to experience a cultural continuity between past and present.   It evokes a co-operation of a kind quite different from the modern corporate partnership of the fishing crew which, through its dependence on outside financial agencies, is itself anathema to the self-sufficiency and mutual interdependency (akin to Friedl's 'Autarky complex' (1974:87) which was implied in traditional co-operation. The spree has no economic value for its participants.   Rather, its significance is symbolic, and is present both in the egalitarian and reciprocal process of the spree, and in its composition.[4]

The Funeral

The introduction of funerary rituals into this discussion could be considered foolhardy, since the anthropological literature on death, burial and mourning practices reveals that they can be shown in one way or another to symbolise (and, indeed, to invert symbolically) almost anything at all.   (See, e.g. Huntington & Metcalf 1979; Danforth 1982;

Hertz 1960; Du Boulay 1982; Drucker-Brown 1982;
esp. pp. 725-6). The risk may be justified,
however, by two rather speculative lines of
interpretation. First, I have suggested that there
is a strong sensitivity to their community
boundaries among people living on the periphery as,
indeed, there may be among the members of any group
who perceive its integrity to be threatened by
incursion. A reasonable, if Durkheimian
demonstration of this claim might be to show that
this sense intrudes even into one of the most
'personal' spheres of life. Secondly, it is a
sense born of a perception of continuous threat to
the community--a threat of so intense a subversion
as to be tantamount to death or, at least, to a
life not worth living. It might therefore be that
in the minds of some people the death of an
individual member is a spectre of the death of the
whole group, particularly since, as has been
extensively shown in comparative ethnography from
Hertz's seminal essay onwards, and, indeed, as I
have reported elsewhere (1978) for Whalsay, people
seem to regard the social identities of the dead
they mourn as being, for those other than the
closest bereaved, indistinguishable from their more
'private' or personal selves. Funerary practices
often seem to qualify the absolute distinction
between the living and the dead, so that, for
example, 'in death there is life.' In Whalsay this
qualification in respect of individuals may extend
also to the community itself, the more strikingly
so since, in my view, it is accomplished by
emphasising the local distinctiveness of the
community's forms and beliefs. Funerary rites thus
themselves become media for the expression of the
new meanings of community evoked by its
continuously changing relationship with the outside
world. The ritual, in reasserting normality, does
more than merely reiterate the past: it responds
to the present and creates fresh meaning. In this

regard, I agree with Bloch and Parry that funerary rituals are 'an occasion for "creating"...society' (1982: 6), and that 'what would seem to be revitalised in funerary practices is that resource which is <u>culturally conceived</u> to be most essential to the reproduction of the social order' (p. 7). In Whalsay, I would argue, that resource is the community's sense of its distinctive self.[5]

When a death occurs in Whalsay, there follows a suspension of normality (marked symbolically by the stopping of clocks in the deceased's house) gradually spreading outwards with a ripple effect in a series of concentric circles from the bereaved household. If the death has been expected, perhaps as the result of debilitating illness, the sick person will already have been accorded a designated status reserved to the dying: <u>a puir aald body</u>. People enquire of each other for news of the illness at every opportunity just as, when the death eventually occurs, they will rehearse repeatedly all they know of its circumstances. Much of this discussion frequently focuses upon the conduct of the doctor and, in my experience, is often critical in tone. Might he not have done more? Should he have said what he did say? Such implicit or explicit criticism is hardly a uniquely local phenomenon. One may suppose that, whatever the actual professional conduct of the doctor, it has something to do with his detachment: he is an integral constituent in the scenario of death, but is not bereaved (cf. Warner 1959: 310-13). Like the priest or minister, he stands on the other side of the boundary (cf. Jorion 1982). But his distance from the bereaved has an added dimension in Whalsay for he is an outsider, a <u>smoothmoother.</u> In commenting about him, then, there is an identification by other islanders with the bereaved family <u>vis-à-vis</u> him: they are <u>all</u> bereaved, while he is not.

The core circle of close mourners, let us call it circle 'A', who occupy a distinctive niche in Whalsay death rites, is defined by the same bases of close social association which marked the deceased's social identity in life: primarily, a nexus of close kin and neighbours, and co-owners or selected crew members in the fishing boat(s) with which he or she may have been especially associated. It is the same nexus as that which is expressed in the composition of the <u>spree</u>. Immediately following the death, the men of this group suspend their normal work. If fishermen, they remain ashore. The women re-order their normal daily routines to focus upon the home of the bereaved widow or mother or daughter. They keep company with her from the time of death until the end of the funeral day itself and, sometimes, for several evenings thereafter.

Two men from circle 'A' may be allocated the task of <u>bidding</u> selected people to the pre-funeral gathering in the home. This, incidentally, mirrors the practice of bidding guests to a wedding. Those invited to this phase of the funeral--circle 'B'- will be acknowledged kinsmen, neighbours and other close associates. Apart from attending domestic prayers and offering condolence to the bereaved, they are also invited to view the body. The bidders are also responsible for posting funeral notices in the local shops.

Two men from the intimate mourning circle 'A' will have been responsible for digging the grave. On the day of the funeral, the ripples reach out beyond close associates to the further shores of the community. The fishing boats owned and crewed by people connected to the deceased remain ashore for the day. If the deceased was a prominent fisherman, or a member of a prominent fishing

family, most of the boats in the fleet will remain
ashore or will return to Whalsay to enable the men
to attend the funeral. Following the death in 1975
of a young fisherman, the entire fleet returned
home. This is a matter of some importance to which
I shall return shortly.

The funeral begins with a short service at the
home, attended by the members of circles 'A' and
'B'. They then proceed to the Church Hall at
Saltness, in the southwest of Whalsay. The service
conducted here may be attended by mourners further
removed from the inner concentric circles. The
main item in this service is a eulogy. This is the
last phase of the funeral which women attend. They
are not present at the burial itself. Before the
construction of a road around the island after the
Second World War, funeral processions went on foot
to the Kirk at Brough, the coffin borne on a wooden
stretcher by relays of bearers, and followed by
mourners joining along the route (cf. Vallee 1955:
124). Today, the delivery van belonging to one of
the local shops is used as a hearse, and other
mourners follow in their cars driving very slowly
with headlights switched on. Most mourners who are
not in circles 'A' or 'B' will be waiting at the
kirkyard for the arrival of the cortege. Everyday
clothes of overalls, jeans and Fair Isle 'garnseys'
give way to dark suits, black ties and high crowned
black caps. Those awaiting the arrival of the
procession may be visiting the graves of relatives,
or musing on stories, recollections and genealogies
of others interred there. When the hearse arrives
two or three men from circle 'A' carry the wreaths
into the kirkyard. Then a further six or eight
circle 'A' men carry the coffin to the graveside.
The pallbearers are prominent members of circle
'A', and they represent each of the three bases of
close association, kin, neighbourhood and crew.
They are followed to the graveside by other members

of circle 'A' and sometimes by a few self-selected
members of circle 'B'. There is, then, a clear
spatial distinction, for the rest of the mourners
stand in an adjoining section of the kirkyard, at
some remove from the gravesite itself. They do not
participate in the burial service, but observe it-
or merely occupy the kirkyard. They talk quietly
among themselves about matters which may or may not
be ostensibly connected with their reason for being
there (cf. O'Neill 1983: 49). Their apparently
anomalous conduct intrigued me and, since it was
usually among this 'peripheral' group that I found
an appropriate place, I paid particular attention
to their conversation. On reflection, I found that
the common denominator of the talk of the dead, of
the war, of last week's fishing, of people and
places and boats was its communal introspection.
The talk I heard invariably had Whalsay as its
referent. It was local discourse predicated on the
boundary.[6] This localism was apparent also in what
I discerned as an embarrassment at the presence
there of outsiders--not just the intrusive
ethnographer but even relatives from other parts of
Shetland well-known in the community. They seemed
to be unacknowledged, commented on but ignored
until and unless the conventions of politeness were
pressed.

For all those other than the members of circle
'A', the interment marks the end of abnormality.
With a rapidity whose logistics I could never quite
work out, the men are at the pier, changed into
everyday clothes, and busily getting the boats
ready for sea again. The normal clamour of life,
whistling, singing, shouting, swearing--until then
silenced--again fills the air. Immediately, also,
critical comments about the deceased, suspended
until he or she has been safely despatched, are
once more to be heard. Life has reasserted itself.

What is there, then, of the expression of the
community and of its boundary in all this? I have
mentioned already my surmises concerning the local
and   introspective   referents   of   cemetery
conversation and demeanour, and the criticism of
the doctor, exacerbated by his non-belonging. Let
me briefly recap some other elements of the
funeral. The obvious demarcation between circles
of mourners is an accurate expression of the
deceased's social relationships: those in the
inner circle 'A' are not selected ascriptively.
Rather, they continue their close relationship to
the deceased which they had in life. As we saw in
the context of the spree, these relationships may
well, indeed often do, cut across ties of kinship.
Some first cousins, or nieces and nephews may be
included; some excluded.   Some affines may be
preferred to some consanguines.   An intimate
friendship   based   on   long   association   in
neighbourhood or fishing crew may take precedence
over kinship.   In this respect, Whalsay funerals
appear to be unusual in sofaras they are maps of
actual,   rather   than   of   ideal   or   normative
relationships and thus differ markedly from
funerary rituals elsewhere (e.g. Douglass 1969: 202
sqq; Mandelbaum 1976; Vallee 1955: 129). Again, as
with the illustrations offered earlier, Whalsay
people are aware of this difference, real or
imagined. Indeed, such an awareness is an inherent
characteristic of their kinship ideology which
resolves tensions over the arbitrary definition of
kin--arbitrary since, owing to the overwhelming
prevalence of local endogamy, the universe of
potential kin within the island is virtually
indefinable--by deferring to a rationale of
closeness-in-actuality.   When Whalsay people
explain their behaviour, they suggest its
distinctiveness: 'We think like this...'; 'here,
we do that...', and often conclude by making the
contrast explicit: 'nor like yon Burra[7] folk',

'not like da folk i' sooth...'

I mentioned also the fishermen's practice of
remaining ashore to attend funerals. This may well
have originated in the days when the opportunity to
stay at home was a welcome relief from the toil of
the haaf fishery and the unceasing demands of the
laird and his bailiff, a rare opportunity to see
wives and children and to sleep at home instead of
in the spartan fishing lodges. After the demise of
the haaf fishing, attendance would not have
involved much inconvenience since relatively few
men fished full time, and those who did returned
home most days anyway. In the lean fishing years
between the wars—indeed, for many years after the
Second World War—the price of fish was so low that
the costs of a day off to the household budget were
fairly inconspicuous. Not so today when boats are
having to gross thousands of pounds weekly just to
meet their expenses. The potential cost of lost
fishing time now is enormous. Moreover, the
Whalsay crews are now fishing well away from home
waters, in the south-west of England or off the
western Isles, so that costs incurred in actually
getting home can be prodigious. It is clear that
their observance of funerals is not just a matter
of personal sentiment except, of course, in the
case of close associates. Rather, it is seen and
explained as an obligation imposed by the fact of
community membership, one of the many
inconveniences attached to such membership but,
yet, willingly borne. For it is recognised that a
failure to honour these obligations would be to
render the community 'less like itself'. That
would be to diminish its very raison d'être and,
thus, to signal its demise. One skipper who had
brought his boat back all the way from the Minch,
arriving an hour before the funeral, and leaving
again with the tide three hours later, said to me:

> Well, we had to try an'wen hame. I mean
> Aald Geordie [the deceased] he wisnae kin,
> like, but he an'me faither were together
> for years, du kens. Ach, it's a bloody
> nuisance, I ken, but if du willna' try
> an'do dese tings, du moit as well bide in
> comfort in Aberdeen or Fraserburgh.

On another occasion, following the death of an old
woman, three fishermen were reflecting ironically
on the economic perversity of their funeral
attendance:

> Man, it's funny ting, dat we're aa' sitting
> here ashore, an'dere's fish i' da sea. I
> never even liked dat aald wife avaa'...Du's
> roit enyoch. Man, she could be sic'a
> witch. But, du kens, du's nae a'funeral
> fer to honour da dead: but da wye I look
> at yon, it's to honour da livin'. Ach,
> it's dis bloody place! If we was Aberdeeny
> men, instead o'frae Whalsa', we'd likely be
> at sea.

These were not isolated cases. But what struck me
more than the explicit statements was the sense
that the question and answer were redundant: they
were tacitly understood.

Funerals have, of course, changed in form:
they are now motorised and, therefore, privatised,
whereas before they were pedestrian and communal;
and they are shorter. Death itself occurs more
frequently away from home than it did in the past
not, as Aries suggests, because it is more
convenient for the living to consign the dying to
hospital (Aries 1976: 88), but because access to
hospital for the sick is so much easier. Also with
modern medical care, death has taken on a new

significance.   Mortuary procedure itself has
changed, with the doctor an invariable participant,
and the district nurse available to wash and lay
out the corpse. As religion has generally declined
into relative insignificance in local social life,
so the religious accoutrements of the funeral are
regarded as almost incidental.   Yet, despite all
such change, people do not think of their modern
observance of funerary rites as making them 'less
like themselves'.   Nor do they invoke customary
practice traditionalistically.   Rather, they adapt
it to the new contingencies.   It carries new
messages.   Indeed, its symbolic potency is still
such that people can read into it whatever messages
may be relevant to themselves.   'Death', as
Humphreys observes, 'provides occasions and
materials for a symbolic discourse on life...'
(1981: 9)--in the present case, on communal life.

     This account of burial in Whalsay has been
intended, not as an interpretive exercise in the
symbolic intricacies of death-related practices and
beliefs, or of the experience of grief and
mourning, or of the meanings of death itself; but
as an attempt to locate in them references to the
community   boundary.   Without   denying   the
inalienable meanings of funerary rituals I concede
that other aspects of life might have served my
purpose just as well.   Indeed, the earlier analysis
of the spree follows closely related lines.   This
does not mean, I hope, that I am engaged in mere
reductionism.   My defence has been that people's
consciousness   of   their   community   and   its
distinctiveness is so sensitised that it informs
their total experience of social life and, thus,
informs the meanings they attach to their symbolic
constructs.   It leads them continually, in Boon's
phrase, to 'play the vis-à-vis'.   'Everything', he
says, 'emerges as a contrastive replaceable for its

complement...' (1982: 213). And, 'Every discourse, like every culture, inclines toward what it is not: toward an implicit negativity'(232).[8]

It may be objected that Whalsay funerals do not differ markedly from those elsewhere in rural Britain or, more generally, in northern Europe. I reply: our prism filters out their differences. Whalsay people think of them as different and that is what matters for that is what motivates the meanings they contrive for or find in the symbolism of the funeral: it is what constitutes their tacit knowledge. It might further be objected that I am guilty of mystifying perfectly ordinary elements of social life. To this, I would reply that my argument is ethnographically warranted by the reflexivity with which Whalsay people appear to endow their procedures. They believe them to be different from those elsewhere. They seem to believe that it is in respect of their tenacious adherence to these differences that they are consigned to a demeaned status of peripherality. Their posture appears to be that if peripherality is to be their imposed identity then so be it: but the laugh is really on them, for they also suppose that such an imposition is an expression of the greater ignorance of those at the centre. They find a wry, if perverse satisfaction in being misread: it keeps the boundary intact, thus preserving their culture from devastating encroachment, and gives them the space to develop their own symbolic means of coping with changed circumstances. To quote Needham again, '...a symbolic aspect can be given to anything that members of a society are interested in' (1979: 14). That such symbolism is expressed in more prosaic forms than we are used to dealing with elsewhere, or is contained in what looks like pragmatic behaviour, should not blind us to its significance.

Leach has argued that, '...the spatial and temporal markers which actually serve as boundaries are themselves <u>abnormal</u>, <u>timeless</u>, <u>ambiguous</u>, <u>at the edge</u>, <u>sacred</u>' (1976: 35). In this respect the boundary marks not only the precise division between categories or states of being: it is also the margin, the in-between, the liminal. It is, therefore, a dangerous place in which to be. When people are confronted by a death they are confronted by a boundary, and all of the proscriptions and prescriptions we know to be associated with it clearly distinguish it as a boundary connoting danger. It may be, as I have suggested earlier, that for Whalsay people the death of an individual speaks metaphorically of the ever-present threat of the death of the community- and, if so, I am in this respect clearly at odds with the assertion of Bloch and Parry (1982: 15) that the marking of death in 'contemporary Western cultures' opposes the individual to society. It seems to me that the danger they confront at this boundary is precisely analogous to that which they see confronting them at the very boundaries of their community. Hence, of course, my claim that an ethnography of death-related practices is an appropriate medium through which to illustrate the way Whalsay people cope with the perception of their relative peripherality. By the same token, both boundaries evoke a similar imperative response. In mortuary practices, the absoluteness of death is disconfirmed: the life of others continues and so, in a sense, does the social life of the deceased since the network of close associates of which he was the centre remains in being to bury, mourn and remember him (cf. Huntington & Metcalf 1979: 93). His interment signals the reassertion of the routines of life, not as a return to the <u>status quo ante</u> (nor by taking the sting out of death) but in circumstances now changed by his decease. The life that ensues

thus accommodates his death, but does not ignore it
for life has been changed by it. Changed, but not
weakened. The threat of the boundary is thus
neutralised by its resonances of vitality.

At the boundaries of the community, I think the
same happens. The boundary is obvious and
undeniable. Each incursion across it threatens, of
course, to make it less so, threatens to blur or
move or otherwise subvert it. The response is to
acknowledge the change wrought by the incursion--
and to master it: to subordinate it to the
indigenous symbolic regime in ways which may be
imperceptible to or misunderstood by those
'outside'. The capacity so to respond revitalises
the boundary as perceived from inside and thereby
signals the renewal of the community.

Conclusion

Taken together, the organisation of both spree
and funeral suggests that the resilience of
customary forms in circumstances which have
diminished their structural significance is more
than the expression of mere traditionalism. The
primacy of these forms is now symbolic and
affective rather than 'instrumental', and their
expression must be seen as a new phenomenon, a
response to the influence of social change without
which they might have been unnecessary. They are
now invested with a new significance. It is as if
people stand at the boundary and witness its
blurring, its fading, feel themselves being tugged
across the line. So they reach in to their
cultural and symbolic reserves to create and assert
an updated sense of distinctiveness, of difference
from the other side. They contrive new meanings
for apparently old forms. They use the very
symbolic devices in virtue of which they imagine

themselves to be regarded as anachronistic, parochial and peripheral: and, by their use, neutralise these perceived implications.[9]   Through such counterpunching[10] the apparent homogeneity of the 'modern' society supposedly creeping out from the centre and insinuating itself into the nooks and crannies of the margin is revealed as a somewhat superficial veneer. Moreover, it is a veneer which, ironically, protects the vitality of the margin and enables it to nurture its new distinguishing features while concealed from the maw of the centre's cultural imperialism.

In the introduction to this article, I wrote that the analysis was based on surmise, but I did not hereby claim freedom from the responsibility to provide ethnographic evidence. On the contrary, I have sought to illustrate the problem of what might count as evidence in the interpretation of other people's often unstated views. This, of course, is a problem with a long philosophical pedigree and is obviously not limited to the anthropology of industrialised societies. But, if I am correct in supposing that a difference between symbolism in industrial and non-industrial societies lies in its degree of explicitness then it is clearly an ethnographic difficulty with which we have to deal in seeking to overcome anthropology's relative inexperience of the industrialised world.

I have claimed--and the ethnography cannot rise above claim to reach anything which might be regarded as 'proof'--that the boundary is so prominent symbolically for Whalsay people that it is brought to their minds by almost any social or physical aspect of their community. In this respect, Whalsay is reminiscent of many other rural communities which have been described in the ethnographic literature and whose members see themselves as in some respects peripheral or marginal to the wider society. The response, the counterpunch, is to emphasise a characteristic of their lives which epitomises that felt marginality, and to assert it positively as a boundary marker, thereby depriving it of its supposed stigma. The Bigouden peasantry of Brittany, for example, felt themselves derided and denigrated by the urban bourgeoisie for their apparent poverty and the simplicity of their technology. But, within their own social world, and unperceived (because unperceivable) by those outside, they delighted in their own greater resourcefulness and their capacity for a non-monetary self-sufficiency. Accordingly, also, they mocked the bourgeois dependency on the ability to buy goods made by others (Helias 1978: 207-10). The Buryat Mongols, a society which might have provided the paradigm case for the early Marxists' despair of the peasantry, gleefully subvert the ceremonial forms imposed on them by their commissars, transforming them through their own greater ritual virtuosity (Humphrey 1983: 373 sqq.). The villagers of Shinohata, for all their increasing affluence, still attribute prestige to each other for the finesse of their rice fields or the size of their silkworm crop--marginal as these products may be in their contribution to the household income--rather than for the number of Toyotas parked outside their houses (Dore 1978). And, returning to one of the major ethnographic themes of this article, the village cognoscenti of Potamia in rural Greece can still read a dead person's moral history in the extent to which his remains decompose during the five years before their exhumation, rather than in the outsider's less worthy criteria of worldly reputation or success (Danforth 1982; also, du Boulay 1982: 222).

This is not to suggest that Whalsay or these other communities have not changed. It is precisely because they have undergone such substantial change, blurring the former edges of their boundaries, that the lines have to be redrawn. The change to industrialised modernity, far from rendering symbolism redundant, gives it new life--even if in old forms.

Notes

Earlier versions of parts of this article have been presented to seminars at the Universities of Oxford and St. Andrews, and to the SSRC Conference on Institutionalised Forms of Co-operation and Reciprocity in Europe. My thanks to members of these audiences--particularly Sandra Ott, Ladislav Holy, Edwin Ardener, Nick Allen, Godfrey Lienhardt and Peter Riviere for their suggestions. A later and much longer draft was imposed on a number of colleagues who responded generously with thorough and incisive criticism and who will, I hope, recognise that I have taken their advice to heart. My thanks to Paul Baxter, Rodney Needham, Robert Paine, Nigel Rapport, David Turton and Peter Worsley.

1. These 'oppositional ideologies' (Schwimmer 1972) often invert or reverse the putative scale of values on which the members of the disadvantaged group suppose themselves to be consigned to the pole of marginality or peripherality by those in the 'centre'-i.e. those on the 'other side' of the boundary. Indeed, one of the potent ways in which they appear to give meaning symbolically to their communality is by reversing the polarities of the scale to make their own values central. Dr. N. Allen has suggested to me in seminar that this argument might usefully be assimilated to the idea of complementary opposition which Dumont porposes

in his theory of hierarchy. My initial response of
scepticism has softened into one of agnosticism,
although I am still reluctant to accept that
Dumont's dichotomous types of 'the encompassing'
and 'the emcompassed' are fully appropriate to the
ethnographic context I deal with here. See Dumont
(1980: exp. 239-45).

2. For a more detailed statement of the
argument, see Cohen (in press).

3. The left-and right-hand sides of this
diagram appear as genealogically unrelated. In
fact, given the high degree of local endogamy over
many generations, it is possible to link
genealogically to each other more than 80 per cent
of the islanders by going back no further than four
generations. But many of these links are either
generally unknown or are considered too distant to
be salient. Kinship, as illustrated in these
diagrams, is a matter of social acknowledgement.
See p. 317.

4. Thus the Whalsay spree must be distinguished
both in form and apparent sigificance from the
alcoholic transactions in the Faroe Islands which
Blehr designates 'token prestations' (1974). He
suggests that the offering of drink is a means of
sustaining long-term economic relations. Indeed,
he goes so far as to say that, '...in not
proffering liquor, the giver would signal that he
intended to account, the very process of inviting
a guest and plying him lavishly with drink without
expecting reciprocation in kind models the value

which the host attributes to his relationship with his guest and, indeed, the deference he pays to him.   Even allowing that Blehr's ethnography is couloured by his commitment to transactional theory it seems clear that social drinking in Whalsay lacks the materially pragmatic character of Faroese drinking.

5.   Robert   Paine   has   suggested   (personal communication)   that   my   argument   if   self-contradictory, maintaining that the death of a member on the one hand signifies the community's death and, and on the other, provides the occasion for its re-assertion.   I agree that there is this ambiguity,   but   ambiguity,   surely,   is   a characteristic of symbolism.

6. Vallee similarly notes the presence of the mundane in Barra funerals. He explains it in terms of their 'normalcy', but also remarks that frequent funeral attendance '...intensifies the awareness of belonging to the community' (1955: 128).

7.   Burra   Isle   is   the   other   major   fishing community in Shetland. There is a long history of contact between the two communities, including considerable intermarriage. However, the members of each frequently contrast themselves favourably to the other.

8. Similarly, Needham points to the eloquence with which symbolic inversion marks not only the divisions among states of being and categories of people, but also social or communal boundaries (Needham 1963: xxxix).

9.   Worsley   correctly   observes   (personal
communication) that a frequent characteristic of
such assertive marginality is that 'what is going
on isn't just a <u>defence</u> of one's own culture, but--
more positively--a <u>critique</u> of the other's.

10. I have previously thought of this process
as symbolic inversion, but have been persuaded by
my critics that I was mistaken.   Nor does it fit
comfortably into any of the twelve varieties of
'reversal' noted by Needham (1983: 93-120).   For
want of inspiration, I therefore resort to the
present clumsy formulation.

References

Aries, P. 1976. <u>Western Attitudes Towards Death from the Middle Ages to the Present</u>. Baltimore: Johns Hopkins Univ. Press.

Babcock, B.A. 1978. "Introduction." <u>In The Reversible World: Symbolic Inversion in Art and Society</u>, ed. B.A. Babcock. London: Cornell Univ. Press.

Beckett, J. 1977. "The Torres Strait Islanders and the Pearling Industry: a Case of Internal Colonialism." <u>Abo. Hist.</u> I, 77-104.

Blehr, O. 1974. "Social Drinking in the Faroe Islands: the Ritual Aspect of Token Prestations." <u>Ethos</u> 1-4, 53-62.

Bloch, M., & J. Parry. 1982. "Introduction: Death and the Regeneration of Life." In <u>Death and the Regeneration of Life</u>, eds. M. Bloch & J. Parry. Cambridge: Univ. Press.

Boon, J.A. 1982. <u>Other Scribes: Symbolic Anthropology in the Comparative Study of Cultures, Histories, Religions, and Texts</u>. Cambridge: Univ. Press.

Cohen, A.P. 1978. "'The Same--but Different!' The Allocation of Identity in Whalsay, Shetland." <u>Sociol. Rev.</u> 26, 449-69.

_____. 1979. "The Whalsay Croft: Traditional Work and Customary Identity in Modern Times." In <u>The Social Anthropology of Work</u>, ed. S. Wallman. London: Academic Press.

_____. 1980. "Oil and the Cultural Account: Reflections on a Shetland Community." In The Social Anthropology of Work, ed. S. Wallman. London: Academic Press.

_____. 1982. "A Sense of Time, a Sense of Place: the Meaning of Close Social Association in Whalsay, Shetland." In Belonging: Identity and Social Organisation in British Rural Cultures, ed. A.P. Cohen. Manchester: Univ. Press.

_____. In press. The Symbolic Construction of Community. London: Tavistock & Ellis Horwood.

Danforth, L.M. 1982. The Death Rituals of Rural Greece. Princeton: Univ. Press.

Dore, R.P. 1978. Shinohata: a Portrait of a Japanese Village. New York: Pantheon.

Douglas, M. 1975. Implicit Meanings: Essays in Anthropology. London: Routledge & Kegan Paul.

Douglas, W.A. 1969. Death in Murelaga: Funerary Ritual in a Spanish Basque Village. Seattle: Univ. of Washington Press.

Drucker-Brown, S. 1982. "Joking at Death: the Mamprusi Grandparent-Grandchild Relationship." Man (N.S.) 17, 714-27.

du Boulay, J. 1982. "The Greek Vampire: a Study of Cyclic Symbolism in Marriage and Death." Man (N.S.) 17, 219-38.

Dumont, L. 1980. Homo Hierarchicus, rev. ed. Chicago: Univ. Press.

Firth, R.   1973.   Symbols, Public and Private.
    London: Allen & Unwin.

Friedl, J.   1974.   Kippel: a Changing Village in
    the Alps. New York: Holt, Rienhart & Winston.

Geertz, C.   1975.   "Thick Description: Toward an
    Interpretive Theory of Culture."   In The
    Interpretation of Cultures. London:
    Hutchinson.

Helias, P.J.   1978.   The Horse of Pride: Life in
    a Breton Village, trans. J. Guicharnaned. New
    Haven: Yale Univ. Press.

Hertz, R.   1980.   Death and the Right Hand, trans.
    R. & C. Needham. New York: Free Press.

Humphrey, C.   1983.   Karl Marx Collective:
    Economy, Society and Religion in a Siberian
    Collective Farm. Cambridge: Univ. Press.

Humphrey, S.C.   1981.   "Introduction: Comparative
    Perspectives on Death."   In Mortality and
    Immortality: the Anthropology and Archaeology
    of Death, eds. S.C. Humphreys & H. King.
    London: Academic Press.

Huntington, R., & P. Metcalf.   1979.   Celebrations
    of Death: the Anthropology of Mortuary Ritual.
    Cambridge: Univ. Press.

Jorion, P.   1982.   "The Priest and the Fishermen:
    Sundays and Weekdays in a Former 'Theocracy'.
    Man (N.S.) 17, 275-86.

Leach, E.R.   1976.   Culture and Communication:
    the Logic by Which Symbols are Connected.
    Cambridge: Univ. Press.

Mandelbaum, D.G.   1976.   "Social Uses of Funeral
    Rites."   In Death and Identity, ed. R. Fulton.
    Maryland: The Charles Press.

Needham, R.   1963.   "Introduction."   In Primitive
    Classification, trans. ed. R. Needham.
    Chicago: Univ. Press.

_____.   1979.   Symbolic Classification.   Santa
    Monica: Goodyear.

_____.   1980.   Reconnaissances.   Toronto:
    Univ. Press.

_____.   1983.   Against the Tranquility of
    Axioms.   Berkeley: Univ. of California Press.

O'Neill, B.J.   1983.   "Dying and Inheriting in
    Rural Tras-os-Montes."   J.A.S.O. 14, 44-74.

Paine, R.P.B.   1982.   Dam a River, Damn a People?
    Saami (Lapp) Livelihood and the Alta Kautokeino
    Hydro-Electric Project and the Norwegian
    Parliament (IWGIA Docum. 45).   Copenhagen:
    IWGIA.

Peacock, J.   1975.   Consciousness and Change:
    Symbolic Anthropology in Evolutionary
    Perspective.   Oxford: Blackwell.

Schwimmer, E.   1972.   "Symbolic Competition."
    Anthropologica 14, 117-55.

Sperber, D.   1975.   Rethinking Symbolism, trans.
    A. Morton.   Cambridge: Univ. Press.

Vallee, F.G.   1955.   "Burial and Mourning Customs
    in a Hebridean Community."   J. R. Anthrop. Inst.
    119-30.

Warner, W.L.   1959.   <u>The Living and the Dead: a Study of the Symbolic Life of Americans</u>.   New Haven: Yale Univ. Press.

GUSII FUNERALS:

MEANINGS OF LIFE AND DEATH

IN AN AFRICAN COMMUNITY

Robert A. LeVine

Introduction

The funerals of the Gusii, like those of other
African peoples, are occasions for dramatic public
statements about the meanings of particular lives
and of life in general. This article attempts to
explicate   those   meanings   on   the   basis   of
observations at Gusii funerals during 1955-1957 and
1974-1976 and interviews conducted then and in
1964. My aim is to describe how Gusii view their
own death rituals and to provide a context for
understanding the place of these rituals in the
personal experience of Gusii individuals.

When I returned to the Gusii in 1974 for a two-
year study of infants and their families, I decided
to make a special investigation of funerals in
order to gain insight into the cultural management
of grief, loss, and mourning and to complement our

Reprinted from Ethos 10, no. 1 (1982):   26-
65. Reproduced by permission of the American
Anthropological Association. Not for further
reproduction.

research on Gusii interpersonal relationships in the early years.   As the fieldwork proceeded, however, I came to realize that Gusii funerals were not only means for dealing with death as social and personal disruption but dramas defining the ultimate meaning of life.   Reading an article by Meyer Fortes (1971) and rereading a book by Monica Wilson (1957), while in the field, also helped bring about this realization and deepened my concentration on these issues.   But it was the Gusii I worked with who convinced me that funerals could provide a key to their perspective on life and death, expressed in a language of ritual action that all Gusii adults understood but which requires lengthy explanation to outsiders.   By eliciting those explanations, attending numerous funerals, and setting what I saw and was told in the context of the Gusii ritual system as a whole, I was able to attain the level of understanding represented by this paper.

Evidence concerning the importance of funerals to Gusii communities and individuals comes from a wide variety of sources.   For example, Philip Mayer, writing in 1949, states:

Every Gusii is conscious of belonging to a group he calls his abanyamatati, 'people of shaving' (cf. amatati, pl. of ritati, head-shaving): we shall call this the 'mourning group.'   At the funeral of a member of the group the other members will be distinguishable by their obligation to shave their heads, to divide up and eat the sacrificial animal, and to wear strips of its hide as mourning rings.

(The) idea of one-ness among abanyamatati, expressed in the joint eating of the funeral sacrifice, finds another reflection in the rules about payment of compensation for killing. The mourning group of a slain man is nominally responsible for payment. [1949: 18-19]

As Mayer describes it, and as I found it in 1955-1957, the mourning group is the nuclear patrilineal group in a society organized on patrilineal or agnatic principles. Their role at funerals, particularly collective head-shaving, becomes the symbol of their solidarity and mutual obligation.

In 1956, I asked a number of senior Gusii women about the differential treatment of and attitude toward girls and boys:

Informant A: If a woman has all girls there is no one to bury her.

Informant B: Both boys and girls are good [to give birth to]. Girls are told that boys should eat [more] because they will always be at home. A mother says, "they [sons] will bury me, but you [daughters] may run off and leave me without the proper cows."

Informant c: Boys are given more food. If the father slaughters a goat, a boy is given three or four ribs, the girl none; she has to eat part of what is given to her mother. A boy is also given more obokima [staple porridge]. We want the boy to be stronger; when his mother and father die he will have to bury them.

This concern with burial, which strikes a Westerner as remarkable, has its parallel in other African societies. Among the Edo of the Benin Kingdom in Nigeria, for example, Bradbury (1965) writes:

To die childless, or sonless, is the most dreaded fate, and when one asks: "Why do you want many children?" the reply is often: "So that they may bury me well." The Edo believe that one who is not properly 'buried' cannot enter the society of his dead kin and associates. For his survival as a social being he is dependent on the performance of the mortuary ritual by his children. Again and again, at the climax of these rites, one hears the song: "This is what we bear children for." In a sense, the funerary ritual is the most potent symbol of the parent-children relationship as it is ideally conceived in Edo culture. [1965: 97-98]

Finally, in 1974 a Gusii schoolteacher who lived in town decided to build his house in the rural area on a pleasantly situated spot within the paternal homestead. When his blind grandfather, who was head of the homestead, heard where the house had been built, he called in his grandson and told him that the spot was not a suitable house site because the ground there was solid rock and would not permit the digging of a grave in which he could be properly buried. Another house was thereupon erected on a site with softer earth.

These examples show that elements of mortuary ritual such as burial and head-shaving are invoked by Gusii in situations of group solidarity, parent-child relationship, and house location. They suggest that Gusii funerals should be seen not merely as actions that occur when someone dies, but (in their representations form) as organized principles in the lives of individuals.

The Location Of Funerals

Gusii funerals take place at the home of the deceased. Each action, from dying to posthumous sacrifice, has a customary location regarded by Gusii (in 1976, as earlier) as an essential part of the ritual. The domestic setting has the same kind of relation to a Gusii funeral that the traditional design of a church, mosque, or synagogue has to the rituals that take place there: where the performance takes place is central to its meaning. In this case, however, it is the same house where life has been lived that is the explicit source of meaning at death.

Although a Gusii homestead belongs to a man, each house within it is identified with a married woman (wife, mother, or daughter-in-law of the owner) who cooks, sleeps, and raises her children there. The house itself is divided into two rooms: enyomba (also the general word for 'house'), which is the woman's room and contains the hearth and sleeping area; and eero, her husband's room, where he entertains his guests with beer and food and where rituals such as sacrifice are normally performed. Outside the entrance to enyomba is a yard where many routing family activities take place; outside the smaller door to eero is (or was) the cattle pen (obweeri). (Cattle are explicitly associated with men in Gusii thought.) Enyomba as the woman's room is considered the left side of the house; a woman is supposed to die in her normal sleeping place there, lying on her left side, and be buried outside it just beyond the yard. Eero is considered the right side of the house, and a man is supposed to die there (though he normally sleeps in his wife's area), lying on his right side, and be buried outside it beyond the cattle pen. (Right is said to be the man's side because he holds his spear in his right hand.) In burial, the woman should remain lying on her left side and the man on his right. Thus, the conceptual division of the house and adjacent external spaces into right and left sections identified with male and female spouses regulates the places and positions of proper death and burial for those spouses.

These are the spatial ideals of Gusii death and burial; persons who die without being spouses are treated as deviations from this model of proper placement. Thus, if an unmarried mother dies at her parents' home, she is buried to the 'left' of her mother's house but as far away as possible-- at the edge of the river in those areas where traditional plots are intact. The left position accords with her gender and the distance with her status as someone who ought to have left home and died at her husband's homestead. Other deviant cases are described in the next section; here the point is that the location of a burial indicates approximation of the deceased to gender-specific norms of marital status.

Contemporary Gusii take these spatial ideals seriously, even when doing so involves inconvenience, discomfort, and expense. They take pains to assure the proper placement of their own bodies and those of their kin in death and burial. Nowadays Gusii sleep in bed rather than on skins, but a dying man is taken from the bed he usually shares with his wife and placed on the floor of eero, so that (as I was told in 1956) he may die 'as a warrior, not a woman.' In the past, an ailing woman would already have been lying on her proper deathbed, next to the hearth. The declining availability of firewood and greater availability of blankets, however, have led some Gusii to build the kitchen separate from the bedroom, but the kitchen--where the hearth is--is still considered

enyomba for ritual purposes. Thus the dying woman
must be moved from the bedroom to her kitchen if
her death is to take place in enyomba, next to her
own hearth. Women are moved before they die and
placed on their left sides. A similar concern for
the   maintenance   of   traditional   standards   of
location is shown in the case of burials. Land
shortage has forced many Gusii to plant crops right
up to the yard on the 'left' side and even closer
on the 'right' side, since cattle pens are rarely
needed.   Thus crops are growing   where burial
should take place. When someone dies, however,
burial takes precedence, and crops are destroyed
to make room for a grave and for the activities
that surround it at the funeral. The rites of
placement remain absolute.

    The   salience   of   these   rules   for   Gusii
individuals is most often discussed by adults in
terms of the fear that one might die without having
a house of one's own. A young man investing his
first earnings in the building of such a house,
even if another house (usually belonging to an
absent older brother) was available for his use and
he had no real intention of living at home, usually
offers the need for a proper burial as a reason: to
be buried properly, no one else's house will do.
There are other compelling reasons for a young man
to build a house at home he has no immediate
prospect of living in: It is a step toward mature
adult status; it makes him more attractive to a
potential bride (this would be her house); it
constitutes a visible claim to his share of the
land. Yet I would not discount the concern for a
proper   burial,   largely   because   it   is   not
independent of these other considerations, all of
which involve his increasing rights as a member of
homestead   and   lineage.   Burial   is   the   final
consideration that subsumes the immediate goals and
can stand for them in speech.   In discussing the

initial phases of marriage, as in discussions of parent-child relations, burial is the condensed symbol of valued goals--the ultimate one that represents all the others. To die without burial (as sometimes happened on the battlefield) is emuma, an abomination, a curse that will bring afflictions to one's homestead and descendants for generations. To die without a house to be buried near is to end life as an incomplete person whose status had not reached that plateau of maturity signified by the establishment of a marital household.

What does in fact happen when a Gusii adult dies without a house of his or her own? In May 1976, an 80-year-old woman, virtually blind but active as a ritual practitioner, died unexpectedly. Long-standing economic disputes among her sons and their belief (widely shared in the community) that she was a witch had resulted the previous year in her house being dismantled, the grass roof sold for cash, and the land on which it stood planted with crops. She was living in the house of an absent grandson at the time of her death. Customary responsibility for the old woman's burial fell to her oldest grandson, who was ready to his duty but perplexed at her houselessness. The issue was resolved by a discussion at which three friends and neighbors of the deceased--an elderly man and an elderly widow from agnatically related homesteads, and a respected elder of less advanced years from a nearby homestead of another clan--argued that a house must be built for her. They were able to draw upon customary precedents for unmarried men who had died houseless; a small structure called egesamo was built for purposes of the mortuary ritual to represent the house 'she would have had in marriage.'

Egesamo simulates the residential house at a
funeral. The word is derived from egesa, referring
to a small hut men used to build for themselves at
home so they could be alone (i.e., apart from their
wives) with their cattle. As a word and concept,
egesa is derived from egesaraate, 'cattle camp,'
where warriors lived away from their families with
the cattle herds before 1913, when the colonial
government outlawed the cattle camps as a source of
interclan violence. Nostalgic for their lives in
the cattle camps, elders prior to 1913 and other
married men after that time, built huts for
themselves at home which were named after the
cattle camp and had some of the same functions.
When a house had to be built for the funeral of a
houseless person, this verbal and conceptual
prototype was drawn upon to designate a small,
impermanent structure built for a more specialized
purpose than an ordinary house (enyomba); hence
egesamo.

The old woman died a 1:00 P.M.; by 11:00 A.M.
of the following day the egesamo for the burial had
been built, and her grandsons were digging a grave
a few feet from its front door (on its 'left,' as
the Gusii view it). Built of grass on a framework
of saplings, the hut was located on the spot where
her house had been. Her woven-wood drying trays
(chingambo, sing. orwambo) for drying grain had
been used for some of the interior walls and
ceiling. Before noon, her corpse was placed in a
coffin and brought from the house where she died
through the 'left' door of the grass hut and set
down there. Her eldest grandson dug a hole for a
small fireplace (egetukora), and his wife brought
embers from the old woman's last cooking fire to
light a fire in the new hut. They spent that night
after the burial in the hut to make sure the fire
did not go out. (Its extinction would have been a
curse and resulted in affliction of the

descendants.) They brought in the old woman's possessions (a blanket, her smoking pipe, and her divination apparatus) and hearthstones for the fireplace, and sacrificed a goat, sharing the meat and millet beer with a neighboring kinsman and his wife, who sat outside the hut. The fire was kept going for a day after the burial, the hut preserved for some days until a second sacrifice was performed. During the lamentation that followed the burial, a granddaughter of the deceased publicly criticized the old woman's sons (including the accuser's own father) for failing to provide her with a house to be buried by, prior to her death. This led to an inconclusive quarrel about who was to blame.

Thus when a Gusii adult dies houseless, a ritual hut must be constructed on the spot where the house was or would have been, the corpse placed in it before burial, and rituals of fire and sacrifice performed to consecrate the hut as a symbolic house. This rule is invariant in its application and cannot be abrogated even when, as in the case described, the deceased is considered a witch and has not been the object of her children's affection. In that case, a good deal of money and effort were expended to give her a proper burial. Without the construction of an egesamo, there would have been no point of reference from which to position the grave--which in Gusii terms makes burial impossible or at least hopelessly improper. With the construction of egesamo, it was possible to place the grave and the corpse on its way to the grave, in its 'left' position appropriate to a woman.

One of the most interesting aspects of these spatial rules is the necessity that each adult have a unique location at burial, one that is not shared with any other adult of the same sex. Hence each

man must have a house that was built for him and
each woman a house in which she has cooked as his
wife; no other available house in the homestead can
serve as substitute point of reference for their
graves. The individual identity of the adult is at
stake here. No matter how much emphasis there is
on the corporate identity of the homestead and the
generational continuity of the lineage in other
parts of the funeral, each person who has reached
maturity is entitled to a unique house-burial site
as a minimal marker of individuality.

The Gusii grave itself is not marked. On the
contrary, informants emphasized the need to smooth
down the earth after burial so that its location
would be invisible to the witches, who are believed
to exhume corpses and eat them. Thus the house is
at the time of death and thereafter the only
visible marker of the deceased as an individual.
For the Gusii, whose bodies are literally incorporated at death into their homesteads and who see
their descendants as their primary evidence of
having lived, the house is an indispensable symbol
of personal identity as an adult individual at the
time of interment. It is also the setting for the
drama of the funeral itself.

The Funeral Ceremony: 1956 And 1976

In describing the sequence of ritual action of
the Gusii funeral, I shall begin with an overview
of the ceremony as it was in the 1950s and as it
changed over the next two decades. Later sections
will describe variations according to social status
and the circumstances of death, and then the place
of emotional expression in funerals.

During 1955-1957, funerals in the Nyansongo
area approximated closely what informants described

as their precolonial form. This can be divided into four phases: (1) death, (2) burial, (3) the public gathering, and (4) subsequent rituals.

1. <u>Death</u>. When a person was thought to be near death, he was put into <u>eero</u> if a man or left in <u>enyomba</u> if a woman, in both cases on the floor so that the death would not contaminate the bed and make it unsuitable for later use. Deathbed confessions were expected from persons suspected of witchcraft, theft, or other serious offenses that might bring afflictions to survivors if restitution was not made. Women in the family started wailing in a stylized singsong before death occurred, which served to notify neighbors that someone was dying. After death, the wailing became louder, and kinsmen were summoned to dig the grave. The corpse was placed on the gender-appropriate side with knees flexed; white clay was put on the face and green leaves on the body. Other treatment of the corpse before burial was contingent on special status attributes and is described below.

2. <u>Burial</u>. The digging of the grave began as soon as the appropriate kin arrived. The preferred person to take charge was the deceased son's son (if there were several, the eldest grandson) but it could be a son if the grandsons were too young or a nephew (brother's son or husband's brother's son) or brother if no son were available. The role of the son's son in giving his grandparents a proper burial was (and is) cherished by elderly Gusii; while an absolute obligation, it gave the grandson a special claim on the grandfather's <u>emonga</u> (personal land, undivided among his wives), livestock, and other property. Other kinsmen, usually agnatically related neighbors of the same generation, helped the grandson or son dig the grave. If these neighbors failed to arrive, it was a sign they believed the deceased to be a thief

whose death was caused by sorcery medicine that would affect them if they touched the corpse. This is one of several instances in which attendance and nonattendance at funeral rites carried with it a great deal of unspoken meaning.

The first break in the earth was made by the hoe of the eldest grandson or son, whoever was in charge. Men whose wives were pregnant were excused from grave-digging on the grounds that the unborn might be adversely affected. Further, pregnant women and their husbands were prohibited from touching the earth of the grave, even after the grave was filled in, for the same reason. The depth of graves was variable and dependent on how seriously is was suspected that the deceased was killed by witches. If the suspicions were serious, the grave would be deeper, more than ten feet; if there were no credible suspicions, it might be as shallow as six feet. If someone was killed by witchcraft, the corpse was believed to be in greater danger of being exhumed and eaten by the murderers but could be protected by greater depth.

The corpse was carried from the house through the door of the gender-specific room in which death had occurred to the grave on the side of the house, and was lowered into the grave and put on its right or left side according to sex. At this point, if the elders of the local patrilineage seriously suspected witchcraft, then the visceral cavity was cut open in the grave while the elders inspected it from above to see if internal organs (spleen, liver, intestines) were swollen, indicating the effects of witchcraft. It was believed that the swelling of organs due to witchcraft would, if the visceral incision were not performed, continue after burial and result in a crack in the surface of the grave, leading the witches to their prey.

With the 'pressure' relieved by the incision, the body was closed and the grave filled in.

Throwing the first handful of earth into the grave had a special significance. It was usually the grandson or son in charge of the digging who did it, but if the preferred kinsman was a child, too small to dig, nevertheless he threw the first earth into the grave although others had done the digging. Other close agnates of the deceased could also throw earth into the grave after the first handful. Women did not unless asked specifically to do so. This happened when the deceased had several wives; had one of them hesitated to throw the earth (fearing subsequent affliction) it would have been assumed she had committed adultery, and a special sacrifice would have been required. Once this ritual throwing of earth was over, the diggers filled up the grave, stamping down the earth as they did. When they were finished, a prepubescent girl had to bring them water to wash their hands and legs with, so that they would not carry earth from the grave away with them; in bringing it, she was forbidden to turn around.

When the deceased was a married man, the exterior roof-stick (egechuri) was removed from the top of the conical roof of the house shortly after his death or during the digging of his grave. This stick symbolized male authority over the women of the house and was later replaced when she took a leviratic husband (omochinyomba). If the deceased's wife had undergone the final wedding ceremony (enyangi) at which iron rings (ebitinge) had been put on her ankles, these were also removed during the grave-digging. These two acts carried the message that a married man had died and his marital relationships, though by no means dissolved, were fundamentally altered.

There was supposed to be a cessation of mournful noise during the grave-digging, interment, and filling-in, but it was expected that the women would not be able to stop themselves from wailing during that time. Once the grave was filled in, however, all expressions of grief were permissible. Widows of the deceased were expected to tear off their clothes, cover themselves with ashes, and put on articles of the dead husband's clothing as they lamented his death and danced on his grave. A widower was also expected to remove his shirt, put ashes on his body, and tie some of his wife's clothing around his waist at this time, a practice called ogokobania. The grave-diggers were supposed to be the first to cry at the grave, but there were usually other close kin present by this time and no rule of precedence was followed. Except when they were dancing on the grave or throwing themselves upon it in grief, women and men clustered separately during this period following the burial, engaging in conventional expressions of grief described below. Kin of the same sex clustered around the bereaved spouse, parent or child of the deceased in order to give comfort in the hours after death. Bereaved women (wife, mother, daughter, sister of the deceased) were expected to mourn continuously on this and the next day, becoming completely exhausted.

When night fell after the burial, a sacrifice had to be performed, 'a goat to cool the house' (embori yogokendia enyomba). This was explicitly interpreted by informants as intended to placate the deceased so that his anger would not result in afflictions for survivors in the homestead. The goat sacrificed was of the same sex as the deceased. It was roasted with the skin on and the whole thing eaten on the spot; unlike other sacrifices, the meat was not allowed to be taken home. Sometimes another goat was sacrificed the next morning, 'so that the dead man will not blame them and send bad spirits to his living kin.' 'A dead man's brothers and sisters stayed in the house during the first night after the burial to give the widows comfort and make sure they do not kill themselves.'

   3. The Public Gathering. It was expected that news of the death would have reached the majority of the deceased's kin on the day of the burial. Members of the deceased's risaga (the community of neighboring homesteads recognizing reciprocal work obligations) abstained from cultivating their fields that day. They and more distantly located kin would come the following day to participate in the mourning. If the deceased were a man, men would bring their cattle and their weapons to the funeral; women would bring food, since widows were forbidden to cook. The deceased's personal possessions were displayed on the grave. For a man it would be his wooden stool, his walking stick, the ankle rings his wife had removed the previous day, and (in 1956-1957) articles of Western clothing (suit jacket, trousers, hat). At some men's funerals their Western-style beds were put on the grave too. For a woman it would be her cooking pots, her stool, her smoking pipe (Gusii women smoked tobacco in pipes), some iron bracelets, and necklaces.

   Large numbers of people came to pay their respects in conventional ways, stayed for a while and then left. Those with closer relationships to the deceased or the immediate surviving kin stayed throughout the day. At a man's funeral, herds of cattle were driven over the grave, often trampling and consuming crops in adjacent fields, as their owners made a display of menacing unseen enemies with poised spears, which they sometimes stuck into nearby trees. All the while they were shouting war

cries, and men accompanying them blew horns and
whistles to add to the din.   Informants said this
custom was intended to show those (unidentified)
enemies who might have brought about the death of
this man that he had warlike supporters who were
prepared to fight them.   They were in effect giving
him a 'warrior's farewell' like a 21-gun salute
rather than seriously intending to identify his
killers and avenge his death.   Nevertheless, in
precolonial times, warriors had their bellicosity
so stirred up by this ritual drama that they
sometimes conducted serious unprovoked raids
against other Gusii clans on their way home from a
funeral.   There was no conscious belief that the
deceased was killed by the people who were attacked
after the funeral. On the contrary, these acts of
violence were more likely to occur at the funerals
of old men who had clearly died at home of
conditions associated with old age.   Gusii
informants who participated in these raids said the
mood established at the funeral impelled them to
conduct a raid on their enemies.

Older men and those without cattle paid their
respects to the deceased by facing the grave, often
a group of men together, and singing an "o-o-o"
sound which they held for as long as they could,
then they dispersed and regathered farther away
from the grave. All men did this at the funeral of
a woman. Women, on the other hand, wailed at great
length, tears pouring down their cheeks, singing
improvised lamentations (described below) and
dancing on and around the grave.   While male
participation in the public mourning was brief and
circumscribed, that of women went on for hours,
with the widows and the mother continually in
evidence near the grave. Each woman did her own
slow, shuffling dance uncoordinated with the
others. If there was a musician playing a Gusii
lyre (obokano), however, then the women were

invariably clustered separately at funerals, and
their activities at and around the grave were
uncoordinated with each other.

This public mourning could go on all day and
even on subsequent days as kinsmen and friends who
lived farther away came to participate. There were
three other rituals that immediate kin had to
conduct on that day: head-shaving, turning the
stool (or cooking pot) upside down, and another
animal sacrifice. At midday the heads were shaved.
This is _amatati_, mentioned above as the symbol of
communion for the _abanyamatati_, the nuclear agnatic
kin group. The shaving group, described by Gusii
as 'people of one grandfather,' actually consisted,
as Mayer (1949: 19) pointed out, of the sons and
grandsons of a deceased man, his father and his
grandfather and their sons and their sons and
grandsons; there were different assortments of kin
for a woman (including her husband and mother) or
a child. In addition, the widows of a man must
have their heads shaved, and in the case of
polygynists, this was usually done on the grave
itself. If a widow had committed adultery, she had
to confess at this time or 'her children would
die'; once she confessed she was shaved on the
grave and a ram was sacrificed.

Once the head-shaving was done, the personal
possessions of the deceased were turned upside down
on the grave (_ogotureka chingambo_); this
particularly applied to a man's stool and a woman's
cooking pots, though anything else that had a
distinguishable top and bottom might also be
inverted. While these articles remained inverted,
widows of the deceased must not go far from the
homestead, cross a river, wash their bodies or
their clothing; a widower was under the same
restrictions. That evening, another goat was
sacrificed: _embori yamatoronge_, the 'goat of the

portions.' The meat of this goat was distributed
to all the houses in the homestead, to permit their
residents to resume cooking, something they had
stopped as soon as death occurred. In its
metaphorical meaning, amatoronge, designating
portions of food shared from a common food basket
(ekee), here refers to the several houses
(chinyomba) of the single homestead. Each house
was likened to a part taken from a whole,
emphasizing the unity of the whole without denying
its segmentation; the message was similar to e
pluribus unum.

4. Subsequent Rituals. With the resumption
of cooking in the homestead of the deceased and the
completion of public mourning by visitors, the most
public aspects of the funeral were over, but the
bereaved spouses remained in a liminal state
initiated by inversion of the deceased's
possessions. This could be terminated as soon as
another sacrifice called okogororokia chingambo
('standing things up straight') was performed.
Since this sacrifice required the brewing of millet
beer and the providing of a feast for neighboring
kinsmen, it could not take place before a week or
two had passed and was more likely to be postponed
for a period of months. One knowledgeable
informant said he had never known a widow who had
performed it before two months, another said it was
frequently done after grass had begun growing on
the grave. It was understood that poor families
would take longer to gather resources for the
feast. The feast was a joyous celebration,
explicitly marking the end of sorrow, the end of
restrictions on widowed spouses, the resumption of
normal life and the establishment of a widow's
leviratic relationships. It can be seen as ending
the customary mourning period for spouses, the
specific length of which could be adjusted by a

spouse on the basis of numerous socially acceptable conditions.

The sacrifice took place in the daytime. With neighboring kinsmen in attendance, a goat of the same sex and roughly equivalent in age to the deceased was led into the gender-appropriate room of the house, then to the grave ('as the dead person was') and back to <u>eero</u> in the house, where all sacrifices are performed. After the goat was ritually slaughtered, the inverted possessions were turned right side up. This lifted the restrictions on widowed spouses. The kinsmen assembled, ate and drank; bits of the goat's stomach contents were smeared on their foreheads and chests and they were given bracelets cut from its hide. They then left the widow (in the case of a deceased man) with her leviratic husband (brother or ortho-cousin to the deceased). The <u>egechuri</u> stick was then replaced on the roof of the house. Life returned to normal.

But there were more sacrifices to be performed. Each married son of a deceased man or woman had to perform a sacrifice in his own house, called 'bringing the patriarch (matriarch) into the house,' <u>okorenta omogaaka</u> (<u>omongina</u>) <u>nyomba</u>. Previous sacrifices had been performed in the house of the deceased, but these subsequent ones were designed as offerings from the houses of the sons to protect them from the potential ill will of the dead person's spirit. Later, each of the married paternal grandsons (sons' sons) had to do the same: 'bringing grandfather (grandmother) into the house,' <u>okorenta esokoro (magokoro) nyomba</u>. When this had been done the spirit of the deceased would have been placated by every house of a married person in the homestead he or she left behind. That marked the end of the normal series of rituals occasioned by one death. When a prosperous old man died leaving numerous married sons and grandsons, the number of sacrifices required was great and so was the likelihood that some of them would be neglected. It was expected that grandsons would postpone this duty for years. But if afflictions struck during that time, the diviner (omoragoori) would attribute it to chisokoro, 'grandfathers,' and would specify the sacrifice that must be done to achieve reconciliation with the neglected spirit. The widespread neglect of sacrificial obligations to one's grandfathers became the primary link between the ancestor cult and the Gusii system of diagnosis and healing managed by diviners.

This account, detailed as it may seem, is no more than a skeletal outline of the Gusii funeral in the middle 1950s, but it can serve as a baseline for comparing with the funerals observed 20 years later. In the interim, the Gusii of the area in which I worked were more intensely missionized, especially by the Roman Catholic Church. By 1974, only a handful of persons remained unaffiliated with that church or the Seventh-Day Adventists. (A few individuals were members of the Swedish Lutheran Church, Church of God, or Pentecostal Assemblies of God.) Schoolgoing, which was rare in 1957, was virtually universal in 1974, and a substantial number of adults had been to secondary school. Many in the area had lived and worked in big cities, read newspapers, and listened to the radio. They seemed to aspire to 'modern' life-styles defined by Western models, which were propagated by the mass media, church, and government. Thus there was every reason to expect that funerals in the area would reflect the effects of social change.

Gusii funerals changed in some respects between 1957 and 1974 and remained the same in many others. I shall review changes in the normative script for the funeral ceremony against the background of the four phases already outlined. The biggest change is in the temporal organization of the four phases. Burial no longer follows rapidly upon death but is postponed until the public gathering can take place. Thus the corpse remains unburied for an extra day. This seems to be an accommodation to the fact that immediate kin who should be involved in the burial are now likely to be working hundreds of miles away and learn of the death over the telephone or through the Gusii language broadcast of the Voice of Kenya radio station; they must be given time to return. Employment also means that many are under pressure to return to work as soon as possible. Thus the phases of burial and the public gatherings are now coterminous, with extended kin and acquaintances attending the burials of persons who in the past they would have mourned only after burial had taken place. This turns the burial into a spectacle and the central drama of the public gathering--which is quite a difference from the past. The other changes can be discussed in relation to each of the four phases.

1. <u>Death</u>. An increasing number of Gusii die away from home, in the Kisii Hospital or at their places of work, but every effort is made to bring the corpse home as soon as possible. Talcum powder has replaced white clay as a facial dressing for the corpse. Men who are bringing a corpse home from the hospital in a pickup truck sometimes put talcum powder on their own faces and silently wave the branches of green leaves that are lain on the corpse.

Coffins, which were never seen at Gusii funerals in the 1950s, are now universal; they are made at home by some of the same men who dig the grave. As soon as the coffin has been built, the corpse is put into it on the correct side, in the proper room of the house. Those who arrive for the funeral before the burial are ushered into that room to view the corpse, something that was not possible when burial followed quickly after death. The coffin is of course the result of Western and Christian influence, but its universal adoption seems to be connected with the new practice of viewing the corpse and having a large number of persons attend the burial. In other words, the coffin can be seen as the response by the immediate kin to the more public nature of the funeral; they are showing an audience of concerned outsiders that they are taking proper care of the corpse. According to new standards of care. We can only speculate as to why these particular new standards were adopted. One plausible speculation is that since the grave itself was conceptualized as affording protection for the corpse from witches, with graves being dug deeper if the threat of witchcraft seemed more imminent, the coffin could have been welcomed as a Western invention that would afford an additional layer of protection for the corpse. I shall return to this interpretation below.

2.   <u>Burial</u>. Burials were conducted in 1974–1976 as described for the earlier period, though before a larger gathering and with coffins. The postmortem examination of the viscera when witchcraft is suspected, for example, continues and was performed at a funeral (of an eight-year-old girl) attended in 1975. The coffin was lowered into a grave 12 feet in depth on ropes made from the cornstalks uprooted to make room for the grave. The coffin was pried open for the operation and nailed shut when the examination was over. Other prescriptive norms concerning who digs the grave and who throws earth into it remain as before. The major new element of ritual is the Christian

liturgy.   At Catholic funerals, a local catechist
reads   prayers   and   leads   the   Catholic   kin   in
reciting them, as the grave is being filled in.
The catechist and others stand at and around the
grave at this time.   The Seventh-Day Adventists
do   the   same   but   hold   a   public   meeting   with
eulogies, prayers, and other speeches some distance
from   the   grave   just   prior   to   the   burial.   In
contrast   to   the   Catholic   pattern,   in   which   the
Christian   prayers   are   simply   inserted   into   a
preexisting   ritual,   the   Seventh-Day   Adventists
create a Westernized occasion, with many attending
in their best clothes, sitting on chairs facing the
deacons and other leaders who address them and lead
them in prayer before the burial takes place.   Once
the grave is filled in, however, the expressions of
grief are much the same at all Gusii funerals, and
the   dancing,   singing,   and   lamentation   remain   the
same as in the past.

        3.   The Public Gathering.   Although the cattle
drive for the funerals of men still occurs in some
parts of Gusiiland, most of the area in which we
worked had no sizable herds, and men no longer make
a display of military activity at funerals.   They
do blow whistles, however, and some bring portable
radios   with   the   volume   turned   up,   to   add   to   the
noise of phonographs already blaring near the grave
and create a din like that of old.   Apart from a
few with a special relationship to the deceased,
men cluster separately from women after burial,
often   drinking   alcoholic   beverages.   The   women
continue   to   behave   more   individually   in   their
emotional expressions, as described below.   Those
attending a funeral nowadays usually give small
sums of money to the bereaved, in place of the food
women used to bring.

        The sacrifice 'to cool the house' is still done
the   night   after   the   burial,   but   that   now   means

after the public gathering rather than before it. Goats were sacrificed for two women who died at 75 and 80 years of age in 1975 and 1976. In the case of men, however, it has become conventional to sacrifice a white cock instead of a goat (the ritual is then called etwoni yogokendia nyomba, 'a cock to cool the house'), and this was done for all men whose funerals were attended in the 1970s, ranging from a 28-year-ald bachelor to an 87-year-old elder. Like the goat roasted in its skin, the cock for this ritual is not cooked in the usual way; its throat is cut and the innards removed, but the bird is put in the fire with the feathers on. When the feathers have burnt off and the chicken is roasted, the participants eat the meat by itself without other food; they must not chew the bones. As with the goat, they must finish the meat there and take none home. Informants said this sacrifice is done for all men who have reached marital age but neglected nowadays for young women.

Since the public gathering now takes place on the day of the burial, before the sacrifice of cooling the house, the head-shaving is no longer temporally associated with the gathering. It is done as in the past, on the following day (now after most visitors have gone).

The second sacrifice, embori yamatoronge, is still done for all adults and the possessions are overturned as before.

4. Subsequent Ritual. The third sacrifice, 'standing the things up straight,' is still done after a variable length of time, but the fourth and fifth, 'bringing the father (and then the grandfather) into the house,' are now frequently postponed until afflictions force the son or grandson to a diviner who diagnoses them as due to

the 'grandfathers' and prescribes the kind of goat or chicken to be sacrificed.

Gusii funerals, then, have changed over a period of two decades: The burial and public gathering take place on the same day rather than on successive days, making the burial later and more public than before. Some specific elements have been added (coffins, Christian prayers), some dropped (the cattle drive), some substituted (talcum powder for white clay, radio music for war cries, a cock for a goat), some neglected (the final sacrifices). The central narrative, however, the 'story' that the funeral tells about the deceased in relation to the survivors, remains the same.

In this central narrative, the deceased as corpse and spirit is initially portrayed as a potential source of danger to surviving kin. Although the corpse is not invariably feared, contact with it or even with the earth of its grave can be harmful to an unborn child in the womb of a pregnant woman or even a grave-digger's pregnant wife; and if the deceased was killed by retaliatory sorcery, the corpse can spread the ill effects to those who touch it. Further, contact with the corpse in bad faith--the adulterous wife who throws earth into the grave--brings physical harm, even death, to a survivor. In other words, Gusii custom does not entail a generalized fear of contact with the corpse but a belief that death places in a state of jeopardy persons involved with incompleted processes--gestation, retaliation, marital betrayal--and that contact with the corpse will bring completion in the form of death. The corpse as a terminal physical condition seems to represent the possibility that the deceased will quickly resolve unfinished business before burial by terminating the lives of survivors. But this possibility is represented in the corpse as an unwilled, automatic, contagious condition-- selective but not intentional.

The portrayal of the deceased as spirit, that is, as the presence for whom sacrifices are performed, brings into focus the intentions and emotional attitudes attributed to a dead person in the Gusii funeral narrative. The deceased is angry and resentful at having died, potentially blaming the survivors for it (regardless of the actual facts) and wanting to wreak vengeance on them. Like the prototypical Gusii adult who has suffered a serious loss (including bereaved persons at funerals), the deceased is portrayed as reacting with a rage that overcomes reason and leads to blame and the desire for vengeance. If the survivors had actually killed the deceased, they would have more to fear--but even if they did not, the facts remain that they are alive and the deceased is dead and that they will benefit from the inheritance; these facts are enough to arouse the deceased's murderous jealousy. Hence the house must be 'cooled'--the idiom is one used in Gusii speech for calming an enraged person--by offering the deceased an animal sacrifice on the first night after burial. If this is not done, the spirit of the deceased (<u>ekerecha</u>) will turn against his or her own survivors and send disaster to them. This is a certainty when the deceased is an adult man of any age or an old woman, but the spirits of young women, like their living counterparts, are less powerful, hence less feared if not placated by sacrifice. Thus the fear of the deceased as spirit to whom mortuary sacrifice is offered corresponds to that person's place in the normative distribution of social power by age and sex.

The narrative of the Gusii funeral includes a story of protection. Before the burial, the corpse is seen as potentially harmful in contacts associated with its unfinished business, and measures of avoidance are taken to protect the living against the deceased. In the burial and treatment of the corpse, however, there is the acknowledgment that the dangerous power attributed to the corpse before burial does not endure after burial; the corpse itself needs protection against the dangers of witches, and this is afforded by the optional postmortem operation, the grave, and the coffin. Once the burial is over, attention shifts to protection of the survivors from the anger of the deceased's spirit, and the entire series of sacrifices is explicitly designed to placate the spirit and ward off the disastrous afflictions it might visit upon the survivors. The policy of protection is enacted not only by sacrifice but by the liminal period of restricted activity for the surviving spouse, which makes the resumption of normal activities and the establishment of a new marital relationship more gradual, and therefore more acceptable to the resentful deceased spouse. By marking this period visibly, particularly its end, the community of kin gives support to the widow or widower in relinquishing a deceased spouse to whom proper respects have been paid and initiating a new life with new relationships. In this new situation, each married son and grandson is required to reconcile its 'house,' that is, family, with the spirit, whose resentment is fading but still dangerous, through a homecoming sacrifice. If this is neglected, the jeopardy of the house is never quite lifted; protective sacrifices will be necessitated at a later time.

This interpretation is one of many possible interpretations of a complex ceremony with multiple layers of meaning. Rather than attempting to decipher all the symbols involved, I have focused on the affects and intentions attributed in Gusii belief to the deceased and the survivors in relation to each other and on the normative prescriptions for action based on these affects and intentions. In the sections that follow, the interpretation is developed further as we explore variations in funerals occasioned by differing status characteristics of the deceased and the affect that is overtly expressed at Gusii funerals.

Variations In Funerals

The funerals of married men and women who have become parents and have living children are the prototypes for all Gusii funerals; those of others are publicly marked as deviant. Thus, Gusii funerals vary in treatment of the corpse, location of the grave, number of people attending, and activity at the funeral, in accordance with the social maturity of the deceased and how death occurred. In this section I examine what these variations indicate about Gusii conceptions of life and its premature termination.

Customary prescriptions for preparation of the corpse and grave location explicitly represent the marital and reproductive progress of the dead person insofar as that person fell short of becoming a mature spouse and parent. An unmarried woman is buried far away from the house, though on homestead land, to represent the sense that she would have been buried elsewhere, at the homestead of the husband she never had, if she had lived on. A woman who was married but had no children is buried with a thorn inserted into each nipple because she had no child to suckle. After the burial, a young chicken, male or female, is trussed and put on her grave 'to cry {i.e., mourn} for her' because 'she had no children of her own to cry for her.' If this were not done, the dead woman would

send affliction to the survivors. When a pregnant
woman dies, the fetus is removed and put beside her
in the coffin. When a young man dies who has been
circumcised but is not ready for marriage yet, an
egesamo hut is built for him, representing the
house he would have lived in had he married. When
a man of marriageable age dies without having
married, he is buried with egechuri, a roof-stick,
beside him in the grave, representing the status he
would have had as a husband with authority over the
house of his wife. (This was done for a 28-year-
old bachelor in 1976; his books and radio were also
put beside him in the coffin, showing his superior
education relative to others in his local age-
cohort.) Finally, in a somewhat different context,
when an old woman dies who has been a diviner
(omoragoori), the iron bracelets known as chindege
worn by diviners must be removed and put beside her
corpse. If she were buried wearing the bracelets,
as one informant said at the funeral of a diviner,
"she might say, 'You put me in a prison with a
chain,' and some afflictions would follow."

These prescriptions show that in treatment of
the corpse and burial, Gusii perform a drama in
which the deceased adult is given a symbolic
fulfillment of marital and reproductive goals that
had not been attained in life. While these
practices give public emphasis to the social
immaturity and incompleteness of the deceased,
their significance is not as criticism or
condemnation. On the contrary, informants left no
doubt that these mortuary practices are addressed
to the deceased, are seen as yielding to his or her
demands, and are performed to prevent the spirit of
the dead person from afflicting the survivors. By
giving the dead posthumous promotions in the
hierarchy of adult statuses based on marriage and
parenthood, the survivors hope to protect
themselves from the resentment of death before

maturity.   As in the case of the diviner whose
bracelets must be properly removed and put beside
her, kin burying a socially immature adult act to
alleviate   the   consequences   of   an   expected
resentment.

Attendance at funerary public gatherings during
1974-1976   ranged   widely,   from   a   dozen   to   a
thousand.   The smallest gatherings were those for
infants, the largest (with some notable exceptions
discussed below) those of elderly men and women.
Thus in a rough way attendance was predictable from
the   level   of   social   maturity   reached   by   the
deceased during his or her lifetime.   The infant is
formally conceptualized as still sharing the social
identity of the mother, who remains alive; the
death is a loss for her and those close to her, but
is   basically   a   domestic   rather   than   community
event.   The elderly person, on the other hand, is
almost   invariably   a   grandparent   and   even   great-
grandparent, thus having reached the most valued
status   in   Gusii   society,   that   of   an   ancestor,
before death.   The identity of such a person is
also   shared   but   by   numerous   descendants   who   have
achieved the status of householders themselves, and
this   in   itself   defines   the   funeral   as   a   public
event   of   broad   significance   in   a   community
organized by kinship.   In addition, however, the
elderly person has lived a long life in which many
other   distinctions   and   widespread   social
connections may have been accumulated--for a man,
leadership   in   war   (before   1908),   government,
community affairs; for a woman, divination and
multiple   associations   formed   through   her   husband
and   her   children's   marriages.   All   of   these
connections and associations engender the desire
to attend the funeral of an old person, a desire
that   goes   beyond   formal   kinship   obligation   and
leads to large public gatherings.

In between the extremes of the infant and the octogenarian, there is also a correspondence, but a much more approximate one, between funeral attendance and the social maturity of the deceased. Those who have been initiated into adult status through circumcision, but have died short of parenthood or even marriage (i.e., those cases cited above as requiring special corpse preparation or burial) are likely to have less well-attended funerals than established householders with children. The latter funerals are obligatory for neighbors in recognition of mutual obligations of support and cooperation among adult householders of a risaga or local community. Attendance at funerals of socially immature adults continues to reflect the social relationships of their parents rather than their own. Thus the funeral of the 28-year-old bachelor previously mentioned was not attended by one major group of closely related neighbors because of a bitter quarrel between them and his parents. Furthermore, the funerals of parents who have borne children bring out many kin and neighbors concerned with the welfare of the children who have lost a parent, particularly their economic future, and this concern leads nowadays to the announcement at the public gathering of a collection of money to help the children. Thus the correspondence between funeral attendance and social maturity for young and middle-aged adults is based less on public evaluations of the amount of maturity achieved by the deceased than it is on the number of ongoing relationships disrupted by the death. Even this approximate correspondence, however, is diminished by the larger gathering for deaths due to accidents and homicide even when the victims are immature, the smaller gatherings for some socially isolated mature persons, and the variable effects of quarrels between homesteads. In other words, for intermediate levels of maturity, many factors other than progress toward more mature status account for the funeral attendance.

There is unmistakable pride in fertility expressed at the funerals of elderly persons who are the ancestors of many living people. At the gathering for a 68-year-old woman, a piece of paper was handed around which listed her dates of birth, marriage and conversion to Christianity, and then her numbers of children, grandchildren, and great-grandchildren (males and females separately), with the total number of progeny at the bottom. At other funerals the summation of accomplished fertility is expressed simply by a large attendance known by everyone to be due to the numerous progeny of the deceased as well as his or her other connections. This interest in quantifying a person's fertility is not exclusive to the funeral situation: an old man of our acquaintance, terminally ill but still active, said he liked to sit on his land and count the number of his descendants and their spouses, the number of people he 'had' in his homestead, of whom he was the patriarch (and for whom he would be the ancestor after death). He was frank enough to reveal what other old people probably do without divulging, namely, counting his descendants. At a funeral, however, this kind of success can be publicly displayed and celebrated by the survivors without concern about jealousy. The mood of such a funeral is one in which everyone is prepared to participate in the enjoyment of the deceased's success; jealousy is attributed to his enemies rather than to those who come to celebrate.

Fertility epitomizes what the Gusii funeral seems designed to celebrate, but several funerals showed that other factors can account for large attendance. One large gathering occurred for a 40-year-old monogamist whose children were not yet married, but he was a high-ranking civil servant in the government of Kenya, a man who resided in Nairobi as part of the elite that current generations aspire to join.   He had also been a member of the Seventh-Day Adventist Church, and his funeral was heavily attended by coreligionists, including pupils in uniform from a nearby SDA school.   Thus the attendance at this man's funeral reflected not his social maturity accomplished through a reproductive and marital career, but his position in a new world of social status outside of kinship and his membership in a new form of community transcending the lineage.

A massive number of people, perhaps 1,000, gathered for the burial of a young unmarried sailor, but he had been murdered at the coast and was buried at home by the Kenya Navy with full military honors.   His murder alone under mysterious circumstances might have been enough too attract a large sympathetic attendance, but the military guard of honor for the corpse, flown in to the rarely used Kisii airstrip, created a public spectacle of unprecedented proportions.   Here again, external recognition compensated for the social immaturity of the deceased in bringing many people to a funeral.   Though funeral attendance is generally correlated with the social maturity and fertility of the person who died--in effect, with that person's status as an ancestor for the living-new forms of social recognition outside of the kinship system can constitute equivalent sources of attraction when the deceased is a man of deficient maturity.

The importance of fertility at funerals of women can be illustrated from another kind of variant life history, that of a co-wife who has died without having children.   As mentioned above, a childless married woman is thought to be

particularly frustrated and resentful at dying in
such an incomplete condition.   If the bridewealth
cattle had been paid for her, her resentment is
intensely shared by her parents and their kin, who
are responsible for returning the bridewealth in
full, since she had borne no children for her
husband's lineage. This amounts to a cancellation
of the implicit wedding contract in which the
bride's family accepted cattle in exchange for her
future offspring.   Her death has brought the
parents a major new economic liability along with
the emotional loss of their daughter.   If their
daughter was married to a polygynist, their
resentment finds a target at the funeral, namely,
the other co-wives, who are typically blamed for
causing her childlessness and her death (through
witchcraft) and wanting to profit from her loss by
taking her property for themselves.   Since the
deceased left no descendants, there is no one to
protect her property from the co-wives after the
funeral is over.   Thus the dead woman's kin (in
1955-1957) came to such a funeral in a state of
rage, attempting to destroy her furniture (if it
was too heavy to carry away) so that the co-wives
would not get it, and sometimes assaulting the co-
wives as well.   Nothing could express more
poignantly the sense of total calamity experienced
at the failure of a woman to become a mother before
death.

The Expression Of Emotion At Funerals

We have seen that many of the ritual actions
of the Gusii funeral are explained by informants
in emotional terms, as ways of preventing harm from
affects attributed to the deceased (e.g., resentment at having died untimely) and as reflecting an
emotional reaction of the survivors to the corpse
(fear of contamination). But as the pride in the

fertility of an old grandparent and the anger at the death of a childless wife suggest, the Gusii funeral is an occasion not only for containing emotion but for expressing it. In fact, at no other Gusii ritual is such a wide range of affects expressed so openly and so intensely. Some affect displays at the funeral are mandatory, some (though not required) are permitted at funerals but on no other occasions, and some exceed the bounds of permissibility even for funerals. All funerary affect displays, including those regarded as excessive, are conventionalized in that they are socially expected and follow recognizable styles of expression. This does not imply that they lack personal meaning, but only that the meanings are conveyed through cultural forms comprehensible to other Gusii attending the funeral. Grief, anger, and fear are the affects most intensely expressed; others are described later.

1. _Grief_. The wailing of Gusii women is long and loud, with a culturally distinctive melodic and rhythmic style that is maintained even when they are sobbing and tears are running down their cheeks. This conventionalized wailing begins when someone is dying and continues on and off for several days, exhausting the close kinswomen of the deceased. There is no distinction between wailing of this sort and what we might think of as 'spontaneous' crying. I was once with a woman when she learned that her four-year-old son had been killed by a car; she immediately began wailing in the standard Gusii style and kept going through the period of most intense grief. On other occasions, too, I observed the most bereaved women wailing this way without lapsing into a style we might consider more 'natural.' I have no reason to believe that conventionalized wailing is not a spontaneous outpouring of grief for Gusii women.

When a wife, mother, sister, or daughter of a
dead person is wailing, anytime between death and
the end of the public gathering, she usually does
a slow shuffling dance in rhythm to the lament,
arms thrust forward and palms turned upward. She
sings an improvised lament sometimes addressed to
the deceased, sometimes to the gathering. To an
outsider, it appears to be a performance directed
toward an audience, but it is not immediately clear
who is the audience or how intentional the
performance. In the first day after death, when
closely related women pour ashes on themselves,
their laments are often addressed to the deceased.
Mothers ask their dead sons, "How could you leave
me?" and beg them to return; they remind the sons
of special treats and favors given them in
childhood, as if to say "Since I was so good to you
then, how can you be so bad to me now?" (This theme
of reciprocation for parental nurturance is a
recurrent one in Gusii cultural narratives about
parent-child relationships.) The dominant affect
is sadness, but it is unmistakably mixed with the
anger of scolding disappointment. In terms of
theories of mourning, it is important to note that
Gusii mourning can and at least sometimes does
include the direct and public expression of anger
to the deceased and the vivid reexperiencing of
affectionate interactions.

Women more distantly related to the dead person
do the same kind of wailing, singing laments and
dancing, often with tears, sobbing and distraught
facial expressions. Wailing becomes subdued during
the grave-digging and filling-in (when it is
theoretically proscribed). Once the grave-diggers
have washed, there is a sudden explosion of grief
as the women hurl themselves onto the grave wailing
loudly, often rolling on the grave, clutching at
the earth, sobbing and singing together. The noise
and sadness of this scene is overwhelming, even to

an observer who knows neither the deceased nor the mourners. After some time, the women begin dancing on the grave, singing laments; this can go on for hours at a large funeral. There can be no question that those women closest to the deceased exhaust themselves in public mourning.

The behavior of men could not be more different. In accordance with Gusii conventions, their expressions of grief are emotionally restrained and circumscribed in time. Men quietly direct the funeral ceremonies, prepare the corpse and dig the grave, read the Christian prayers, deliver formal eulogies at Seventh-Day Adventist funerals, and attentively observe the women express grief. Adult married men rarely weep or sob; the only occasion on which I witnessed it was at a 1974 funeral of a two-year-old boy where his father wept openly. The cattle drive and group intoning at the public gathering have been described above, and the cattle drive is no longer performed in the area of my research. Thus Gusii men are largely quiet participants in an occasion the emotional tone of which is defined by women. This does not mean that men are emotionally untouched by the grief of funerals; on the contrary, several men reported that the women's wailing made them feel mournful and that it was important to them to pay attention to the women's expressions of grief. This helps account for the fact that men do not turn away when women are grieving but watch them carefully.

Gusii men claim they need prompting and external stimulation to overcome their inhibitions enough for even conventional displays of grief. They find this in the women's wailing, the collective encouragement of the group (of men) that stands together to intone, and (in 1974-1976) in the blaring transistor radios and record players. The loud rock music constitutes a din they experience as equivalent to the war cries of the cattle drive and as putting them in the mournful mood appropriate to a funeral. In reporting this, they merge the sadness concerning the loss of the deceased with the vengeful anger of the cattle drive--a merger which apparently reflects both personal experience and social expectation.

By the time of the burial and public gathering, the kinswomen closest to the deceased are often so exhausted that their public display of grief is somewhat subdued, and other women--recent arrivals-are more conspicuous mourners. The outpouring on the grave itself is often their last burst of energetic mourning, as they let others take over for them. The mourning that follows is varied not only by sex but by the individual mourner's relationship to the deceased. At two funerals of elderly women, the most conspicuous mourners, who were dancing on the grave long after others had stopped and weeping and wailing more grievously than anyone else, were some young women and men who I discovered were the deceased's daughter's children. Having worked themselves into an almost frenzied grief, these young people showed by their prolonged and intense display how much their maternal grandmother had meant to them. This is particularly interesting because Gusii children are raised at their father's home and have only intermittent contact with their maternal grandmother who is known in Gusii lore as the primary joking partner for her grandson and the one who calls her daughter's children by their praise-names, that is, the names they are called only at their mother's home and which connote so much warmth and affection that informants report their use brings tears to their eyes. As in other patrilineal and patrilocal societies, so in Gusii the mother's kin, particularly her own mother, symbolize the unalloyed indulgence and emotional warmth that is superseded at (the father's) home by formal authority relations. The result seems to be that these grandchildren mourn with a greater intensity than others at the funeral of an old woman, an intensity which, in the case of her male grandchildren, overcomes their masculine inhibitions about public weeping. Informants confirmed that observed behavior of maternal grandchildren at the two funerals was common and expected.

2.   <u>Anger</u>.   The expression of anger plays an important part at a Gusii funeral. The laments that women sing, before and after the burial, include accusations against alleged murderers and enemies of the deceased and criticism of how the deceased (especially if an elderly widow) had been neglected by her children. In other words, in singing a lament, a woman displays concern for and solidarity with the deceased <u>against</u> others, toward whom righteous anger and moral outrage are expressed. All of these accusations and criticisms would constitute extreme breaches of social convention if uttered on any occasion other than a funeral. Thus the funeral gives license to the public declaration of suspicion and hostile criticism that are normally withheld from all but the most confidential conversations.

At most funerals a mother, daughter, or wife of the deceased publicly claims that the death was caused by other persons, and this is expected. She may sing that the dead man had enemies who were jealous of his cattle or land and who killed him. Sometimes there is a conspiracy theme: When a young woman died in Kisii Hospital (in 1956) after I had taken her there for a cesarean section, her mother sang at the funeral that perhaps I had plotted her death with the hospital attendants (whom I had reported to the authorities for attempting to extract a bribe from the mother at the time of admission). Although I was upset at being accused, the assurances offered me that such funeral allegations were not to be taken seriously proved true; in fact, the woman who made them was never unfriendly to me thereafter. Men attributed this apparent inconsistency to the emotional volatility of women: When they are upset, they make irresponsible charges that are discounted then and forgotten soon afterwards. If a man were to say such things at a funeral, they could not be ignored or forgotten. While it is true that Gusii men are far more restrained in their public statements generally and their funeral expressions in particular, the truth behind female accusations that are not taken seriously is more complex.

The drama of accusation at a Gusii funeral has a public surface that may be consistent or inconsistent with the actual sentiments and beliefs of the local lineage elders who form public opinion and make decisions about actions to be taken. In the public drama the deceased must be portrayed as a victim, killed by the willful intentions of others. Kinswomen close to the deceased make these allegations in histrionic laments because (I believe) they think the deceased is listening and would want to hear it that way. They are giving voice to what they construe as the dead person's reaction to his or her own death, that is, to blame it on enemies or on hitherto unknown conspirators. They do not feel free to blame the deceased for his or her own death, although (as shown below) the elders may believe he or she is responsible for it, or even to claim publicly that the death is attributable to neutral causes that make blame irrelevant--this would seem to them a betrayal of the dead person. The female accusers see their role as making a display of loyalty to the deceased, one that keeps the individual's public image blameless, attributes the death to the evil intent of others, and thereby assures the deceased that they are on his or her side. Having made this gesture at the time they believe the deceased's spirit is nearby--that is, before the house has been 'cooled' by sacrifice--they feel protected against the harm that the spirit's resentment could bring. But they do not necessarily expect that their accusation, formulated for the benefit of the deceased, will be given credence by the others present or lead to action.

This interpretation makes sense of otherwise puzzling material, for example, accusations at the funerals of octogenarians that they were killed by their enemies, when most Gusii generally believe that people can die natural deaths in old age. If the purpose of the women making the accusations is to demonstrate their loyalty to the deceased by aligning themselves with what they believe to be the individual's own view of his or her demise, then the puzzle is removed. The accusations are offered not as a realistic explanation of death, but as comfort for the dead person's spirit and protection for the survivors. This also explains why a well-known Gusii proverb expresses skepticism about funerary witchcraft allegations, which are portrayed as universal but not always believable occurrences. In essence, the claim that a person was killed by the malevolence of others is a last tribute to the deceased, something that everyone is regarded as deserving regardless of the facts of the matter.

When the facts are believed to show that the deceased is responsible for his or her own death, they are not publicly mentioned at the funeral; here the discrepancy between the inevitable public accusations and the actual beliefs of the elders (and others) is unmistakable. In 1957, for

example, a 50-year-old man was dying. The elders,
who believed him to be suffering from the effects
of antitheft medicine that killed his son the year
before, tried to persuade the man to admit his
son's crime and permit counter-magical measures to
be performed. He refused and died. At the
funeral, none of this was mentioned, as his widows
accused a neighbor with whom he had been having a
boundary dispute of having killed him through
witchcraft.   In public, the deceased was
represented as an innocent victim rather than
someone whose own errors or culpability might have
brought death upon him; the latter possibility was
discussed only privately among the senior men of
the neighborhood. Similarly, in 1976 a man said to
be 100 years old fell asleep, drunk, and was
fatally burned in the cooking fire. While we have
no record of what was publicly said at his funeral,
we know from informants that the violent and
painful way he died was believed by funeral
participants to be retribution by the spirits for
several major abominations (chimuma) by the
deceased, and that none of this was openly
discussed at the burial or public gathering. Three
days later the survivors were preparing to perform
the ritual remedies for the deceased's wrongdoings,
but the latter had been concealed at the funeral
itself.

There are limits to the public representation
of the deceased as a victim of wrongdoing by
others. These were reached at the funeral in 1975
of a 69-year-old diabetic man who had been drinking
heavily, against medical advice. The story
circulated during the funeral that a rat from his
grass roof had bitten him on the toe while he was
asleep, that the wound had not healed, and he had
died from it. People are rarely bitten by rats in
Gusiiland, and since rats are associated with
witches in Gusii belief, women sang at the funeral

that a witch had sent a rat to kill him.   In this
case, however, the adult sons of the deceased, who
feared that someone within the homestead would be
accused, causing strife among the survivors (four
co-wives and their children), intervened publicly
to reject the witchcraft explanation and declare
that he had died of diabetes.   This shows that the
witchcraft accusations at funerals are not always
taken simply as gestures to placate the deceased
that can be discounted in terms of their
interpersonal consequences for the living.   When
adult men responsible for the welfare of the
survivors decide that funeral accusations will lead
to division within the family, they will refute a
divisive explanation in favor of one that is free
of blame.

In other instances, however, the death gives
rise to so much blame and division before the
burial that there is no realistic possibility of
pragmatically suppressing or refuting the
accusations of malevolence.   In 1975, an eight-
year-old girl died, allegedly the victim of
poisoning by her paternal grandfather's wife (not
the girl's grandmother, who was dead), who had been
involved in serious disputes with the parents of
the girl.   The deceased was said to have told the
story of her poisoning just before she died.
Shortly afterward, the accused woman disappeared,
an act interpreted as proving her guilt.   For the
burial of an immature girl, the funeral was heavily
attended with perhaps 75 kin present, and the
atmosphere was unusually tense.   The grave was dug
to a depth of 12 feet, indicating the prevalent
opinion that the dead girl had been the victim of
witchcraft and would be the target of cannibalistic
attack after burial.   One woman sang a lament
accusing the grandfather of being an accomplice in
the killing, since he permitted his wife to escape.
No one argued with this claim.   After the coffin

was placed in the grave, the grandfather descended with a knife and opened the abdomen of the corpse to relieve the swelling and permit inspection by the elders, who stood at the head of the grave. Although the grandfather did this to prove his innocence and demonstrate his protective concern for the deceased, his act did not assuage the anger of the girl's mother, who shortly thereafter set fire to the house of the accused woman.   The grandfather himself disappeared, rejoining his wife at this land in a settlement scheme in the Rift Valley.   In this case, the public accusation at the funeral expressed anger that was consistent with actual community opinion and led to violent action and the dissolution of the homestead as an intergenerational domestic group.

The possibility of such cataclysmic outcomes from blame assigned at funerals is never completely out of mind, particularly for those men who assume responsibility for the care of survivors. Seventh-Day Adventists deal with this problem by preventive denial: At the funeral of a high-ranking civil servant described in an earlier section, leaders of the Adventist community explicitly stated in their speeches that the deceased had died of disease and no one should be blamed for his death.   Their intent was that of the traditional Gusii leader seeking to preserve unity and prevent division, but their style--attempting to suppress the opposing voices of the fractious women--contrasts sharply with the pluralistic expressive style of the Gusii funeral.

The description of anger as an affect expressed at funerals has carried us more deeply into the meaning of death for the Gusii. The accusations uttered by lamenting women leave no doubt that they view the deceased in the following terms: He (or she) believes himself to have been singled out for deprivation, is jealous of those not so deprived, wants to hear that his deprivation was an attack by others (primarily those he had previously suspected of wishing him ill), seeks retaliation against them, welcomes demonstrations of loyalty from allies in this retaliatory intent. This can be seen as selectively interpreting death in the idiom of segmentary opposition, a model of intergroup and interpersonal relations that is pervasive in Gusii social life and was a source of pride for men in precolonial patterns of feuding and warfare. When warriors retaliated against the attacks of other clans or lineages, they mobilized kin against the attackers, acting to protect the interests of the local agnatic group. In this context, retaliation was a form of moral action, associated with collective ideals. Thus when a man died, the warriors who came to pay their respects to him brought their cattle and weapons, enacting a drama of military retaliation as a means of identifying the deceased with this worthy cause regardless of the actual conditions of his death. Brandishing their spears against his invisible and unidentified killers, they publicly asserted his claim to the status of a group martyr whose death should be avenged. Awarding him this honor, they showed their loyalty in the way that mattered most in the segmentary Gusii context--by opposing his enemies.

The women's funeral accusations echo this traditional theme of martyrdom, assimilated to the more mundane (and nowadays more dangerous) realm of domestic and neighborhood relationships. Invoking actual persons and ongoing disputes, their attempts to portray the deceased as a victim of external attack involve the risk of exacerbating conflicts between persons and segments and must be dealt with by the men, who discount or contradict them as much as the situation permits. The women, taking advantage of their low status and low credibility, feel freer to sing openly what everyone suspects, leaving those in authority with the task of assessing the validity of these claims and acting upon them. In funerals as in other Gusii rites, women play the role of the Shakespearean fool, expressing emotions that men disavow. But men and women are united in offering to the deceased the comfort of a martyr's death in the narrative drama of the funeral. Indeed, the Gusii funeral embodies a code for interpreting death in terms of opposition and vengeance.

3. Fear. Unlike grief and anger, which are publicly expressed at Gusii funerals, fear has no place in the ritual performance—it is assumed to be the motivation that lies behind it. In conventional belief, all of the prescribed burial practices, sacrifices, and other propitiatory measures of the funeral are explained as motivated by fear of the corpse's danger or the spirit's vengeful wrath, but their enactment normally proceeds without direct reference to that affect, as if it were precluded from experience by participation in the ritual. From this perspective, the standard funeral ritual consists of a series of precautionary responses to a potentially fearful situation.

Sometimes, however, the potential for fear arousal is realized at a funeral. In 1976, a mother of ten children died two years after her husband was killed in a motor accident; in the interim his brother, residing next door, had died. It was widely believed that the brother, jealous of the academic success of his nieces, had engaged in sorcery which killed the couple but also backfired on him. The rapid succession of deaths suggested to the survivors, as to others, that the sorcery medicines threatened to exterminate the entire homestead and perhaps that of the uncle as well.

At her mother's funeral, the eldest daughter was distraught; she appeared grief-stricken in the extreme. Conversation with her indicated, however, that the intensity of her distress was due to fear that her brothers and sister, if left at home, would be killed; within a week, she had moved them out of the homestead to kin living in distant places.

This case exemplifies a general principle, namely, that when a death is classified as affliction (sent by ancestors, witches, or sorcerers), it is seen as a sign that the homestead of the deceased will be annihilated and therefore arouses great fear as well as grief. During the funeral ritual, the distress of the mourners, particularly the survivors themselves, reflects their feelings of terror concerning the future embedded in conventional expressions of grief but understood to communicate their fear and sadness. In Gusii belief, afflictions (<u>emechando</u>) threaten the lives not of a single individual but all who share his or her fate, particularly spouses and children. The common fate of homestead members, those who share a domestic community of production, reproduction, and distribution, is nowhere more starkly illustrated than in their belief that the death of one may mean the death of all. The fear that a person's death signifies group extinction lies behind much of contemporary Gusii reliance on ritual, not only in funerals but in divination, healing, and sacrifice outside the mortuary setting.

Affects other than grief, anger, and fear are in evidence at Gusii funerals, though they may not be as overtly or frequently expressed in word and action. The emotional moods of pride and shame at funerals of those who died after complete or incomplete reproductive careers, respectively, have

been described above.   Except at Seventh-Day
Adventist funerals, with their eulogies explicitly
based on American models, however, these feelings
were expressed largely in the numbers of people
attending, the collective mood they generated, and
their private conversations about the deceased
afterwards. For the participants, these implicit
messages conveyed by the selective attendance and
nonattendance of particular persons and their
behavior at the public gathering, are unequivocal.
In addition to pride and shame, there is the
expression of love through grief, particularly by
maternal grandchildren or adult sisters of the
deceased, that is, persons who no longer reside in
the homestead and are not part of the group whose
mourning is most prescribed by convention.   They
come to the funeral from a distance and voluntarily
convey their emotional attachment through intense
and demonstrative grieving over the loss.   The
conventional structure of the Gusii funeral
requires the expression of grief but permits other
affects to be communicated in largely indirect ways
that are nonetheless noticed and understood by the
mourners themselves. Thus, each funeral, though
following a cultural formula, is a unique event in
terms of which emotions are expressed and by whom.

Summary And Conclusion

In this article I have approached Gusii
funerals as dramas communicating the terms in which
life and death are collectively experienced in a
Gusii community.   Description of the dramas
included their prescribed physical setting, the
standard script for ritual action, variations in
script and performance according to individual life
histories and circumstances of death, and the
performance as a vehicle of emotional expression.
In seeking meanings, I have used exegetical,

operational, and positional evidence as conceptualized by Turner (1967: 50-52), and I have also been guided by the advice of Huntington and Metcalf (1979: 53-54) that 'close attention to the symbolic attributes of the dead body provides an avenue into a culture's understanding of the nature of death.'

Despite the Gusii funeral's abundance of elements suitable for analysis of symbols in the styles established by Durkheim, Freud, or Levi-Strauss (representations of social groups and positions, phallic and vaginal images, binary oppositions and inversions, respectively), my focus has been on the characters of the drama, particularly the emotions and intentions attributed to them, as accounting for the central narrative action of the ritual. A ritual thus described and interpreted can be seen as embodying a narrative about self and others in interaction--one of numerous cultural narratives about the self that communities transmit and revise in accordance with their current sense of self. I found Gusii funerals, despite some structural changes in their script, to have retained their basic narrative content (i.e., the emotions and intentions attributed to the deceased and survivors in interaction) over a 20-year period, and I proceeded on the assumption that this content represented collectively shared concepts and expectations of the self and of relationships between the self and others.

The Gusii funeral takes place entirely at the home of the deceased, is conducted by closely related kin and is permeated in its narrative content by imagery derived from domestic architecture and domestic kinship, which retains many of the meanings it has in everyday life. In the funeral narrative, relationships with deceased persons are represented as though they were living kin, with emphasis given to attributes associated with their social positions and genealogical connections rather than those associated with their personal idiosyncrasies.   Kopytoff (1971) has argued that a distinction between living elders and dead ancestors is not made in the indigenous verbal categories of many African (particularly Bantu) societies and is denied by the continuity of ritual attitudes toward elders, dead or alive.   So it is with the Gusii, who refer to the spiritually active dead elders as <u>chisokoro</u>, 'grandfathers,' a term referring to living kinsmen as well.   Their funeral narrative, however, portrays the deceased of any age or status in continuity with expectations of him or her as a living member of the homestead, and the rituals are explained as prescribed ways of coping with the expectable response such a person would have at suffering a major misfortune.   Thus the Gusii funeral narrative does not depict a distinctive world of spirits but is directly constructed from the expectancies of domestic relationships.

The interpretive summary that follows gives emphasis to those parts of the funeral narrative I believe to be particularly revealing of the sense of self in the Gusii community studied.

1. As soon as a person is defined as dying, his or her positional identity (as a man or woman of a particular stage of social maturity, identi-fied with a particular house in a particular home-stead and in certain kin relationships) becomes the salient focus of attention, determining location of dying, placement and treatment of the corpse, location of the grave and who digs it, who attends the funeral, and so forth.   The drama of social identity, largely predictable from background facts about the deceased, constitutes the setting in

which many more variable themes and feelings are
expressed, but is also of great personal significance in itself. Contemporary Gusii feel strongly
about dying at home in the proper place with a
proper house and with grandsons to dig the grave;
they go to great lengths and considerable expense
to locate their deaths and funerals in the
appropriate social space.

2. The representation of the deceased in the
funeral narrative is split: corpse and spirit of
the same deceased person have different properties.
The corpse is dangerous to those associated with
pregnancy and retaliatory processes, processes
regarded as incomplete in Gusii belief, and it can
kill them (thus terminating those processes)
through contact with the earth in which it is
buried. But the corpse's dangers act automatically
(and only until the burial is over) rather than as
the represented outcome of the deceased's intention
or emotional response. Furthermore, the corpse is,
itself, dangerously vulnerable, and ritual measures
at the grave are directed to its protection from
harm. The spirit, by contrast, is never portrayed
as vulnerable, only dangerous to all the survivors
in the homestead, and is represented as angry,
resentful, and intending to kill them. Its dangers
are prolonged and must be dealt with through
sacrifice over an extended period. The attribution
of persistent emotion to the spirit is particularly
evident in the ritual transition of a widow from
the state of mourning to a leviratic union with her
husband's brother or (patrilineal) cousin: they
reveal a concern that someone (presumably the
deceased) considers the new relationship to be
adultery, despite the fact that it is a public
obligation inherent in bridewealth marriage.
Though everyone knows the levirate to be customary
and obligatory, the ritual deals with the
possibility that it could be interpreted as

adulterous, a possibility based (I believe) on the
idea that the deceased remains a sexually jealous
presence, unwilling to relinquish control over his
wives' sexuality.   The split between corpse and
spirit as images of the deceased reveals two
stories of vengefulness, in one case emanating from
weakness and automatically threatening an immediate
termination to ongoing activity; in the other,
vengeance emanating from authority and deliberately
threatening   long-term   destruction   unless
appropriate placation is offered.

3. Variations in treatment of the corpse and
burial by age and reproductive maturity are
particularly revealing of Gusii expectancies
concerning the life goals of adult men and women.
Every deceased is represented as deprived and
vengeful, but those who had not achieved parenthood
are given symbolic substitutes to compensate for
what is believed to be their greatest deprivation.
In response to the imagined disappointment of the
dead person, he or she is awarded in the burial a
state of social maturity higher than that actually
achieved: the unmarried woman is buried farther
away (to symbolize her husband's home), the
pregnant woman is buried with the fetus beside her
like a child, the person without a house is built
a hut to be buried by, etc.   The mortuary ritual
thus embodies an empathic response to the dead
person's sense of frustration at not becoming a
householder, spouse, or parent, based on the
assumption that each person wants that progress
along the Gusii stages of social maturity more than
anything else.   The only exceptions are those men
whose visible pubic positions in the national
society are viewed as compensating for their
deficiencies in reproductive progress toward
ancestorhood.

4. Although the emotional expressiveness of men and women at funerals is polarized in the extreme, the messages they intend to communicate to the deceased are remarkably concordant. Men, in the customary cattle drive and show of weapons, gave a dead man a warrior's farewell by feigning an attack on his imagined (but unidentified) enemies; in precolonial days, this sometimes led to an attack on other Gusii clans. Women, in their contemporary accusations at funerals (to which the men pay close attention), strive for the same end, namely to display loyalty to the deceased by publicly opposing his or her imagined enemies--even when the deceased is very old and not a plausible murder victim. Here again the survivors empathize with what they imagine to be the deceased's emotional reaction to his or her own death, namely, the sense that he or she was done in by enemies, and they attempt to placate the deceased's spirit at the public gathering by 'feuding' on his or her behalf. Since this feuding is potentially dangerous, now more than ever, it has devolved upon women, whose accusations can be more easily contradicted or subsequently discounted, to engage in this form of public expression. The general posture of survivors toward the deceased, and the assumption on which it is based--namely, that the dead consider themselves murder victims and are comforted by displays of promised vengeance--remain salient among the Gusii.

This interpretative summary of narratives contained in Gusii funerals is offered as a series of hypotheses about the meanings Gusii assign to life, death, and the central relationships involved in both. These meanings are central to social processes in contemporary Gusii communities, and I am proposing that they are also central to the psychological well-being of contemporary Gusii individuals. They reveal the terms in which loss, separation, and deprivation are construed and the ideas chosen to compensate for the emotional disruption that begins at death.   These hypotheses about the generality of the meanings in funeral narratives can be tested by examining other Gusii rituals that deal with different threats to psychological well-being and by examining how individuals use rituals in coping with stress--in material to be presented elsewhere.

References

Bradbury, R.E. 1965. Father and Senior Son
    in Edo Mortuary Ritual. African Systems of
    Thought, eds. M. Fortes and G. Dieterlen.
    London: Oxford University Press.

Fortes, M. 1971. On the Concept of the Person
    Among the Tallensi. La Notion de Personne en
    Afrique Noire. Paris: Colloques de la
    Recherche Scientifique. 544: 284-319.

Huntington, R., and P. Metcalf. 1979.
    Celebrations of Death: The Anthropology of
    Mortuary Ritual. Cambridge: Cambridge
    University Press.

Kopytoff, I. 1971. Ancestors as Elders.
    Africa 41: 129-142.

Mayer, P. 1949. The Lineage Principle in Gusii
    Society. International African Institute
    Memorandum No. XV.

Turner, V.W. 1967. The Forest of Symbols.
    Ithaca, N.Y.: Cornell University Press.

Wilson, M.H. 1957. Rituals of Kinship Among the
    Nyakyusa. London: Oxford University Press.

II. RELATIONSHIP BETWEEN THE DECEASED AND THE SURVIVOR

GUILT AND POLLUTION IN
SEBEI MORTUARY RITUALS

Walter Goldschmidt

Introduction

In this paper I examine the rituals surrounding
death among the Sebei of Uganda. I want in
particular to show that these customs relate on the
one hand to the structural characteristics of Sebei
society and on the other to the individual
motivations and the intrapsychic tensions of the
mourners. These internal attitudes of the actors
in the recurrent drama of death are seen to involve
generalizable qualities of personal motivation and
emotions as they are evoked by the social situation
that a death creates. I am aware that causal
explanations cannot be established on the basis of
single instances and, in fact, I have no interest
in extrapolating from Sebei ritual behavior to
funerary practices in general. My aim is at once
more modest and more ambitious: in seeking an
understanding of the particular character of Sebei
customs I am suggesting a paradigm for the
understanding of ritual in terms of the
contrapuntal relationship between individual
motivation and structural context. Like all
single-instance analyses, the principles involved
are illustrated, rather than proved.

Reprinted from Ethos 1, no. 1 (1973): 75-
105. Reproduction by permission of the American
Anthropological Association. Not for further
reproduction.

131

The customary procedures with respect to Sebei funerals described here are based on informants' statements and five funerals I observed. The general description will be followed by a detailed presentation of the funeral of a man I shall call Cherkut, so that we may see the expressions of interpersonal sentiments in the context of these customary procedures. This will give substance to the theoretical discussion at the close, in which I relate the ritual content to the guilt-provoking behavior that a funeral induces.

The Sebei are a Kalenjin-speaking people living on the north slope of Mount Elgon. Some two or three centuries ago the ancestors of modern Sebei were a predominantly (though not exclusively) pastoral people who, after they reached the well-watered slopes of Mount Elgon, added to the traditional millet, sorghum, and root crops the use of plantains, which they learned from their Bantu neighbors to the west, and thus became increasingly sedentary. A process of cultural adaptation to the new ecologic situation was going on when European overrule brought a new set of circumstances early in this century, influencing all aspects of their social and economic life, but not destroying their domestic institutions and patterned attitudes. The Sebei terrain offers varied environmental opportunities, and my research was particularly concerned with the differential character of cultural adjustment to the diverse ecological circumstances (Goldschmidt 1965). Thus we must take cognizance of the differentials in funeral practices that developed in response to both European influence and ecological adaptation.

Sebei society is acephalous, organized into agnatic clans subdivided into shallow lineages that form corporate groups for legal but not property-controlling activities. They have a cycling age-set system comparable to the Nandi and other Kalenjin tribes, and recognize spatial units consisting of the 'sangta', a dispersed village, and the 'pororyet', a larger region. Marriage is clan exogamous, polygynous, and involves a bride price in cattle and other goods; in many respects the wife is viewed as a member of her husband's clan, with leviratic inheritance of widows ideally by the next junior brother but subject to diverse specific considerations.

Customary Funerary Rituals

General Features

Death rituals are more important when a man dies than when a woman or child dies. The major events subsequent to a man's death are: (1) the burial itself, which takes place on the day of death or the morning following; (2) the ceremony of chasing away death (<u>kopuntoyet ap met</u>), or purification rite, which normally takes place on the fourth day after the death; and (3) a final release of the widows from mourning, involving ritual sexual intercourse between the widow or widows and the man who is to inherit them, which takes place some time after the purification rite. If both the deceased and the man who inherits his widows have cattle, there will be a fourth ceremony a month or more later which establishes amity between the two herds. Legal matters integrated into these ceremonies involve a public hearing of all indebtedness claimed against the estate, the determination of the person or persons who are to inherit the widows, and the allocation of the deceased's stock and personal possessions among the heirs.

The persons chiefly involved with the death are

the widows, full brothers, and sons of the man, but involvement extends to all his clansmen, the wives of his brothers, his mother's clan, and the people of the village, in diminishing importance as the relationship becomes more remote. One man, properly the next full brother, or, if he is an old man, the first son of the first wife, may be thought of as a chief mourner; he is spoken of as the one who 'buries' the deceased. This expression may be used in ordinary conversation while both are still living, as a means of pointing up the close social relationships between the two men. It is he who should receive the body in the grave, engage in the ceremonial sexual intercourse with the widows and inherit them, and serve as custodian of the estate held in trust for the minor sons of the dead man, though he may in fact do none of these things or only some of them. Other special functionaries in the performance of the funeral rites can best be discussed in the context of the roles they perform. All clansmen (whether in the area or not) and all the people of the village (whether kin or not) are expected to observe a period of mourning by refraining from all work, except milking and herding cattle, and no ceremonies are to be held 'as far as the next stream in either direction.' Clansmen but not fellow villagers are also expected to refrain from sexual intercourse. Both categories of people are expected to attend the rituals of interment and purification; failure to do so would suggest hatred toward the deceased and this in turn would rouse the suspicion of responsibility for the death.

Disposal of the Body

If a man dies early in the mourning, he may be buried in the same day; but if it is later in the day it will be delayed until the following morning, as the stock should not be released from the <u>kraal</u> until his body has been disposed of and because it is desirable that his brothers and sons have an opportunity to view the body, if witchcraft is suspected. The body is supposed to be placed in that part of the house of the first wife set aside for visitors, though some informants say that it is "dangerous" to take the body inside if the man was not already in the house at the time of death.

The Sebei formerly disposed of the body by placing it on the ground in an open area and letting the hyenas devour the cadaver, as did many of their Kalenjin neighbors.[1] Two brothers or sons carried the body to a satisfactory location, laying it on its right side (left for a woman) with its face to the west. The bones of prophets and twins were later recovered and buried in a cave or a crevice in the rocks; but there was no further interest in the bodily remains of others. This custom was replaced under European influence with interment, which is now universally practiced. As might be expected with respect to a relatively recent innovation, there is some flexibility and uncertainty regarding some of the details of interment.

People arriving at a funeral exchange no greetings with one another or with the family of the deceased, though they may speak freely of other matters. The relatives, particularly the women, may keen before the body or at the grave, especially on first arrival, and some women fling themselves on the ground and beat it while expressing their grief, or (I was told) kiss the face of the deceased.

The grave is dug near the house of the first wife, in that area where they throw refuse. The gravediggers (<u>bolik ap mwenet</u>) are preferably brothers or clan brothers of the deceased, but may be either the sisters' husbands or the wives' brothers, and may be from the mother's clan or merely friends. They must be married men whose wives are not pregnant, and "the people who are most affected are the real brothers and they <u>should</u> do it; if they are available and don't do it, people would criticize them."

The personal ornaments of the deceased, arm and neck rings and the like (except one bracelet), are removed and placed in the house of the first wife. Before interment nowadays the body is washed. I was given conflicting information of the kin who were expected to do this, and was also told that the custom is so new "that we don't have a name for that." After washing, the clothes are replaced and the body is wrapped in white sheeting of the kind known in East Africa as 'americani.'

Two persons enter the grave to receive the body. These functionaries (<u>tupik ap musto</u>) may not be the same individuals who dug the grave, but the same categories of kin are drawn upon and they, like the gravediggers, become ritually unclean. The man at the head should be the inheriting kin, but the matter is not consistent. The body is placed on the sleeping mats of the deceased (formerly his stool was placed in the grave with him), he is covered with blankets, cloth, banana fronds, or the like, and the grave is covered and carefully tamped. I was told that it was particularly bad luck for the earth on the grave to form cracks. The implements used for digging and covering the grave are set aside and must be ritually cleansed. The grave is unmarked, except the grave of a twin, when a piece of hard wood is placed on the grave so that it can be located for subsequent rituals or for disinterment. Some modern Christians mark the grave with a wooden cross, but these disappear in time.

After the interment, the widows of the deceased remain in the house of the first wife, attended by a woman who must herself be a widow. No other persons should enter it. They are under special ritual restrictions, and no ashes may be removed from the house. The men who dug the grave and the two who received the body are under lesser ritual restrictions; they may not greet people (but can enter into conversations), may not go to where there is beer (but may drink what is brought to them) and they may not have sexual intercourse.

The Ceremony of 'Chasing Away Death'

The ceremony of 'chasing away death' (<u>kopuntoyet ap met</u>) takes place on the fourth day after the burial (or on the third day for a twin or the father of a twin). If the man is wealthy in stock, his herd bull (<u>kintet</u>) should be slaughtered, the chyme strewn on the path to the stream or (in the case of twins only) smeared on the body of the deceased, and the meat distributed in accordance with clearly prescribed rules. In both funerals for cattle-rich men witnessed by me, the actual herd bull was not killed but, for practical reasons, a substitute bull was provided. In cattle-poor areas no bull is slaughtered, but a ram (uncastrated and with horns) is substituted; nobody discussed a division of meat under such circumstances. When a bull is slaughtered, this is done by spear and the person who does the spearing should be compensated by the family of the deceased. The ram is suffocated.

After the slaughter but before the distribution of the meat the mourners are shaved. The man who has 'buried' the deceased, other brothers (especially those who have been in the grave to receive the body) and their wives, and the widows are expected to be shaved; others may do so if they wish. Formerly, many relatives were shaved, but since the Sebei have been dropping the style of shaved heads, fewer undergo this part of the ritual. Persons standing in the relationship of mother or father, brother, brother's wife or unmarried sister, and son, son's wife, and unmarried daughter may be shaved; sisters and daughters who are married may not be shaved; ritually, a woman is associated with her husband's clan.

All persons except widows are cleanly shaved in the open by anyone; but the widows must be shaved behind a screen, where they cannot be seen, by a woman who has lost her husband, with tufts of hair left so that people will know they are in mourning. They are also sprinkled on the head and down the right side with ashes, taken not from the hearth but from where they have been discarded. Ashes are placed in her vagina.

All those who have been shaved next file to the stream to bathe, preceded by two persons who go to warn others away, as it is extremely bad luck for anyone to see them during this mission. They go by way of a 'left hand' path and return by a different route, on the 'right' side. There is a strong interdiction against their looking behind them at any time on this journey. En route, they scatter their hair in the bushes. At the stream the men go upstream and the women downstream to bathe, and when all are finished they return to the house of the deceased.[2] The widows are no longer screened from sight after their bath. (At a funeral in Benet, high up on Mount Elgon, they did not go to the stream but washed in water brought to the site and placed in a cowhide because, they say, "they have been going to the river all the time and the people continue to die," and therefore have stopped that custom.)

The mourners now turn to matters regarding the property of the deceased. His personal belongings are brought out, an elder of the clan smears them with fat (tail fat of a ram or kidney fat of a bull) and spews beer on them. They may now be taken by others; normally the spear and shield by the oldest son of the first wife, the panga (machete) and beer tube (the Sebei drink beer from a common pot) by a widow, and other items in accordance with private arrangements. A moot is held, under the leadership of the senior member of the clan or lineage, in which all claims against the estate are made public by the creditors. These may be discussed, clarified, or disputed and should be resolved when possible, though I have seen disgruntled claimants leave muttering threats to take a case to court. At any rate, making the public statement establishes a legal claim, and a debt not stated at this time is, in principle at least, no longer legally recognized. This normally ends the activities involved in chasing the death away.

                    The Release of the Widows

The widows remain under restriction for a period called sororo. The man who has 'buried' the deceased and is to inherit the widows moves into the house of the first wife, together with the other widows, if any. They are not to be seen by others, engage in any work nor sexual relations, and are under dietary restrictions with respect to meat and certain foods. (Those foods specifically mentioned were all wild plants and fungi, not cultigens.) Their meals are prepared for them.

They may not use sleeping mats, but sleep on leaves; they are not supposed to scratch themselves with their fingers but must use sticks; they are not allowed to touch their food but must use a pointed stick or leaves. The ashes should not be removed from the hearth. These restrictions are quite like those applicable to initiates after their circumcision, though presumably the analogy is the other way about; that is, the ritual of circumcision is likened to the consequences of death.

The final ritual involves the ceremonial eating of the meat and vegetable foods that have been interdicted and the sexual intercourse, which is referred to as 'cleaning out the ashes.' Just when it takes place is variable, whether because of differences in time, place, acculturation or circumstance, I am not entirely sure. Some said it takes place on the third day after the purification ritual, others said that for an important man it takes place on the second dark of the moon after the death. What is clear and consistent is, first, that there should be prepared a kind of stew involving each of the foods that were taboo, together with a bit of each part of the meat of an animal (bull or ram), and that these should be partaken of by the widows, their children, and the man who is to inherit them. Second, the man who is to inherit the widows is to have sexual intercourse with each of the wives successively, in order of their marital priority, to make them keyanyiny, good, clean.

Some Variant Funeral Practices

Funeral practices are subject to variation; they have changed over the years, they are somewhat variant in different parts of Sebei, and they vary

in accordance with the social circumstances of the
deceased. Women, twins and the parents of twins,
old people, and infants are socially different from
men; this difference is reflected in their
funerals.

The funeral of a woman, though ritually in a
similar manner, lacks many of the features
attendant upon the death of a man. As she has no
property other than a few personal belongings, it
is not necessary to hold a moot. As the husband's
status is far less changed by a woman's death,
there is less ritual involvement.   I did not
witness a funeral for a woman or a child.

The woman's funeral is handled by the clansmen
of her husband, for in all matters pertaining to
death there is a reaffirmation of her membership in
her husband's clan. The corpse is handled in the
same way as a man's except that she lies on her
left rather than on her right side. If she is
pregnant, the fetus is removed and either buried
beside her or, if after the seventh month, in a
separate grave. (If it is a first child and a son,
I was told, the father must pay an extra cow in
bride price, as his 'spear' had killed the mother.)
The husband is under restriction and the cleansing
ceremony held after four days, with the shaving,
the bathing, and the rest. Someone must be
appointed to cook for him, as his other wives
should not do so. "But if he has no wives, he may
take care of himself; it is not important."

Twins and the parents of twins evoke certain
considerations. The community does not cease to
work during the period of mourning, but only those
quite closely related; the personal ornaments are
not removed but are buried with a twin; the shaving
ceremony takes place on the third day rather than
on the fourth; a ram is slaughtered and tail fat

placed in the mouth of the dead twin, he is smeared with its chyme. Most important of all, as already noted, the grave is marked, the bones are subsequently removed and placed in a cave. Furthermore, surviving twins and parents of twins cannot take any principal role in the rites connected with funerals: "They are free of everything; they cannot even weep." During the night of the circumcision, a surviving twin, or the child following the twins (kisa) if both are dead, goes to the grave of the dead twin and smears earth from it on his face.

A man or woman who dies at a very old age (so old that he no longer engages in active affairs) has what is known as a sweet death (kelil), and under such circumstances none of the funeral rites described above is performed. Rather, the body is laid out in an open place or under a tree, on his sleeping skin, with his beer straw, his spear and, if he was a smoker, his pipe beside him. His grandchildren and great-grandchildren are told to go and see him, that they may enjoy a long life such as he has had; they may laugh and enjoy themselves; they sing the song of welcome as at a wedding or after a circumcision.

Infants who die in childbirth or shortly after childbirth are buried unceremoniously by the mother near her house or within it, in that part where the goats and calves are kept. Older children are, however, buried with more ceremony. When a child of nursing age dies, the father digs the grave and the mother is the one to step inside and arrange the body. There is crying, as for an adult, but not many attend and strict mourning is not kept. The father remains with the mother at night, but they do not have sexual intercourse, and the cooking is done by another wife or a young girl.

The Funeral of Cherkut

The generalized account of Sebei funerary
practices can be better understood, and some of the
attitudes and sentiments involved may be better
seen, if we examine in detail the actions of one
particular event. For this purpose I describe the
funeral of a neighbor, whom I will call Cherkut,
living near Sasur in the plantain-growing area of
western Sebeiland.   Cherkut had been ill as the
result of an injury and I had driven him to the
dispensary at the Sipi Mission a few days earlier.
A man in his forties, he had one wife and his
oldest child was an as yet uncircumcised teen-age
boy.   His father had been a local chief, was
apparently quite well off and had had eight wives,
so there was a large family of close relatives.   I
was discussing clan matters with a group of
neighbors when news came of Cherkut's death, and
with that news came speculation as to its cause.
By the next morning this discussion had reduced
itself to three theories: (1) that he had drunk
beer (more likely warage, the native-made gin) and
later been given an injection at the dispensary, a
combination thought to be lethal; (2) that he had
been in a fight with one of his brothers who had
kicked him in the chest, and that this blow had
caused the death; and (3) that a relative, who
disappeared when the death was announced, had
engaged in magic. As we shall see, these theories
are not mutually exclusive.

As I went with my interpreter to Cherkut's house
the morning after the death, I was told of a new
custom of requesting money from those present; when
I made my donation, I noticed that most had given
a standard two shillings, as recorded in a booklet.
The body was laid out on a cot under the veranda of
the house, and the women were standing near it or

sitting on the grassy slope. Most of the men were watching the four gravediggers, who used an ordinary hoe and a pan to remove the earth. Some of the brothers asked me to take pictures of them together with the corpse. While I was doing so, a lorry stopped on the nearby road, and one of Cherkut's sisters came running and wailing and flailed herself about on the grass in front of the corpse. From time to time other women also wailed. (Ngumui, one of Cherkut's brothers, said with disgust: "What's the use of that?" But later, when they were lowering the body, he muttered something about being afraid and unable to watch, and he absented himself until the grave was nearly covered.) There had been no formalized wailing during the preceding night, but I was told that the sisters and brothers' wives had sat with the body.

In a short time one brother returned from the shop with white sheeting, sewn into an envelope large enough to receive the body. Cherkut's body was taken to the head of the grave and placed on banana fronds; they put on his trousers and removed his kansu. Two of his sisters then washed his body with soap and water, as far down as his waist and up his legs as far as possible without removing the trousers. (A woman nearby remarked: "What's the use of that?") The kansu was replaced, the body was placed in the cloth envelope and was bound with strips of the same cloth, beginning at the legs. After a delay, waiting for the lay reader of the Protestant Church (who proved unavailable), a prayer book was produced and one of the brothers and my interpreter read in unison a prayer in Luganda (the language of the Baganda; no religious material has been translated into Sebei).

By this time the grave, dug by two of Cherkut's brothers to a depth of about four feet, had been lined with banana fronds, over which was placed

Cherkut's sleeping mat and a new inexpensive mattress. The body was passed to the brothers, he was covered with his blankets, banana stalk sections were placed around him "to make him comfortable," and the whole was covered with fronds. The two brothers then got out of the grave and went to wash, while other brothers and sisters began replacing the earth, one man carefully tamping down the earth with his feet.

The grave was completely covered and many people were beginning to leave when an argument flared up. One of the brothers pointed to a man, asking angrily what he was doing sitting among Cherkut's clansmen inasmuch as he had killed a man of that clan. (He had served a prison sentence for the killing, and thus had not paid indemnity to the clan which would have erased the enmity.)

When I arrived at the ceremony on the fourth day, the mother of Cherkut was haranguing the large group sitting on the grassy slope in front of the house, regarding M. She claimed M had run away when her husband died, that he comes back at night and they "find broken roots on the grave" the next morning. One brother: "When our father was [a government-appointed] chief, he brought M here from the plains and kept him as a servant. When he married, our father even paid for his wife, who is here now, and he should be here concerned about the cause of the death and not run away." But another brother brought up the matter of the combination of injections and beer.

The discussion was being led by a full brother of Cherkut's father, who was head of the lineage. He turned the discussion to the question of who would shave the widow and it was decided it should be the woman who had been staying with her during this period of mourning.

After a lengthy delay he raised the issue as to who should be 'guardian of the family,' noting that this formerly would not have been spoken of at this time but only after beer had been brewed.   He suggested that the proper person was the full brother who followed Cherkut.   An old woman (Cherkut's father's first wife) made reference to earlier suggestions that nobody was to inherit the widow: "If they say that, who will look after the children?" she concluded. Cherkut's son rose and responded heatedly with: "What you are saying is a nuisance; nobody will inherit my mother." Several members of the clan put the boy down: "Do you think this young boy is old enough to look after the cows and this other property?" and "You are too young to decide. It's up to us. It's not your wife, it's our wife and we are responsible for her and for you, too."

The name of Kamudjnok was brought up, as well as that of S. A part of the discussion follows:

S: The one following the deceased [i.e., the next younger full brother, namely himself] is the right person to inherit the woman and look after the children. Men have suggested my name, but I am not interested. Kamudjnok is the right person. As for myself, I agree that I should support the children, but I do not want the wife.

Yakobo [another brother]: Another thing is to ask the widow. There are so many brothers from the same father from whom to choose. [He then listed a number of precedents of selecting half-brothers.] Ask her whom she wants.

A woman: S should be the right person and she shouldn't refuse him. If she doesn't like him, all he must do is to wash the ashes from his brother's wife and eat the vegetables with the wife and

children.   If he refused, Aribasi [oldest son by
the father's next wife] should be the one to do
this.

Aribasi: This is a bad thing.   I can't do it.
There was a ceremony for a <u>kisa</u> [a child who
follows after twins] here and I performed it.
[This reason seemed to satisfy all as a basis for
exclusion.]

A woman: Who knows this man Kamudjnok?   We have
never seen him until the deceased died.

Clan leader: Listen, you sheep.   S is the one
to wash the ashes and eat the vegetables with the
children.   After that Kamudjnok is the right person
to live with the woman.

The discussion continued, but it seemed agreed
that the ceremonial act should be performed by S
and the widow be permitted to choose among those
eligible to live with.   I later learned that the
discussion had eliminated Kamudjnok on the grounds
that he was the son of a mother who had been
inherited, and therefore should not himself be an
inheritor.

There followed in quick succession the
discussion of eight separate claims against the
estate, all but one of which was satisfactorily
agreed upon:

1.   A complicated matter involving a three-way
     exchange of a goat

2.   The use of a cow as security on a loan of
     100 shillings for the son's school fees

3.   Loans received from two men, using the same

plot of land as security

4. Sale of land to the deceased for which full payment had not been received

5. Loan of 100 shillings by Cherkut with land as security

6. Claim by a Mugisu man on a dispute between him and father of deceased over the exchange of a cow that had been allocated to the mother of Cherkut. (While the debt was not denied, it was maintained that it did not fall on Cherkut's estate. This was the only unsatisfied claim.)

7. A claim of 100 shillings loaned to Cherkut by Ngumui (the brother who could not bear watching the interment), who forfeited this claim.

8. A matter of a broken beer pot.

About a week after this ceremony, the widow called on my wife, looking troubled and sad and saying that she was unhappy because S was insisting that she permit herself to be inherited by him. He had, she said, asked her to sleep with him some weeks before Cherkut's death, but she had refused him and this, apparently, led to a fight between him and her husband in which Cherkut had been severely beaten and kicked in the chest, the injury which was seen as one possible cause of his death. She said that S had tried to kill her husband (though she was still inclined to credit the witchcraft of M as the real cause), and that she did not wish to marry S because he was a very fierce man, stubborn, lazy, and bad. There was a younger brother whom she wanted to marry, but he had not come forward and asked for her. When asked what recourse she might have in the matter, she stated that she could complain about S to neighbors or to the clan head, but that if they insisted that it was his "right," she would have no recourse. She claimed that S wants to "spoil her life" because she has more property than he, including coffee, and that he wants the money from her trees and she is afraid he will try to sell them. "This land doesn't belong to him or to me, but to my children, and if the money from it isn't used for my children I have a case against him."

She said that S had not come to "clean out the ashes" when he should have, and that she was therefore forced to cook the ceremonial food for her children before this cleansing, which she regarded as bad. At night, after the door was shut, she could hear spirits crying outside, and on the third day after the ceremony some neighbors passing saw Cherkut in front of the house smoking, and they ran away in fright. After S came several days later and washed out the ashes, the spirits stopped coming at night. When S did come, she went on, he did not stay the whole night, but left in the middle of the night and returned to his own house. He wants her to come to his house to live, as he is afraid of her son (who had vehemently objected to her being inherited at all) and doesn't want him to know that he sleeps with her. (He comes like a thief in the night.) Her son does not want her to accept because he is afraid S will beat her when he is not present, and because as a full-grown boy he would feel ashamed that she married somebody else. Other boys would tease him: "Your mother has so many husbands!" She feels, however, that the real reason is the quality of S; if he were rich and respected, the son would feel differently.

The discussion of the causes of Cherkut's death

is of interest. Suspicion centered around M. The
first wife of Cherkut's father discussed the matter
at some length. M was the son of a woman whom her
husband called _senge_ (father's sister), and when
M's parents died, her husband brought M to his
house and arranged for his bride price and paid it.
"When M came of circumcision age [she went on], I
had no child old enough to be circumcised, so I
acted as his mother and arranged the circumcision
feast for him. This was wrong, for by arranging a
circumcision feast for the first time for somebody
else's child instead of my own, all the children of
my oldest son have died." The evidence against M
consisted in the belief that he stayed away five
times at a death in this family, that he was
related to others who were generally suspected of
sorcery, that on the morning Cherkut died he had
been seen going to Sipi Falls where he was
suspected of keeping his medicine, and that in
"tightening" it he caused Cherkut to be very
thirsty (and hence to drink beer), and finally that
it is always dangerous, according to the Sebei, to
give the privileges of a clansman to a man not of
that clan.

Major Features of Sebei Funerary Behavior

In the context of other aspects of Sebei
culture, several major elements emerge that
characterize Sebei funeral practices: (1) the
rearrangement of social and economic matters that
takes place in association with funerals, (2) the
almost total absence of ritual involvement with the
soul of the deceased, and (3) the ritual focus on
the survivors, with particular reference to their
purification.

Social Rearrangements

The Sebei demonstrate both kin-based and spatially based loyalties in the restrictions placed upon economic and social activities and by the presence of kinsmen and neighbors at the funeral rites--a matter so general in its occurrence and so in accord with established theory that it hardly warrants further comment. Far more important to the Sebei and more unusual in occurrence is the Sebei utilization of the heightened emotional ambiance following upon a death to settle important legal and social matters.

To appreciate this situation it is necessary to know a few facts of Sebei law. First, the Sebei regularly engage in elaborate contractual arrangements regarding primarily cattle, but also small stock, land, and other property. These contracts, which I discussed in detail in Sebei Law (Goldschmidt 1967: chap. 11), have complex traditionally established codicils that may lead to diverse complications. The usefulness of contracts in spreading risk, obscuring wealth, and firming social ties is such that any man of property will be both creditor and debtor in a number of contracts at any one time. The obligations incurred may continue over many years, and they devolve upon the heirs when a man dies. It is incumbent upon a creditor to assert his demand upon the estate at the funeral moot of the man who owes him something; if he fails to do so he forfeits his claim. We saw several claims settled at the funeral of Cherkut; in Kambuya's Cattle (Goldschmidt 1969) many more were brought forward and others were held over to a more propitious time.

The second legal aspect has to do with the

regulations of inheritance. Formally, each Sebei man is expected to pay the bride price for his son's first marriage and some time subsequently give him his share of the stock, after which the son has no further claim on his father's herd. As each son successively reaches maturity he serves as his father's herdsman, and the last to do so inherits the residual stock, keeping a portion for any as yet uncircumcised (legally minor) brothers. The matter is further complicated, however, when a man allocates some of his cattle to his wives, who then hold a subsidiary right that has its chief importance in that these cows (including their progeny) go to her sons. A comparable pattern with respect to land has been developed. These arrangements, which are fully described in Sebei Law (Goldschmidt 1967: chap. 3), are further complicated by debts both due and receivable; this means that for a man of substance the inheritance of property, particularly livestock, becomes a matter of difficult and often tedious decision-making. Even for a man of moderate means and few debts, such as Cherkut, there had to be fairly extensive hearings involving nice decisions.

There is one further legal involvement, the inheritance of a man's widows. While the standard rule is that the wives are taken by the next younger brother, there are many complicating factors. There are the matters of personal preference, perhaps more important now that (according to modern laws) nobody is supposed to force a woman into an unwanted marriage, but I believe that they always played some role. There are many subsidiary rules governing inheritance of widows (as for instance a man should not have two wives of the same clan) and we saw in the case of Cherkut two ceremonial reasons why certain potential heirs could not take his widow--or used them as an excuse to avoid the obligation. This

aspect of the inheritance pattern takes on more
salience in the farming sector, where the control
of the land (though nominally held in trust for her
sons by the first husband) is placed in the hands
of the man who inherits the wife.

The ritual of chasing away the death and the
subsequent one involving the freeing of the widow
to remarry are therefore occasions for the making
of a wide variety of decisions regarding both
property and social rearrangement, and this secular
aspect of the funeral ceremony becomes a major
element in the mortuary procedures.

The Body and Soul of the Deceased

The traditional mode for the disposal of the
dead for these Kalenjin people was, to say the
least, summary. Disposal is still quick and
peremptory, despite the addition of washing and
putting the body in a winding sheet.

But what seems to me to be far more important is
that so little attention is paid to the soul.
Among the closely related Nandi, the portal to the
spirit world was the intestines of the hyena
(Hollis 1909: 7). Even this concern was not heard
to be expressed by Sebei. Nor have the changes in
burial customs brought about any greater concern
with the spirit of the deceased. When the body is
placed in the grave it is made comfortable as a
body, but nothing is made available for the soul;
there is no libation of beer or bit of meat or
words of encouragement (save those now read from
the Book of Common Prayer in an alien language).
The items placed in the grave are those most
intimately associated with the living body--his
clothes and bedding; they are not the things he
might wish to possess in some postmortem existence-

-not even the beer straw he had always carried with him.[3] No path was laid out for the soul to take; nor even an expressed request to the soul to leave in peace. The fear of heat cracks on the surface of the grave might be interpreted as fear that the soul would escape, but it was not so interpreted for me. Cherkut was heard and seen after his death, but this was perceived as a result of the failure to have fulfilled the ritual function of sexual intercourse--a ritual that certainly would do nothing to give Cherkut's soul personal satisfaction if it retained the emotions of the living. This manifestation of Cherkut's spirit is the only reference in my notes to the soul of the dead in funerals I witnessed or in informants' discussion of mortuary customs. One could watch Sebei funerals and never know that the Sebei had any belief in a human soul.

The Sebei do, in fact, believe that each man has a soul (oynatet, pl. oyik), and that the spirits of the dead take an active, and essentially malevolent, interest in the living. No ceremony, large or small, is without some recognition of this belief in the form of libations of beer, bits of food, the dedication of an animal, or other consideration. Indeed, I believe the funeral is the only ceremony that makes no reference to the oyik. The spirits of the dead are chiefly concerned with their own clansmen, but a person may be afflicted by actions of the spirits of his mother's clan as well. The fate of the soul is most dimly and inarticulately described; informants regularly shied away from discussion of the abode of the dead, which was vaguely seen as being underground, or the fate of the soul, which was always conceptualized in highly impersonal terms.

But the ceremonies of the funeral are not concerned with the soul of the deceased, either in word, in symbol, or in act. The very name of the ritual, <u>kopuntoyet ap met</u>, refers to death, <u>met</u>, not to the human spirit of the deceased.

Ritual Purification

The character of the funeral rites indicates that death is perceived as essentially a pollution, for the ritual acts serve to cleanse the survivors.[4] The ceremonial is replete with symbols of cleansing: general ones such as washing, running streams, fire and ashes, the right and left paths, and the removal of that most obvious human growth, hair; culture-specific ones, such as the chyme and fat of slaughtered animals, the use of certain medicinal roots and vines. Even the ritual of sexual intercourse (which might have been viewed as defiling) is expressed in the idiom of cleansing. I would also see that ancient symbol of Orpheus and Job, the taboo against looking back, as being in this context a fear of the evil inherent in death, not the spirit of the deceased, that is the focus of concern.

That death is seen as polluting is not the unusual element in ritual practices; it is so recurrent as to suggest universality in some form or another. But the Sebei focus on pollution, which infects not only the mourners but the possessions of the dead, including his livestock, has the special characteristic of putting the entire focus of the ritual procedure upon the living. This is, of course, the obverse of the lack of concern for the deceased himself.

Other Considerations

There are several other elements that emerge

from the death practices which should briefly be
brought forward. First, the extensiveness of the
ritual stands in direct relation to the importance
of the deceased, particularly to the measure that
he was in control of property. Second, the degree
of ceremonial involvement of the several mourners
stands in direct relation to his proximity to the
deceased--a proximity that again is measured in
terms of the likelihood that he will be involved
in the transfer of property. These elements are in
no way unusual, but deserve notice.

On the third item I can speak with less
certainty. It is my belief, however, that the
Sebei find the demands of the funeral rites,
whether they involve a major role or a minor one,
highly distasteful. I do not mean merely that they
dislike or fear to be in the presence of death, but
that they do not want to dig the grave or bury the
body or be shaved or engage in the ritual sexual
intercourse with the widow. This perception
derives from the form in which certain remarks were
made, such as "twins are _freed from_" the mourning
customs, and "if the brothers do not bury a man
they will be criticized," as well as the expression
that there is an obligation to appear at a funeral
sanctioned not only by moral suasion but by the
possibility that they will be suspected of
witchcraft.

The Structuring of Guilt-Provoking Behavior

The Sebei data have been brought forward not to
contribute to an understanding of death rituals in
general, but to the illumination of the specific
problem as to why among the Sebei they take the
particular form that they do. In this section I
want to show that because the Sebei utilize the

emotional ambiance[5] of death to resolve the
complicated matters of personal rights that derive
from their legal codes, the ritual leads to a
heightened concern with the survivors, who must
therefore necessarily each direct his attention to
his personal interests in the estate of the
deceased, and this in turn quickens a sense of
guilt which is expressed as pollution requiring
acts of ritual purification.

The point of view that sees the death rituals as
being concerned with the rearrangement and
reaffirmation of the social order has been
expressed in general terms by Durkheim himself:

> The foundation of mourning is the
> impression of a loss which the group feels
> when it loses one of its members. But this
> very impression results in bringing them
> into closer relation with one another, in
> associating them all in the same mental
> state, and therefore in disengaging a
> sensation of comfort which compensates the
> original loss. Since they weep together,
> they hold to one another and the group is
> not weakened, in spite of the blow which
> has fallen upon it. (Durkheim 1915:   401)

After the mourning is over, the domestic group
is recalmed by the mourning itself; it regains
confidence; the painful pressure which they felt
exercised over them is relieved; they feel more at
their ease (Durkheim 1915:   413).

The Durkhemian view has been reiterated and
elaborated by Van Gennep[6] (1960: chapter 7), Hertz
(1960), Radcliffe-Brown (1933:   285), and more
recently by Monica Wilson (1957:   226-233), Goody
(1962:   432-435), Douglass (1969:   211-212), and

Orenstein (1970:   1370-1375).   That the Sebei
reaffirm both the spatial and the kinship groupings
is evident from the data presented and is in
conformity with this point of view; it therefore
needs no further adumbration here.

What does require further examination, however,
are the processes of social rearrangement.   When
Radcliffe-Brown expresses this phenomenon in the
passive mode ("the social sentiments of the
survivors are slowly reorganized and adapted to the
new conditions," 1933:   288), he is unconsciously
expressing that reification of society which is
characteristic of Durkheimian thought, and in the
process he reduces the persons involved to mere
objects. The attitude is reflected by Wilson when,
after noting that the "anthropologist cannot look
into men's minds; he is not concerned with personal
religion" (Wilson 1957:226), she steps gingerly
around the problem of Nyakyusa motivation.

This reordering of the social world is not a
passive phenomenon. On the contrary, the active,
aggressive press on the part of each individual to
protect and further his personal interests brings
it about.   The mourners are principals in legal
encounters of diverse kinds; they engage in acts
designed to further their individual causes and in
so doing reshape the social sentiments. The social
order is not reshaped for them.

Consider the actions of S.   If he was not
dissembling his motives, he was at the very least
suspected of doing so, and in either case, we find
evidence of attitudes expressive of hostility and
suspicion, with the explicit fear for the
protection of rights in the land. The events that
took place at the death of Kambuya (Goldschmidt
1969) are replete with evidence of unseemly
behavior directed toward the protection and

furtherance of private interests.   These actions
resulted   in   openly   displayed   hostility,   the
evocation of ancient quarrels, accusations, and
intimations of engaging in forcery, adultery,
family   disloyalty,   and   other   dishonest   and
reprehensible acts.   Such actions not only are
taken by the direct heirs, but by all those present
who have some claim upon the deceased, to the
degree that these claims are viable and their
interests   are   cogent.   In   addition,   these
individuals further their aims by rhetorical
devices, by dissemblance of motives, and by other
means that they can hardly conceal from themselves,
however effectively they are hidden from others.
It is important to appreciate that, by attending to
the behavior of individuals in the social context,
we can get expressions of personal motivation and
individual emotions, even if we cannot "look into
men's minds."

    Not all the matters that arise at a funeral have
to do with property and personal gain in the
economic sense of the term.   There are what may be
called emotional stakes as well.   Both the widows
and their potential heirs are concerned with the
implications for their future emotional and sexual
lives when they are determining this aspect of the
social rearrangements attendant upon a death.   In
this context, the strong sentiment of Cherkut's
teen-age son is certainly relevant.   That he did
not want his mother to be remarried was clear not
only from what he said and the vehemence with which
he said it, but from his certain knowledge that his
expression of these sentiments exceeded the bounds
of appropriate role behavior.   I myself see his
behavior in terms of an oedipal attachment, but it
might well have been a fear of losing control of
the coffee lands; in either case, however, it was
an expression of personal motivation.   Had Cherkut
died a few years later, the son's wish would have

prevailed (I learned subsequently that it did), as it is said that widows with grown sons are usually not inherited. Indeed, this very fact, together with the ready recognition of the boy's sentiment by his mother, suggests that the attitude was not peculiar to him, but characteristic of young Sebei men.

The behavior of Ngumui, the man who could not bear to watch the interment of his brother, is also instructive in this context. His calm visibly and admittedly shaken by the situation, he renounced his claim to a piece of property that was his right, rather than engage in self-serving actions. It would seem as if he could not face the guilt that such actions evoke because he could not accept the rite of purification, toward which he had been derogatory. His was the only instance of such action that came to my attention, and it was recognized as generous, though, so far as I could tell, not particularly laudatory.

We see, therefore, that the rearrangments that take place in the affairs of the survivors of a death are not automatic adjustments of a hypostatized social order, but are the results of the active prosecution of individuals in pursuit of private aims, whether economic or sentimental. Paradoxically the several actors must harbor socially inappropriate sentiments in the performance of socially appropriate roles. It must be emphasized that these sentiments and actions are not merely chance occurrences, but are structured into the situation by the legal demands and the customary procedures of Sebei funerals. The mourners are forced into this paradoxical situation by the particularities of Sebei economics and law[7] and by the character of the funeral rites themselves.[8]

Mary Douglas (1966, 1968) would have us believe
that a sense of defilement derives from a kind of
structural disorientation, that pollution is dirt,
and that dirt is matter out of place, and thus, a
people feel a sense of pollution when the normal
world is disoriented--as by a death. This again
(as with Monica Wilson) is an effort to avoid
facing the existence of human emotions.   For
pollution is to dirt as anxiety is to fear, which
is to say that it contains an emotional load that
is not adequately accounted for by external
reality; thus clearly it must relate to
intrapsychic events. Where there is a generalized
sense of pollution (as is implicitly the case when
matters must be ritually taken care of), then the
intrapsychic events of those involved must be a
common response to a generalized situation.

Paul Ricoeur provides us the necessary clue to
the meaning of pollution. Ricoeur argues that the
sense of defilement is a more primitive form of
moral order than the concept of sin--"a more
archaic conception of fault" (1967: 7) to use his
phrasing. The notion of guilt, he feels, is
implicit in the concept of defilement. "Dread of
the impure and rites of purification," he says,
"are in the background of all our behavior relating
to fault" (1967: 25). As Freud has said: "Least
of all will [a person] permit himself to think of
the death of another if with that event some gain
to himself in freedom, means or position is
connected" (1956a: 305). Yet as I have shown,
Sebei mourners not only are advantaged by the
death, but are forced to behave in a way that
furthers such advantages.

We are constrained, however, not merely to
understand why the Sebei place emphasis upon
defilement and hence upon the protection of the
mourners, but also why they place such small weight

upon the deceased himself. Since the association between pollution and death is so widespread as to seem universal, what makes the Sebei instance exceptional is its essential disregard for the person who died.

It is necessary as background to an understanding of this matter to realize that the thrust of Sebei culture is toward individual independence. This is not only true in the economic sense where, for instance, the sons are given their inheritance and placed on their own in early adulthood, and where widows readily find subsitute husbands, but it is also true in an emotional sense, for the Sebei do not characteristically form strong personal attachemtns to others, whether these be parents, children, siblings, or spouses. (That exceptions can be found goes without saying, but the essential emotional independence of the Sebei individual is impressive.) Thus a death does not provoke that sense of personal loss which, for instance, Freud (1956a: 154) expresses in his analogy between malancholia as a psychic state and mourning as a patterned form of social behavior. In the absence of these ties, that ambivalence of attitude, the latent hostility, and hence the projection of which Freud writes in Totem and Tabu (1950: 51-63) does not retain the salience that would otherwise be the case.[9]

The essential point is that while the Sebei act in ways unseemly in the face of death, these actions are not taken against the deceased as such, but are acts against those who remain among the living. The social drama that takes place on the occasion of a funeral involves conflicts between heirs or potential heirs, and between these and creditors. Such conflicts directly involve the living--not the deceased--and provoke feelings of

guilt and fears of retribution. But to the death
is not irrelevant; it is the death as a social fact
and as a symbolic and emotional event that brings
these unseemly actions into play, and thus it is
death, the abstraction rather than the dead man,
that is the source of the defilement against which
prophylactic action must be taken. Again we may
take our clue from Ricoeur:

> The anticipation of punishment, at the
> heart of the fear of the impure,
> strengthens this bond between evil and
> misfortune: punishment falls on man in the
> guise of misfortune and transforms all
> possible sufferings, all diseases, all
> death, all failure into a sign of
> defilement. (Ricoeur 1967:   27)

The bond between vengeance and defilement is the
essence of the case. Each funeral is a reenactment
of the dilemma of proper Sebei behavior: the quest
for personal advantage as a social requisite; the
consequent fear of the hatred of those against whom
one must act; the sense of guilt that is aroused
for the sentiments one holds and the acts one
engages in; and the ultimate resolution through
ritual purification.

Conclusion

If my analysis of Sebei death ceremonials has
cogency, it does so precisely because it deals
directly with the interplay between the private
motivations of the individuals and the structural
context within which they operate. The symbolic
meaning of the rituals themselves is thus seen as
mediating between the private and internal
psychological tensions of the individual and the
public demands that are made upon these persons.

I want to conclude this essay with some
reflections on the relation between motivation and
social structure; between the individual and the
society. In this I am in agreement with Victor
Turner, who also argues that rituals are expressive
of the inner psychological tensions created by the
structure of the society, when "the structurally
inferior aspire to symbolic superiority in ritual,
the structurally superior aspire to symbolic
communitas and undergo penance to achieve it"
(Turner 1969: 203). Both of us take cognizance of
personal and private motives and both of us
recognize that these are--or may be--in conflict
with normal role demands, as these are structured
into the situation. But I differ from Turner in
several respects. First, Turner appears to be
seeking some broad and general thesis that accounts
for recurrent, if not actually universal, features
in ritual activity, whereas I seek to demonstrate
only the particular structural-motivational tie in
a single instance. Second, and not unrelated to
the first, Turner evokes what seems to me to be
both vague and mystic individual motivations,
whereas I would look for more mundane and
demonstrable ones such as jealousy, guilt, and the
like. Finally, I am not certain that Turner is
willing to admit that he is imputing individual
motivation as a systemic element in his
explanations,[10] whereas it is my major purpose to
show that ritual can be understood only when we
take into account the individual as a motivated and
emotion-laden unit.

Note has already been taken of the manner in
which Wilson has backed away from the psychological
aspects of Nyakyusa funerary rites, though she too
is aware of the ambivalence of some of the mourners
with respect to the death.[11] In contrast, Jack
Goody (1962) takes cognizance of the roles played

by individual motivation for personal gain and by
tensions between kinsmen over property in
explaining the differences in funerary practices
between the two communities of the LoDagaa he
studied. The major thrust of his argument is that
the ritual behavior varies in response to the
differing importance in matters of property between
the matrilineal and the patrilineal kin groups in
these societies with dual descent. It is a thesis
that the LoDagaa themselves endorse. The
importance of his analysis lies in his
demonstration that these changes are responsive to
the differential locus of interpersonal tensions,
in accordance with the institutional variation in
the control of property rights--though he is not
always as explicit as one might wish.

Goody also recognizes the existence of the
intervening variable of psychological elements that
stand between social institutions that are
functionally related. Spiro argues for a
recognition of such involvement of psychological
needs as they relate specifically to religion:

A third set of desires which, I would
suggest, constitutes a motivational source
of religious behavior consists of painful
drives which seek reduction and painful
motives which seek satisfaction. . . . In
the absence of other, or of more efficient
means, religion is the vehicle--in some
societies, perhaps, the most important
vehicle--by which, symbolically, they can
be handled and expressed. (Spiro 1966:
114-115)

This recognition of the psychological dimension
does not mean, as it largely did for an earlier
generation of anthropologists, that we must seek
our insights solely from the psychoanalytic mode,

or that the psychologists' analyses of behavior satisfactorily explains the phenomena that come to the anthropologist's attention. The difficulty inherent in the psychologists' approach lies in its application to a single cultural situation, with the result that psychologists either explain the particulars of some specific pathology or they endeavor to find universalistic characteristics. The psychoanalyst, for instance, begins with the perception of pathological mourning, which he reasonably sees in terms of overdependency and/or guilt feelings and, if he endeavors to generalize at all, extrapolates from such observations and analyses to mankind as a whole.   Thus Bowlby (1961: 328-331) in his examination of the subject relates his observation to generalized instinctive drives, seeking support in a long-since-discredited fashion from random ethological observations and anecdotes on diverse species of animals and birds. Bowlby's analysis does not help us to understand the normative behavior, let alone the customs and rituals surrounding death. In these matters, Freud remains the master and is more useful for our purposes; he takes cognizance of the projection of unconscious hostility (1950: 64), the ambivalence with respect to the object of the mourning (1956a: 161), and the impact of guilt feelings that arise because an individual may find himself advantaged by the death of another (1956b: 305). These dynamic qualities inherent in the mourning situation must, however, be examined in the context of the specific structural situation in which they occur--a level of sociological sophistication that could hardly be expected of Freud writing more than half a century ago.

It may reasonably be argued that motivation and emotion pertain necessarily to _individual_ acts, while ritual events are institutionalized forms of _social_ behavior, and must therefore relate to

social states.   The point, however, is that though
the former are intrapsychic, and hence necessarily
individual,   they   are   consistent   responses   to
institutionally created situations and hence are
shared   responses.   Where   rituals   serve   to
ameliorate intrapsychic states, we must presume
that a social situation creates a common pattern
of sentiments.   Some rituals, such as war dances,
are aimed at promoting common sentiments.   It was
to   show   that   the   mourners   were   consistently
provoked   to   a   common   emotional   state   that   I
described the social pressures on their psychic
state.   There is, I believe, a normative emotional
state   of   guilt   which   the   cleansing   rituals
ameliorate.   This   normative   level   is   set   into
relief by the culturally abnormal action of Ngumui:
because he could not accept the meaningfulness of
the   purifying   activities,   he   could   not   indulge
himself in the guilt feelings and hence forfeited
his rightful claim against the state.[12]   It lies
beyond the scope of this paper to show why the
Sebei have placed these emotional burdens upon
mourners, though enough has been said to indicate
that   these   legal   institutions   have   their   own
rationale.   It might also be noted that the strong
sense of individuation that generally characterizes
pastoral   life   (Goldschmidt   1971),   and   the
importance of private ownership of property is of
relevance to these considerations.

    The institutional structure provides the matrix
in which social, economic, and sexual needs are
gratified and establishes procedures by means of
which such gratification may legitimately (and, in
fact,   nonlegitimately)   be   sought,   as   well   as
providing for collaborative activity through which
sustenance and reproduction are achieved.   But even
the legitimate efforts for self-fulfillment create
a tension between the individual and the social
order,   for   the   essence   of   an   orderly   social   life

requires a curbing of the individual's personal appetitive desires, even those shaped by the culture. There are structured situations in which these tensions are particularly manifested. One recurrent example of such a structural 'problem' is the transfer of rights between the generations and the tensions that these transfers create between the senior and the junior members. Consider for instance the recurrent problem with respect to the transfer of farms in peasant societies where land is scarce or relatively so (Goldschmidt and Kunkel 1971). It is one of the tasks of religion to relieve such tensions, either by reinforcing the psychological support for the existing order or, as Spiro indicates, by reduction of the painful drives. Fortes has exemplified such a use of ritual roles between fathers and sons in his discussion of the Tallensi: "The ancestor cult is the transposition to the religious plane of the relationships of parents and children; and that is what I mean by describing it as the ritualization of filial piety" (Fortes 1959: 30).

Structural situations may exacerbate these 'natural' tensions as, for example, when the road to success in economic and social life is through attainment of professional competence under circumstances of limited opportunity. Such a pattern has for generations created a heightened tension for postadolescent middle-class Europeans and for upwardly mobile minorities in America. The Sebei funeral ritual is such an exacerbation. Deaths normally involve the transfer of rights and this transfer is, at least, one source of conflict (both interpersonal and internal) that emerges recurrently, if not universally. The Sebei load this situation by raising diverse economic and legal issues on the occasion of a death. Viewed from the standpoint of Sebei contractual law, the public hearings regarding debts at the time of

death can be seen as a functionally effective
device for preserving the record in a nonliterate
community; the existence of such contractual
arrangements is, in turn, a functionally effective
device for spreading risks, sharing resources, and
establishing collaborative action in legal as well
as economic matters (Goldschmidt 1967:   191-192).
Viewed, however, from the perspective provided by
the occasion of a death, it can be seen that this
custom places a particular emotional burden on the
mourners, provoking their cupidity and rousing them
to engage in behavior that invokes a sense of
guilt--guilt that the ritual elements of Sebei
funerary practices are designed to allay.

The functional understanding of society makes
the basic assumption that institutions are formed
to provide for orderly human relationships and the
maintenance of the social system.   Implicit in this
assumption, though rarely voiced, is an underlying
notion that man is not by nature orderly and
cooperative, else these institutional devices for
orderly social systems would be unnecessary.   Thus
there inevitably exists a tension between the
individual and his private desires and emotions and
the society with its demands for conformity.   One
function of rituals is to dispel this tension, to
disarm the potential disruption created by such
structural conflict.   If a ritual is to perform
this function, it must relate realistically to the
private, though culturally induced, desires of the
individual and the structural requirements of the
social order.   This, I believe, is what the Sebei
funeral rites are designed to accomplish.   That is,
they serve to ameliorate the specific psychological
tensions that are the product of the peculiar
situation in which a death places the survivors.

Notes

1. The data are not always consistent, but most dispose of some or all the bodies in this way: Dorobo of Tindoret Forest (Huntingford 1953b: 68); Elgeyo (Huntingford 1953b: 74); Hadzapi (Huntingford 1953b: 126); Iraqw (Huntingford 1953b: 131); Masai (Huntingford 1953b: 126); Nandi (Huntingford 1953a: 137; Hollis 1909: 71); Pokot (Huntingford 1953b: 90); Sandawe (Huntingford 1953b: 139); Toposa (Gulliver and Gulliver 1953: 92).

2. There are several times in Sebei daily life when behavior is restricted because it is something that is done at a funeral. Thus I was told that a man's wives must never undress and bathe at the same time, because they will do this at his funeral.

3. There are some exceptions, notably with respect to twins and the very old. The special treatment of the former, in funerals and elsewhere, reflects a special status that remains enigmatic to me. That of the latter is of particular interest in that clearly neither the legal nor the emotional situation, which is discussed below, has relevance for a man whose active life is behind him.

4. Of course, the rituals serve the survivors, not the dead, as Firth has pointed out: "It is rather as a framework for activity in _this_ world and for positive experiences in _life_ that concepts about the continuity and fate of the soul are developed rather than as a protection against death. In the ritual behavior where crude fear of the dead seems to be the salient theme, the concern for freedom of action of the _living_ is most marked" (Firth 1967: 334, emphasis in original). But this does not mean that the ritual will not be overtly

concerned with the deceased, or with the relationship between the living and the deceased.

5. There appears to be a heightened emotional ambiance attendant upon a death in all societies; certainly it is among the Sebei. Why this should happen is not a point at issue, but a separate problem. The Sebei display an inordinate fear of death (Edgerton 1971: 119).

6. "[Mourning] is a transitional period for the survivors, and they enter it through rites of separation and emerge from it through rites of reintegration into society" (Van Gennep 1960: 147).

7. It is reasonable to raise the question as to why this situation occurs among the Sebei. A proper answer to this question would take us too far afield, but I believe it lies in certain aspects of the ecology, the demands of pastoral economic life (Goldschmidt 1971), and the historic processes of adaptation to a new environmental situation.

8. Though not expressed in this form at the time, the description of the Hupa White Deerskin Dance (Goldschmidt and Driver 1940) indicates that world renewal ritual had the purpose of removing the accumulated sins of mankind, and these are derived from the aggressive act in Hupa legal bargaining (see also Goldschmidt 1951). Something similar is also indicated by Turner (1969) in his concluding chapter dealing with humility and hierarchy.

9. Edgerton (1971) finds that the Sebei have an inordinate fear of death, as already noted, and this fear is supported by the character of Sebei rituals generally, as well as by the funeral rituals. It is perhaps the sense of death as a

total annihilation, that derives from loose affective ties, together with the very poorly articulated notions of postmortem existence, that accounts for this obsessive dread of death--though admittedly the matter remains enigmatic.

10. Note the uneasiness in the following: "There would seem to be--if one can use such a controversial term--a human 'need' to participate in both modalities [Societas and Communitas]" (Turner 1969: 203).

11. One is tempted to expand the ancient saying De mortuis nil nisi bonum to include the mourners as well.

12. William Torrey (in personal communication) said that the Gabrra delayed discussions of inheritance for two years precisely to avoid the sentiments that would be provoked during the time of mourning.

References

Bowlby,   John.   1961.   Processes   of   Mourning.
    International Journal of Psycho-Analysis 42:
    317-340.

Douglas,   Mary.   1966.   *Purity   and   Danger: A*
    Comparative Study of Concepts of Pollution and
    Tabu. London: Routledge and Kegan Paul.

_____. 1968. Pollution. *International*
    Ecyclopedia of the Social Sciences 12:   336-
    341. Macmillan.

Douglass,   Wiliam   A.   1969.   *Death   in   Murelaga:*
    Funerary Ritual in a Spanish Basque Village.
    American   Ethnological   Society   Monograph   49.
    University of Washington Press.

Durkheim,   Emile.   1915.   *The   Elementary   Form   of*
    Religious   Life,   trans.   Joseph   Ward   Swain.
    George Allen and Unwin.

Edgerton,   Robert.   1971.   *The   Individual   in   Cultural*
    Adaptation: A   Study   of   Four   East   African
    Peoples. University of California Press.

Firth,   Raymond.   1967.   *The   Fate   of   the   Soul   in*
    Tikopia   Ritual   and   Belief.   George   Allen   and
    Unwin. (Originally published in 1955.)

Fortes,   Meyer.   1959.   *Oedipus   and   Job   in   West*
    African Religion. Cambridge University Press.

Freud,   Sigmund.   1950.   *Totem   and   Tabu: Some   Points*
    of   Agreement   Between   the   Ritual   Lives   of
    Savages   and   Neurotics,   trans.   James   Strachey.
    Norton. (First published in *Imago*, 1912-1913.)

_____. 1956a. Mourning and Melancholia, trans. by Joan Riviere. Collected Papers 4. London: Hogarth Press and Institute of Psycho-Analysis. (First published in Zeitschrift 4, 1911.)

_____. 1956b. Thoughts for the Times on War and Death, trans. Joan Riviere. Collected Papers 4. London: Hogarth Press and Institute of Psycho-Analysis. (First published in Imago 5, 1915.)

Goldschmidt, Walter. 1951. Ethics and Structure of Society; an Ethnological Contribution to the Sociology of Knowledge. American Anthropologist 53: 506-524.

_____. 1965. Theory and Strategy in the Study of Culture Adaptability. American Anthropologist 67: 402-408.

_____. 1967. Sebei Law. University of California Press.

_____. 1969. Kambuya's Cattle: The Legacy of an African Herdsman. University of California Press.

_____. 1971. Independence as an Element in Pastoral Social Systems. Anthropological Quarterly.

_____. 1972. An Ethnography of Encounters: A Methodology for the Enquiry into the Relation between the Individual and Society. Current Anthropology 13: 59-78.

Goldschmidt, Walter, and Harold E. Driver. 1940. The Hupa White Deerskin Dance. University of California Publications in American Archaeology and Ethnology 34, no. 8: 103-131. University of California Press.

Goldschmidt, Walter, and Evalyn Kunkel. 1971. The Structure of the Peasant Family. American Anthropologist 73: 424.

Goody, Jack. 1962. Death, Property and the Ancestors: A Study of Mortuary Customs of the LoDagaa of West Africa. Stanford: Stanford University Press.

Gulliver, Pamela, and P.H. Gulliver. 1953. The Central Nilo-Hamites. Ethnographic Survey of Africa. East Central Africa 7. International African Institute.

Hertz, Robert. 1960. A Contribution to the Study of the Collective Representation of Death. Death and the Right Hand. The Free Press. (Originally published in L'Anée sociologique, 1907.)

Hollis, A.C. 1909. The Nandi, Their Language and Folk-lore. Clarendon Press.

Huntingford, F.W.B. 1953a. The Nandi of Kenya: Tribal Control in a Pastoral Society. London: Routledge and Kegan Paul.

_____. 1953b. The Southern Nilo-Hamites. Ethnographic Survey of Africa. East Central Africa 8. International African Institute.

176   Sebei

Orenstein, Henry. 1970. Death and Kinship in Hinduism: Structural and Functional Interpretation. <u>American Anthropologist</u> 72: 1357-1377.

Radcliffe-Brown, A.R. 1933. <u>The Andaman Isalanders</u> (2d ed.). Cambridge University Press.

Ricouer, Paul. 1969. <u>The Symbolism of Evil</u>. New York: Harper and Row.

Spiro, Melford E. 1966. Religion: Problems of Definition and Explanation. <u>Anthropological Approaches to the Study of Religion</u>, ed. Michael Banton. Association for Social Anthropology Monographs 3 and Tavistock Institute.

Turner, Victor W. 1969. <u>The Ritual Process: Structure and Anti-Structure</u>. Lewis Henry Morgan Lectures, 1966. Aldine Publishing Co.

Van Gennep, Arnold. 1960. <u>The Rites of Passage</u>, trans. Monika B. Vizedom and Gabrielle L. Caffee. Chicago: University of Chicago Press. (Originally published in 1908.)

Wilson, Monica. 1957. <u>Rituals of Kinship Among the Nyakyusa</u>. Published for the International African Institute. Oxford University Press.

DEATH AND THE SOCIAL ORDER:
BARA FUNERAL CUSTOMS (MADAGASCAR)

W. R. Huntington

The Importance of Mortuary Customs

The central importance of tombs, burial customs, and related rites to Malagasy culture is affirmed by almost every account of the island's customs. Even a casual visitor to Madagascar quickly becomes aware of the large role burial customs play in the lives of the people. In many parts of the island, tombs, whose elaborate and solid construction far exceeds the care given to the houses of the living, dominate the landscape. During the cool season, the roads are full of people travelling to their ancestral villages to participate in elaborate exhumation rites at their family tombs. Best known are the exhumation rites (fadamihana) of the dominant Merina people at which hundreds of kinsmen gather and celebrate for several days with drinking, feasting, and dancing to the music of professional performers. The expenditures of time and resources for the maintenance of tombs and the production of these ceremonies are considerable, especially in light of the meager economic base. The conspicuous burial of the dead is the ultimate activity of Malagasy systems of religion, economics, and social prestige.

This paper focuses on the funeral customs of the Bara people who inhabit most of the interior of southern Madagascar. The Bara are essentially

Reprinted from African Studies 32, no. 2 (1973): 65-84. Witwatersand University Press, Johannesburg.

pastoralists, tending their ample herds of zebu cattle in this dry and sparsely-populated region. Although cattle are their prime concern, the Bara also practice subsistence production of rice. The basic unit of Bara social organization is a local agnatic kin group whose members generally reside together in one hamlet and share a common tomb. I did field research for eighteen months (1970-1971) in eastern Bara land, residing in a small village called Anosibe. During my stay at Anosibe I attended funeral ceremonies, of which ten were burials and nine were secondary funeral events. All research was conducted in the Bara dialect of the Malagasy language, no other language being spoken in the village.

Although Bara tombs and funeral rites are less visible than those of many other Malagasy groups, customs relating to burial are no less important. The Bara rarely construct tombs but bury the dead in caves hidden in the hills. Nor do they perform large-scale, periodic general exhumations, but rather carry out more simple secondary burial of individual corpses. Still, vast resources are consumed in the three-stage process of providing the final resting place for the dead. And although the observer sees no tombs, the Bara know where the dead lie. In the village of Anosibe, the mountain containing the burial caves dominates the landscape even more impressively than do the man-made tombs in other parts of Madagascar. This mountain is entirely associated with burial and the ancestors: no one goes there for any other purpose or refers to it in any other context.

Since funerals are the focal point of the social, economic, and religious aspects of Bara culture, there are several useful analytical approaches. In interpreting Malagasy funeral rites, several French investigators have followed in the tradition associated with Van Gennep and Hertz, emphasizing death as a period of transition in a rite de passage (Dubois 1938, Decary 1958, Faublee 1954).   Others have emphasized the sociological role of tombs and burial in defining and reinforcing individuals' membership ties in kin groups through participation in and contribution toward these communal activities (Bloch 1971).   In addition to being a rite of passage and an event of social integration, the funeral is also a ritual expressive of the fundamental organizational principles of Bara social life by virtue of its symbolic emphasis of a conceptual unity of the life of the group with the individual lives of its members.   This paper will focus on this aspect of the funeral as a 'ritual of kinship' which symbolically expresses the basic Bara notions about the nature of human existence both in its aggregate and individual manifestations.

Burial (Fandevana)

Death is not immediately acknowledged or announced.   When a person stops breathing, preparation of the body and house are quickly and silently begun.   All visible signs of grief are forbidden.   In spite of the interdiction, women often lose control and begin to sob but they are sternly ordered to be silent and to wait.   The preparation of the body is not elaborate.   It is washed with warm water.   The jaw is closed and temporarily held in place with a cloth tied under the chin and over the head.   The eyelids are closed and the arms and legs are straightened.   The body is clothed simply and minimally.   A man is dressed in just a pair of shorts or a loincloth.   A woman is dressed in a siky, the toga-like cloth worn by men and women all over Madagascar, and her hair is braided in the usual fashion.   All of these preparations are done by close kin of the same sex as the deceased.

During this initial period, two huts are silently and hastily cleared and made ready for the reception of callers. One house is for the men (<u>tranadahy</u>--'male house'), and one is for the women (<u>trano be ranomaso</u>--'house of many tears'). In the north-east corner of the women's hut, a place is made for the body which is laid on its back, its head to the east. They often place a partition around the body for it is considered somewhat shameful (<u>mahamegnatsy</u>) to have non-kin stare at the body. Only after all these preparations have been completed and those who have touched the body have washed, is wailing permitted. This outbreak of wails and cries is the first notice to the village at large that death has occurred. Messengers are sent out to inform officially each hamlet of the village and all the hamlets of kin in neighboring villages.

Co-villagers, kin and non-kin, converge on the unhappy hamlet to offer condolences and to participate in the rites. The men of the stricken family receive male visitors in the 'male house.' Each new group of arrivals enters, sits, is greeted by the hosts, and then offers condolences in a very stylized address used only at funerals. The <u>tompom-paty</u> (lords or owners of the body) accept these condolences with a similarly stylized reply. Since there is usually more than one new visitor and more than one <u>tompom-paty</u>, the condolences and then the reply are each given in a round-robin fashion in order of seniority. The length and elaboration of the statements vary directly with the status of the speaker.

The scene is similar in the women's 'house of many tears', but with the addition of ritual wailing. The women go through the same formal

condolences and responses as the men, but with less
elaboration. As each set of verbal exchanges is
completed, a parallel cycle of wailing begins. The
closest kinswomen begin to cry and the others
gradually join in, the most recently arrived
mourners joining earliest and most vehemently. As
they wail, the women cover their heads and faces
and put their hands on one another's backs. They
stop wailing in reverse order until finally the one
woman most closely related to the deceased is again
crying alone as in the beginning. The crying women
keep watch on the corpse for three days and two
nights and no men enter the 'house of many tears'
until they come to take away the body for burial.

   The most important part of funeral activities
takes place at night. People gather and enter the
hut appropriate to their sex and await the start of
the festivities. As the night progresses, the
girls leave the 'house of many tears' to sing and
dance outdoors. Gradually, the young men leave
their hut, first to watch and then to join in. Rum
is served, and perhaps a meal of beef and rice.
The local accordian player is hired to provide
music. At best, the funeral nights generate an
orgy of sorts. The girls taunt the boys with
extremely ribald songs and sensuous dancing. The
boys watch in little clusters, excitedly discussing
who will get which girl before the night is over.
The level of drunkenness increases; more and more
boys join in the dancing which becomes quite
spirited. Finally the affair breaks up at about
four o'clock in the morning. Those couples who
have arranged liaisons then go off to bring the
night to its logical conclusion, while the less
fornunate youths sleep alone. Those having sex
must saparate from their partners before sunrise.

   Day-time is devoted to catching up on sleep and
making preparations for the night and for burial.

The most necessary activity is the construction of
a coffin. About twenty men go off into the woods
to cut down a large, soft-wooded tree and scoop it
out into a coffin. A little rum and perhaps some
beef is taken along and consumed while making the
coffin.   While this is being done in the woods,
others are slaughtering and butchering beef,
purchasing rum, and preparing a meal for the
helpers. Close kin and the elderly continue to sit
in   the   male   and   female   huts   while   these
preparations are organized largely by affines.
Sons-in-law of the deceased, in particular, are
obliged to provide not only their services, but
also cattle, rum, or money. The amount of goods
consumed at funerals varies, but for the death of
an adult, one hundred litres of rum, four cattle,
plus much rice, would not be at all extraordinary.
This expense is carried by the immediate family of
the deceased with major contributions from sons-
in-law.

Although the length of time between death and
burial is ideally three days (two nights), this is
subject to variation according to several factors.
Most obviously, the funeral of a senior person is
more elaborate than that of a young person or a
child.   Weather is also important since bodies
decompose much too rapidly during the hottest
season to allow a lengthy funeral. The material
circumstances of the family are also a factor, but
less important then one might think.   Even when
cash and rice are in short supply, cattle can be
traded for rice, sold to pay for rum, or simply
slaughtered and distributed more generously to
compensate for the lack of rum.   Astrology also
plays a role in determining the length of the
funeral.   If one dies three days before an
inauspicious day, the funeral may well be
shortened.

Be it the third day or only the second, after great expense or minimal outlay, burial in the tomb hidden on the mountain finally separates the corpse from the living, and people are able to return to their routine affairs. Although burial takes place during the day, its general temper and active symbolism clearly relate it to the night-time festivities. In terms of the consumption of rum and beef, burial is the highlight of the several days of activity. A poorer family will conserve its resources in order, at least, to be able to provide for a spirited burial. This festive burial with drinking, dancing, and playing with the coffin, first strikes the Western observer as being somewhat perversely irreverent, at best. The Bara find it to be an interesting paradox to sing and dance at the burial of a loved one: so wrong and yet so right.[1]

The men enter the 'house of many tears', put the body in the coffin, and take it outdoors over the tearful protestations of the women. The coffin is covered with a cloth (siky) which must be new and in an unsewn, unfinished state. At this point the coffin is carried around and around the 'house of many tears' while unpounded, still fertile rice is sprinkled in its wake. Several gunshots may be fired and the procession heads toward the burial mountain several miles away. The funeral procession stretches out over the countryside with the youths and young girls quickly leading the way with the coffin, followed at a distance by adult men, then women and children, and finally the family cattle herded at the rear. The youths with the coffin pull farther and farther in advance, running all the way, carrying the coffin in relays. Only those youths who have had sexual experience can take part in this episode which is essentially a sexual contest between the girls and the boys for possession of the corpse.

The procession halts and regroups at a prearranged place about half-way to the mountain. At this point, the cattle are brought up and stampeded around and around the coffin while the young men vie with one another in the somewhat risky sport of cattle wrestling (<u>mitolo aomby</u>) which consists of leaping up onto the hump of one of the members of the stampeding herd and holding on as long as possible. When this is over, the young men and girls go on with the coffin to the tomb, accompanied by two or three older men to perform proper burial. Those that go up to the mountain are called the 'strong birds' (<u>voro mahery</u>). The remainder of the people sit and wait several hours for the return of the 'strong birds' and make minor preparations for the final celebration.

At the tomb, an older man acting as <u>tompom-paty</u> approaches, sprinkles rum on the entrance, and announces their presence to the ancestors. Only a few of the group participate in any of the real activity of the tomb. The rocks are all taken away from the entrance and the principal workers and sometimes everyone present are served rum. The coffin is opened, the cloth is placed on the body inside--head uncovered--and then the lid is replaced and nailed shut. The coffin is slid head first into the small opening of the tomb-cave. Most of the assistants feel safer entering the tomb feet first, in contrast to the corpse. After the coffin is properly placed inside, the assistants come out and the entrance is carefully closed and covered with large rocks. The elder then addresses the ancestors within:

"<u>Ao jafinao, da teraky ao, da tsy ahilakilaky, ndre ao</u>."

("Here is your grandchild. Born here. Do
not push him away, even from here.")

Then the elder picks up a green branch, <u>hazo le</u>
(wet tree) and raps the entrance to the tomb
several times, addressing the newly deceased:

> "<u>Da ato ianao, lahy. Laha hoatsy agny
> namoriky anao, dia hiremby ity hazo ity.
> Ka ny Janahary nangalany anao, iya handidy
> Janahary, lahy? Laha hoatsy vonorikiny olo
> avao, da alainao, mamorikinao</u>."

("There you are, brother. If someone has
bewitched you, then look for this tree. If
it is God(s) who has taken you, who can
command Gos, brother? But if it is merely
a person (who has bewitched you), then you
take him, you bewitch him.")

Informants state that the wet branch is like the
new corpse, cut off but still wet. Before they
become dry (<u>malazo</u>) the witch too will die.

The 'strong birds' then return down the mountain
to where the rest of the people are waiting. The
pace is fast, but the girls now hold themselves
quite aloof and the sexual gestures and joking are
clearly finished. When everyone has regrouped, rum
is served. It is a pleasant and merry party at
which each enjoys his intoxication for its own
sake. At the end of the rum supply, the beef is
distributed according to a rather complicated set
of principles, and everyone heads for home. The
funeral is over, although the female relatives may
continue to meet each day for a while to mourn in
the 'house of tears'. Those men who have shaved
their heads as a sign of mourning, let their hair
grow back at its own speed. Other men who have
made the opposite variety of the same gesture

(letting their hair and beard grow so that they look like wild men--omba) and women who have left their hair unbraided, will wait a week or so before rearranging themselves.

This description of the activities leading up to burial is but an introduction to these events which are the main subject of this investigation. Before describing the two remaining funeral rites, I should emphasize certain characteristics of this first burial rite. It is a ritual of extremes. At normal Bara gatherings, members of opposite sexes sit separately. In a hut, the men sit along the east and south walls while the women sit to the west by the door. But at this preburial activity, this separation is extremely rigid and men and women cannot enter the same hut. On the other hand, the night-time festivities exhibit a very close licentious relationship between males and females which is most unlike the normal cross-sex behaviour of the Bara. During this pre-burial period there is no middle ground; the sexes are absolutely separated by day and enjoined to an obscene, boisterous togetherness by night. There is also the contrast in sound. Funeral activities are separated from the preceding normality by total silence at the time of death which is then followed by loud wailing, singing, shouting, and gun shooting. Finally, these events take place in the village proper and all the way up the mountain by the tomb. Only after the burial is completed does a celebration take place between these two extremes.

The Gathering (Havoria)

One cannot control or predict when a death will take place and the expense of a burial ceremony cannot be prepared for in advance. Only with time and planning can a Bara family fully mobilize and exhibit its resources.   Partly for this reason, a family often puts on a _havoria_ ('gathering') after the rice harvest following a death.   This is a huge affair at which several hundreds of neighbors and kin are housed, feasted, intoxicated, and entertained for three days and two nights.   In general, the _havoria_ is a better organized, more opulent, less frenzied version of the celebrations that take place at burial.   Each afternoon, everyone gathers at a place outside of the village to drink, dance, wrestle, and watch the hired troupe of dancers.   Each evening, they gather in the village to drink, eat, and dance all night. Mornings are for sleeping, although many couples are otherwise occupied between the end of the dancing and the rising of the sun.

The 'gathering' is the biggest, most important, and most elaborate event in Bara social life. Whereas at the pre-burial ceremony there may be fifty to one hundred people, as many as five hundred people may attend a _havoria_.   Whole families walk ten, twenty, or thirty miles and then move into the village for several days.   A hundred litres of rum is considered very adequate for a burial ceremony, but at a 'gathering' there are often five hundred litres.   Ten or twelve cattle are slaughtered providing abundant beef for people who as a rule are too poor to eat a chicken or drink a cup of coffee, both of which they love. The _havoria_ is essentially a conspicuous display of wealth.   The rum is paraded before the people to be counted, admired, and anticipated, likewise the cattle.   And even the girls, dressed in their finest clothes (plastic raincoats were the ubiquitous fashion of 1970) and costume jewellery, are paraded single file before the crowd.   All expenditures are announced to the public: the fee for the dance specialists, the amounts of money given to the wrestlers and cattle riders, the

number of slaughtered cattle, and most important,
the amount of rum.   Normally, the Bara are quite
modest about their material success. They never
boast of or even admit to the size of their herds
or the success of their harvests. But a <u>havoria</u> is
not a time for modesty.

Although these activities are largely a grand
extension of the earlier burial ritual, the <u>havoria</u>
does not exhibit the extreme polarities that
characterize the burial.   In particular, the
relations between the sexes are more normal. There
is a women's hut and a men's hut as at the burial,
but now women and men often enter the opposite hut
for a variety of reasons. The young men and girls
dance together at night, form liaisons, and couple
discreetly; but their public demeanour is quite
reserved. The bawdy songs and sexual taunts are
notably absent. The location of the 'gathering' is
also less extreme as people gather in the village
proper by night and out in the near savannah by
day. There is a pragmatic alternation between the
two locations. Also, the paradox of extreme grief
and great celebration is diminished with the
passage of time.   Death and burial are sudden,
unplanned for, shocking events. <u>Havoria</u>, on the
other hand, are prepared, organized celebrations
that occur each year at the same season. So, in
spite of the huge consumption of resources and its
association with the activities surrounding death,
the <u>havoria</u> partakes of a regularity and normality
which clearly distinguish it from the burial
ritual.

There is, however, a dark side to the Bara
<u>havoria</u> celebration which is due to the great
danger of witchcraft.   A witch (<u>pamoriky</u> or
<u>pamosavy</u>) causes illness or death by deftly
slipping a minute amount of evil medicine into rum
or food while serving it to his victim.   Rum is

considered to be especially dangerous in this regard, and I have seen Bara order that a litre bottle of valuable rum be poured out because its cork seemed to have been disturbed. Also witchcraft medicine is transferred from one person to another by being placed on the genitals before sexual intercourse. In cases of adultery, incest, and witchcraft, the victim suffers from the same malady: a grotesque and fatal swelling of the stomach. It is no wonder, given this analogy between witchcraft, sexual excess, and gluttony, that a ceremony at which hundreds of people eat, drink rum, and copulate should generate a degree of inquietude regarding witches. Additionally, it is the dry season: the 'wet branch' and the corpse are drying out fast. If the man was killed by witchcraft, time is running out for the responsible party. A <u>havoria</u>, then, is particularly dangerous, both because it is a perfect opportunity for witches in general, and because it is seen as the logical time for specific witchcraft attacks in retaliation for the death that has already occurred.

Although I attended numerous <u>havoria</u>, only one took place in the village where I lived and knew all of the participants well. For about a week before the event, numerous friends warned me to be very careful and to watch the fingers of the rum servers. I was to stay close to my friends and only accept rum from people from whom they would accept it. At the very beginning of this <u>havoria</u>, a son-in-law of the deceased brought up a large barrel of water in his ox cart to save people the long trips to the river. Amid much shouting and confusion, this much-needed water was dumped out while people shouted that drinking it would kill one. Later, when the same son-in-law was dutifully helping to serve the rum, several people refused to drink it because they felt he had bewitched his

wife's father. It was insisted upon, later that
night, that two young men accompany me home. These
fellows, who normally wander about at night to meet
their girlfriends were so clearly frightened on
this <u>havoria</u> night, that I had little trouble
persuading them to let me be the one to walk them
home.

The gathering ends on the afternoon of the third
day. If rum still remains, it is served. People
watch the dance specialists for the last time.
Wrestling matches are staged between the boys of
different villages.   Girls dance to accordian
music. In short, the entertainment of the previous
days continues. Finally the family herd is brought
in and, as at the burial ritual, it is stampeded
around and around. In the middle gather the ill
and infirm. Young men display their courage by
leaping up and hanging onto the humps of the
stampeding cattle for as long as possible. Several
more cows are slaughtered, butchered, and
distributed. The women go through one more wailing
scene and the <u>tompom-paty</u> makes his final address.
The expenses are tallied, the distribution of beef
is stated, and most important, the death name is
announced. The deceased is given an elaborate new
name and his old name is often given to a
grandchild.

In summary, the <u>havoria</u> is characterized by
multiple but related dangers. Wrestling (<u>ringa</u>),
cattle riding (<u>mitolo aomby</u>), and specialized
dancing (<u>sery</u> or <u>panao karitaky</u>) are all believed
to be extremely dangerous to the practitioners who
must carry protective charms (<u>aody</u>) and observe
numerous taboos (<u>fady</u>). The risks of witchcraft,
sex, incest, and adultery have already been
explained. Rum is considered extremely dangerous,
not only as a vehicle for witchcraft, but also
because of its power of intoxication. I have seen

havoria which ended in large-scale fighting or individual hatchet attacks. At more prudent havoria, all of the spears, clubs, walking sticks, and rifles, which Bara men always carry to these affairs, are collected and placed in a large pile some distance away before the rum is served. The occasion is beset by what the Western observer would classify as both natural and supernatural dangers. But the Bara do not seem to make such a distinction. They are concerned with the danger of unrestrained, excessive vitality, whether it comes as a hatchet attack or a witchcraft attack.

Reburial (Fanaovam-paty)

At the first burial ritual, the deceased is placed in an individual coffin (sondry-dazo) and put in the family tomb or in some other temporary location. After the flesh has decayed, the body is exhumed, the bones are cleaned and then put in the final resting place in the tomb. This reburial ritual, which like the havoria takes place during the dry season following the harvest, is referred to by several names: fanaovam-paty (doing the corpse), mandatsaka kazo (dropping the tree or branch), and mamindra haraka (moving the dried-out one). This activity lasts one day only and although there is usually rum, beef, music, and dancing, it is a smaller affair than the havoria. But it is much more important than the 'gathering' which, in spite of its lavishness, is essentially an optional event. Although reburial can be delayed for many years, it is an absolute obligation of the descendants toward the deceased.

Inside the tomb are numerous large decorated, communal caskets (tamango), each containing the dried bones of perhaps ten persons. The number of caskets varies, but the tomb of a well-established family at Anosibe (three generations) contains between ten and fifteen of these caskets. To the north are grouped the caskets containing the bones of all the male ancestors. Each skeleton is placed in its rightful position with that of its father. At the south, by the door, are grouped the caskets holding the bones of the female agnates. The bones of a woman are grouped with those of her sister, father's sister, and brother's daughter. Also, in the female casket are the bones of young children of female agnates. These skeletons properly belong to the tomb of the father, but are given to their mother's family as an affinal prestation. Women are always buried in the tomb of the father, never with the husband. This common custom of <u>mizara zaza</u> ('dividing or sharing the children') is the only way a woman can be buried with immediate kin. Otherwise, a woman is cut off in death from her father, mother, husband, and children. The male caskets embody a lineal order of grandfather, son, and grandson; whereas the female caskets are sort of collection boxes for the skeletal residue of this system.

If a corpse is to be moved from another location to the official tomb, then the 'strong birds' leave early in the morning to exhume the body. The composition of the group of 'strong birds' is very much like that at burial but now there are more senior male relatives of the deceased. At the opening of the temporary tomb, care is taken to announce themselves, sprinkle a little rum on the rocks, and then drink the remainder. The old coffin is pulled out and opened and then the bones are scraped clean, rubbed with cow grease, and placed in a new cloth. All signs of grief are forbidden during these preparations just as they are forbidden during the preparations immediately following death. The return down the mountain is also much like the burial procession with everyone running and the boys carrying the remains in relays. They do not return to the village, but join the rest of the people already gathered at a prearranged location out on the savannah. There is one last wailing scene with both male and female kin joining in, and then the 'strong birds' pick up the remains, perhaps a new casket, as well as clothing for the deceased, and start on the merry run up to the final tomb.

The tomb is opened with the usual rum sprinkling and drinking; the remains and other objects are taken inside and arranged. At reburial, new clothing is placed near the corpse to replace the now rotted unfinished cloth that he was originally buried in. The clothes are his 'best' and often include Western items such as long trousers, shoes, used military uniforms, and even an occasional umbrella.[2] One additional item brought to the tomb is the horns of a newly-slaughtered ox to be placed with those from previous reburials. At some tombs, there are as many as one hundred pairs of ox horns placed in front of the wall opposite where the male caskets are grouped. When these arrangements are completed, the 'strong birds' rejoin the group down in the savannah for a celebration with more beef and rum.

At the reburial celebration there are special obligations for the grandchildren of the deceased. One other object taken to the tomb is a very expensive cloth (siky), usually one of the lovely, handwoven, colourfully dyed cloths made by the neighboring Betsileo out of native cotton or raw silk. At the tomb, this siky is thrown on the ground with shouts of, "Throw it away, throw it away!" Then all of the grandchildren pounce on it and rip it into strips, each of which becomes a colourful new loin-cloth (sadia) for a grandchild. Afterward, both males and females are obliged to dance at the celebration for their grandparent.

They are also expected to get a bit drunk and act somewhat silly but without any of the sexual overtones characteristic of earlier phases of Bara funeral rites. Otherwise, it is a rather orderly party at which people become sedately intoxicated and enjoy watching the cavorting of the grandchildren.

In short, the Bara reburial rites are much like the burial and 'gathering' ceremonies. In spite of the similarity of the feasting, drinking, dancing, running, and general merry-making, there are important differences. The reburial activities take place entirely by day and entirely out of the village. There is little of the extreme polarity and paradox of the original burial, and little of the dangerous element so important at the gathering. Bawdy songs, professional dance troupes, wrestling matches, and cattle riding contests would all be out of place at a reburial. Not surprisingly, the reburial signals a return to normality, one important aspect of which is that the deceased's widow is finally free to remarry. In terms of comparative Malagasy ethnography, it is important to note that the Bara reburial contrasts markedly with the well-known orgiastic nature of the exhumation rites (_famadihana_) of the Merina people.

Rite de Passage

Any anthropological discussion of funeral ritual must give consideration to those ideas about transition and burial first expounded by Hertz (1907) and Van Gennep (1909). Both authors view mortuary ritual generally as a symbolic emphasis of the ambiguous state of the deceased while in passage between life and some fixed eternal state. The death of an individual alters the usual order that prevails in the relationships between the ancestors and the living, between this particualr individual and his survivors, and among the living themselves. The solution to this ambiguity is seen as resting in the ritual manipulation of essentially eschatalogical conceptions.

The reconsideration of the Van Gennep-Hertz approach is particularly relevant with regard to Bara funerals. Both authors were quite familiar with Malagasy ethnography and the funeral rites of the Betsileo neighbors to the Bara figure in the original formulations of the hypothesis (Van Gennep 1960: 148-49; Hertz 1960: 47-48). Also Malagasy funeral rites have since been explained from this general viewpoint, somewhat unsuccessfully, by authors with first-hand experience with the Bara and their northern and southern neighbors (Faublee, Dubois, Decary). The spririt of the deceased is described as being isolated and lonely during the several-day period following death, and the purpose of the funeral revelry is to facilitate his difficult transition by providing amusement and distraction (Dubois 1938: 662-63; Decary 1958: 9).

But Dubois and Decary do not question why these particular forms of activity (drunken incest, bawdy songs, cattle wrestling, etc.) should be seen as appropriate ways to entertain the soul of a departed relative; and Faublee, in a similar fashion, fails to explain the important sexual component of Bara funeral symbolism. He reports the following song of the youths during the procession to the tomb, but offers not a word of explanation:

> Andeso apasy, sasao fa matsy, o mena.
> Andeso angebo, sasao fa membo, o mena.
> Tsy matify. Ino-n-io? O mena.
> Homea siky, o mena.

Tamango fandraky, tamango vy, o mena.
Ditiny n-apela tekofy ny trandraky, o
mena.
Sapan-andala boak-ambony, o mena.
Sapana ny dity boak-apory, o mena.
Tana, tana, tanandrotsy, nioriky an Isalo,
o mena.
Tanany panotsy nita renisango, o mena.
(Faublee 1954: 19)[3]

Carry on to the sand, wash it for it rots,
o red.[4]
Carry on to the plain, wash it for it
stinks, o red.
It is not light. What is it? o red.
Give a siky, o red.
Casket of wood, casket of iron, o red.
Stickiness of woman pricked by the
hedgehog, o red.
Fork in the path coming from above, o red.
Fork in the stickiness coming from the
anus, o red.
Branch of the rotsy tree bewitching on the
mountain, o red.
The tickling hand touching the clitoris, o
red.

An adequate analysis of Bara funerals must attempt
some explanation of how the tickling of a clitoris
helps a departed kinsman move on to his next
status.

   The notion that funeral rituals can be seen as
a transition which begins with the separation of
the deceased from life and ends with his
incorporation into the world of the dead is merely
a vague truism unless it is positively related to
the values of a particular culture. The continued
relevance of Van Gennep and Hertz is not due to the
tripartite   analytical   schema   (separation-

transition-reincorporation) itself, but to the creative process by which they combined the schema with cultural values to grasp the conceptual vitality of each ritual. And so too, in following this approach, it is necessary not merely to apply an old formula to new rituals, but in a sense to create anew the rite de passage in a dynamic relationship among the logic of the schema (transitions need beginnings and ends), biological facts (corpses rot), and culture specific symbolizations (whatever).

The first part of this chapter related the funeral activity to the logic of the rite de passage schema and to the biological facts, presenting the material almost entirely in terms of trans-cultural universals. It is a tribute to the insight of Van Gennep that these funeral events can be understood to such a large degree with a minimal consideration of their specifically Bara attributes. Yet, as indicated earlier, certain crucial aspects of these rites remain inexplicable unless they are related to that system of values that is uniquely Bara. A difficulty in the analysis of Bara and Malagasy funerals stems from the fact that there is an apparent contradiction in these two modes of ordering the data. The extra-cultural, sequential approach emphasizes the ambiguous and transitory aspect of dying, and rightly so. But this approach can obscure important Bara values which stress that it is life which is transitional and dying that is tragically unambiguous.

Order and Vitality

In terms of the Bara phenomenology of the person, life is maintained by a tenuously balanced combination of what can be referred to as 'order' and 'vitality'. As a biological object, a person is formed when the 'fertile blood' (<u>ra</u>) of the mother is ordered by the semen (<u>rano-mamboatsy</u>-- literally, 'water that arranges') of the father during sexual intercourse. To be socially and economically successful, an individual must balance out his relationships with his mother's and father's families. Bara kin groups, if they are to survive, must balance their desire for agnatic solidarity against the need to maintain affinal alliances. Dying, tombs, ancestors, father, social and moral order are all explicitly associated together by the Bara. Keeping this in mind, I seek to further explain Bara funeral behaviour with the hypothesis that they view death as an overdose of order upsetting the life-sustaining balance, and that much of the funeral behaviour is an attempt to redress the imbalance through a symbolic increase in vitality.

By formalizing these Bara notions of order and vitality into a table of oppositions and extensions, it is possible to begin to understand how such conceptions articulate with the ritual behaviour.

ORDER	VITALITY
male	female
father	mother
semen	blood
bone	flesh
sterility	fecundity
dying	birth
tomb	womb

In his study of <u>Polarity and Analogy</u> in early Greek thought, G.E.R. Lloyd reminds us that oppositions include relationships of many different natures. As an example, he suggests that we,

Consider the pairs black and white, and odd

and even...The first pair admits intermediates
(grey and other colours), but the second pair
does not. It is not the case that all colours
are either black or white, but every whole
number is either odd or even. (Lloyd 1966: 87)

Additionally, some terms admit only one opposition
whereas others may be opposed to several terms.
'Male' can only be opposed to 'female'; but
'father' can be as easily opposed to 'son' or
'mother's brother' as to 'mother', depending upon
the context. By examining the above list of
opposed pairs in terms of the varying natures of
the oppositions, it is possible to begin to see in
what ways the notion of death as a transition
relates specifically to Bara culture.

As one moves down the above columns, the
relationships of opposition become more and more
extreme. The upper pairs are each complementary
with the two poles combining to produce viable
existence (male/female, father/mother, semen/blood,
bone/flesh). But for the last three pairs, this
complementarity is replaced by a profound
antagonism. In fact, this antagonism is so
pronounced as to be almost inexpressible since as
the one column progresses toward the maximum order
of the tomb, the other column progresses toward
maximum vitality and chaos. I have used the terms
'fecundity', birth', and 'womb' merely to indicate
the sorts of attributes the Bara view in opposition
to death. But actually, the opposite of pure order
cannot be expressed in an orderly fashion. In
reconsideration of the above table of symbolic
oppositions and extensions, it is clear that there
are two different relationships of opposition
represented, one complementary and one
antagonistic. The pair flesh/bone partakes of both
these forms of opposition. Bone and flesh are

complementary in the human body but become antagonistic when breath has ceased. The two columns presented earlier can be elaborated to express the change in the nature of the symbolic opposition which accompanies dying.

ORDER/VITALITY

male	female
father	mother
semen	blood
bone	flesh
death	'birth'
sterility	'fecundity'
tomb	'womb'
ABSOLUTE	ABSOLUTE
ORDER	VITALITY

The corpse clearly occupies a 'liminal' state between that conjunction of bone and flesh which is considered 'life' and that separation of these substances which is considered 'death'. And, as Hertz and Van Gennep explained long ago, this understanding of the liminal nature of the corpse does much to explain the rites of burial, exhumation, and reburial which mark both Malagasy and Indonesian funeral customs.

But the sexual aspects of these funeral rituals relate more to the consequences of this liminality than to the liminality per se. These consequences are that the dead, sterile order of bone is taking dominion over the ebbing vitality of the decomposing flesh. Reality as the Bara perceive it has moved from a state of mediated equilibrium between order and vitality to a state of pure,

fatal order. This extreme aspect of order cannot
be mediated, but can only be opposed by the most
extreme aspects of vitality. The sex and sex-
related activities of the funeral nights and the
'gathering' are symbolic ammunition in the open
warfare between the extreme ends of the polar
continuum of reality.

The Representation of Vitality

Many of the funeral activities express aspects
of the Bara notion of vitality. In particular, the
songs, dances, and contests of the preburial period
all express the inter-related themes of sex, birth,
life, disorder, incest, danger, war, and fertility.
These powerful themes are most explicitly presented
in the lyrics of the girls' songs which continue
throughout the preburial night-time festivities.
New songs come into fashion every year and the most
popular songs of even recent years are rarely
heard. Like popular music in much of the world,
new songs rapidly replace old, but the themes
remain the same from year to year. The most
popular funeral of 1970 is a clever piece of ribald
double entendre.

Jay magnambara	Now hide it
Jay magnambara jalahy	Now hide it, boys
Jay magnambara da maty	Now hide it because there is a death
Itsika hilele	Together let us copulate
Itsika hilele jalahy	Together let us copulate, boys
Jay magnambara	Now hide it
Jay magnambara da maty	Now hide it because there

	is a death
Brroo kibo	"Brroo" goes the quail
Ho votraky andoha sely	To perch at the head of the sely tree
Masony te-hatory?	The eye wants to sleep?
Masony te-hilele	The eye wants to copulate
Brroo kibo	"Brroo" goes the quail
Votraky antrongony sakoa	To perch on a bump of a sakoa tree
Masony te-hilele	The eye wants to copulate
Masony te ho voa soa	The eye wants to ejaculate
Brroo kibo	"Brroo" goes the quail
Votraky andoha fotaky	To perch at the head of the mud
Magnambara	Hide it!
Magnambara jalahy	Hide it, boys!
Jay magnambara da maty	Now hide it because there is a death
Itsika hilele	Together let us copulate
Itsika hilele	Together let us copulate
Ndre madinky	whether big
Ndre lahibe	whether little
Jay magnambara	Now hide it!

The onomatopoeic 'brroo' of the quail is an expression commonly used to refer to ejaculation in sexual intercourse. The word for quail is also the

word for belly (<u>kibo</u>). The word for eye (<u>maso</u>)
also refers generally to any centre, hole, circle,
or vortex; in this case, the vagina. The vagina is
also suggested by the word for mud (<u>fotaky</u>) which
refers generally to any wet slime or slipperiness.
And the quail, according to the Bara, is quite
incapable of perching either at the head or on the
knob of a tree. There is the suggestive image of
the quivering quail looking for the appropriate
place to hide. First it tries the head of a tree,
then a lower knob of a tree, and finally settles
into the stickiness below.

Another popular funeral song takes up a more
serious theme as the girls sing a lament on the
difficulties of child-birth. This song too is sung
at funerals and at no other time.

<u>O mena manja</u>	O bright red
<u>O marary aho amjao</u>	O I am hurting now
<u>O mena manja</u>	O bright red
<u>Da marary ny terak'io</u>	I am hurting from this birth
<u>O mena manja</u>	O bright red
<u>Alavo moto nono</u>	My breasts have fallen heavily
<u>O marary aho, o nene</u>	O I hurt, mother
<u>Tanetanihy ny fagnola</u>	Massage my stomach
<u>Tanatanana ny pagnotsy</u>	Make it easier

When referring to participation in these
preburial vigils, the Bara say they are going to
<u>miandry</u> (await) <u>faha</u>. The word <u>faha</u> is difficult
to translate, but its various usages and
connotations include: nourishment, ration, a live
prestation to a visitor, rifle cartridge, the
winding of a clock, elasticity,[5] rebound,

resiliency, and energy (Abinal and Malzac).   The
Bara in the village of Anosibe most commonly use
the word in referring to a thin cow (lack _faha_) and
as a name for those curing ceremonies that aim to
strengthen one who has been weakened by illness.
In   general,   _faha_   signifies   vitality,   but   the
emphasis is on a potential, stored-up vitality
rather than on the dissipation of energy in
activity.

The concept of storing up vitality is perhaps
evident in the mode of dancing associated with
funeral activities.   The meaning of a dance style
is less explicit than that of the lyrics of a song
and perhaps less amenable to analysis.   However,
there is a definite contrast in style between
funeral dancing and all other Bara dancing.   In
addition to the three funeral ceremonies, Bara also
dance   at   circumcision   and   spirit   possession
ceremonies. On these occasions the dancing is wild
and unrestrained with dancers individually showing
off their skills, At funerals, the girls dance in
a slow, tight circle in front of the 'house of many
tears'.   One by one the boys join so that there are
often two or three circles, one inside another.
The dancers in the innermost circle move very
slowly forward in a tense double time while those
in the larger outer ring come down hard on the
beat.   Often one or two pre-adolescent boys dance
in a languid half-rhythm very quickly around the
outside of the other circles.   Each succeeding
circle (from outside) is tighter, faster rhythmed,
and slower moving.   The dance gives the appearance
of the winding up of a human clock-spring.   It is
this dancing combined with the girls' running
(while singing) round and round the hut containing
the body, which is seen by the Bara as the epitome
of _faha_.

Cattle play important roles in Bara funeral

events in two respects. First, there is the cattle wrestling (<u>mitolo   aomby</u>) at the burial and gathering ceremonies. This sport of stampeding the herd round and round resembles a bovine version of the funeral dances. When describing the event, Bara boys always emphasize the snorting, panting, and bucking of the cattle as signs of intense vitality. This sport is practiced at only one other occasion and that is at the sowing of the rice fields when the trampling hooves perform a plough-like function. The association of cattle with the fertility of the earth is also clear in a number of Bara legends. In one reported by Faublee, the cow states:

> When I die do not bury me in a tomb but your stomachs shall be my tomb. My head you shall not eat but bury it in the earth. After one week corn sprouts and rice, manioc, and sweet potatoes. And the head too shall give you life. And this is why you must offer up the first fruits in thanksgiving. (Faublee 1947: 381)

Another legend recounts how God was once about to give all the animals a potion of life so that death would be eradicated. The cow accidentally drank the entire supply and since there was no more to be had God advised the other animals to kill the cow during times of danger and eat of its flesh which contains the force of life. This relates to the second role of cattle in the funeral events, namely the slaughter of numerous cattle to provide for the feasting. The killing of cattle is done differently at funeral events than at all other ceremonies. The killing of a cow at a marriage or circumcision is a complicated process calling for a formal address to the ancestors, plus special positioning and washing of the cow. At funerals, however, the animals' skulls are simply bashed with an axe. Whereas in other ceremonies cattle are sacrificed to facilitate communication with the ancestors, at funerals it seems as though cattle are slaughtered so that the living can protect themselves by absorbing the force of life inherent in beef.

An important aspect of the representation of vitality is the idea that it is in a sense chaotic as opposed to the order of the ancestor cult. In one of the songs, the girls call upon the boys to be _maola_ (to act crazy, unrestrained, and shameless) during the funeral fete. It is in this regard that rum takes on special significance. A drunken person is generally referred to as being _maola_ or a _biby_ (a wild, undomesticated animal). Rum is served not merely because intoxication is pleasant, but because disorderly conduct is essential.

The most important mode of generating a sense of disorder is through incest. For the Betsileo funerals, Father Dubois describes what he considers "the moment of horrors" when everyone copulates incognito with a total disregard for incest regulations (1938: 666). The Bara do not tolerate unexpiated incestuous intercourse, not even at funerals; but the songs, dances, and bawdy remarks exchanged among kin at a funeral would at any other time require the sacrifice of a cow in expiation. An actual attempt at intercourse with a relative at a funeral celebration constitutes a wrong and must be expiated. But, the attitude of the Bara toward such incest is that it is an inevitable part of funeral fetes and the offender should pay the penalty (one cow, bony) with good humour. The incestuous behaviour of the participants in the preburial and the 'gathering' celebrations is in opposition to the fundamental Bara principle of moral and social order.

The semi-professional dance troupes, the _sery_, are also viewed as possessing dangerous asocial qualities. The _sery_ are hired for virtually every 'gathering' and occasionally for a burial if the family can afford it, but they are prohibited from singing or dancing at most other functions. Should a _sery_ sing to a sick person, the patient will die. At the 'gathering' celebration, the _sery_ perform only during daylight to stimulate and amuse the guests. At night, with the occasional exception of early in the first evening, it is considered far too dangerous to have the _sery_ perform. They may not enter the village before the start of the 'gathering' celebration and must be permanently out of the village before the final closing ceremony. The _sery_ dress outrageously. The men wear their hair in long braids entwined with coins and bells. They are explicitly dressed in the symbols of warriorhood and no _sery_ ever dances without his/her elaborate spear. The dancing is wild and sexual with particular energetic dances being done to entice even more money from members of the audience. In her study of the status of musical specialists, Norma McLeod (1964) ably describes how the _sery_ must build their huts outside of the village and in the inauspicious directions of south and west.

Resolution: Intercourse and Rebirth

During the time following death, extreme vitality is generated through the various excesses of the funeral celebration in an effort to counterbalance the extreme order of death. But this unstable situation cannot persist and the funeral activities become directed toward effecting a return to normality. Since the instability of the situation derives from the antagonism between the bone and the flesh of the corpse, the resolution depends upon removing the corpse from the world of the living.   For as long as the corpse in which bone (order) is taking dominion over flesh (vitality) remains, then the life-giving balance or order and vitality is impossible.   In another Bara legend, a man with ten cows asks the king for advice because his cows are barren.   The king says this is because the man did not bury his father who died when he was young.   The man then holds a funeral, builds a tomb, kills cattle and buries his father.   Soon there are many new calves and his wife also gives birth (Faublee 1947:   377).

The actual burial takes the form of a double metaphor of sexual intercourse and birth.   First the competition between order and vitality is intensified during the removal of the corpse from the village to the tomb on the mountain.   This funeral procession resembles a 'burial by capture' as the men enter (for the first time) the 'house of many tears' and take away the coffin over the tearful protests of the women.   The young men then run, carrying the coffin relays, toward the mountain of the ancestors.   A group of young girls, often with their hair and clothes dishevelled, run and catch up to the coffin-bearers to distract and detain them from their task.   Often the girls intervene physically to stop the journey to the tomb and there ensues a tug-of-war over the coffin as the girls try to pull it back to the village. When this fails, the girls may run ahead and line up across the boys' path.   The boys charge using the coffin as a battering ram to penetrate this female barrier and continue toward the tomb.

This sexual symbolism is continued at the tomb itself as the coffin is poked head first into the small hole at the mouth of the cave.   But the symbolism shifts as attention focuses on the arrival of the deceased among his ancestors.   The dominant theme becomes that of birth with the deceased entering the world of the dead head-first like a foetus. When asked to comment on the meaning of burial, the Bara invariably use the metaphor of birth.[6] This theme is evident as well in the song cited earlier and in the tomb-side address to the ancestors: "Here is your grandchild, born here. Do not push him away, even from here." Just as one must be born into the world of the living, so must one also be born out of it and into the world of the dead.

Bara burial is indeed concerned with the transition of the deceased from the world of the living to the realm of the dead just as Van Gennep and Hertz would maintain. But the Bara recognize only one mode of transition that is adequate for changing the state of being for a human: sexual intercourse and birth.   Not unexpectedly, the process of being born into the world of the dead is the inverse of the process of entering the world of the living. Biological conception begins with the chaotic fecundity of the mother's womb and menstrual blood to which must be added the ordering power of father's semen. Order is added to fertile vitality. Entering the tomb, however, is quite the reverse. The cessation of life and breath in the deceased has created a situation of sterile order to which must be added a massive dose of vitality to accomplish the difficult birth into the world of the ancestors. Vitality is added to sterile order. It is not enough merely to bury someone, merely to dispose of the body. The survivors must bring about the successful conception and rebirth of their deceased kinsman into the world of the ancestors. This process, like the conception and birth of an infant, is a difficult and risky endeavour for both the deceased and his survivors. Should this transition fail, the consequence is nothing short of catastrophic infertility, with the deceased remaining like a dead fetus in the womb of his survivors' world.

Epilogue

For the burial ceremony itself, then, the deceased, the living, and even the cosmos go through a period of transition; beginning with the separation from normality (the silence at the moment of death) and ending with a reintegration (rebirth at burial). This almost universal sequential ordering of a rite de passage is expressed through a uniquely Bara configuration of values relating to the two modes of structural opposition between flesh and bone. Because the notions of flesh and bone are closely associated with ideas of male and female, father's line and mother's line, ancestors and affines, and the ultimate human problem of reconciling unchanging order with the disruption of necessary renewal; the corpse is what Victor Turner (1967) would call a dominant and multireferential symbol. The imbalance of the male and female components of the corpse threaten the balance of the components of the Bara social and moral universe. And it is only through the symbolic manipulation of these essentially sexual components that the corpse with its inherent imbalance can be removed.

But this burial rite de passage is not the end of Bara mortuary customs. Two ceremonies remain. For a situation as complex as death, there is not just one transition to be made, but several. Each of the three Bara funeral ceremonies concentrates on a transition of a different nature. The burial is largely concerned with the transition of the corpse. The 'gathering' is the least structured of the three ceremonies and the only one that is optional. It is distinguished from the other ceremonies by the concern shown toward the reordering of social relationships which have been altered by the loss of a kinsman. This is manifest in the witchcraft fears and accusations which are largely concerned with the settling of social scores, especially with regard to the death of the man in whose honour the 'gathering' is held. The affair closes with the granting of a new name to the deceased and to some of the living, which is followed by a short speech stating that it is time to leave off yearning for the departed.

The reburial focuses explicitly on the transition of the remains from the individual coffin to the final resting place in the communal casket containing the ordered bones of agnatic kin. The ritual itself is a miniature and subdued replication of the original burial. The exhumation is marked by the same mandatory silence and prohibition of weeping that mark the moment of death itself. There is a festive procession between the temporary burial place and the family tomb, ending with the placement of the bones in their proper place and the closing of the tomb. Separation, transition, incorporation: It is a <u>rite de passage</u> concerned with arranging the ambiguities that death creates in the organization of the ancestors. The proper relationship between the worlds of the living and the dead is also re-established.

Additionally, one can view the whole funeral sequence as a single rite of passage with the original burial as a rite of separation, the 'gathering' as an unstructured period of liminality, and the reburial as the ritual of reintegration. It is a question of how wide a perspective one takes. There are transitions within transitions within transitions. For the Bara, all of life is ultimately a transition and

only a perspective wide enough to include birth
allows an understanding of death.

Acknowledgements

Field research was supported by fellowships from
the Shell Foundation and Duke University.

I would like to thank Robin Carter, Christopher
Crocker, James Fox, Robin Hallett, Peter Huber, and
Monica Wilson for their helpful comments on earlier
drafts of this paper.

Notes

1. Informants often asked if my people sing and dance at funerals. They pondered over my negative answer and admitted it was sensible. "But we Bara are strange, we are sad about the death, but we sing and dance anyway."

2. When cloth was scarce during the war, young men often robbed tombs under the pretense of, "Oh sleeping Indian merchant, how much for your wares?" To alert their kin to this desecration, the ancestors caused the deaths of innocent descendants so as to bring the family to the tomb. And of course, all of the thieves are reported to have died. Today the Bara find the anecdote of the sleeping Indian merchant very amusing.

3. I have standardized Faublee's idiosyncratic orthography and substituted an English translation for his French.

4. Bara colour symbolism is important but too complex to be discussed in this paper.

5. Many Bara Boys claim that if an elastic 'undershirt' (a popular European item) is worn to a funeral, the close contact with death will cause the stretchy material to disintegrate. This applies only to stretchy material and not to European goods in general.

6. See Althabe 1969: 142, for similar usage among the Betsimisaraka.

References

Abinal, R.P., and Malzac, R.P. 1888. Dictionnaire
    Malgache-Francais. Paris: Editions Maritimes
    et Coloniales.

Althabe, Gerard. 1969. Oppression et Liberation
    dans l'Imaginaire. Paris: François Maspero.

Bloch, Maurice. 1971. Placing the Dead: Tombs,
    Ancestral Villages, and Kinship Organization
    in Madagascar. London and New York: Seminar
    Press.

Decary, Raymond. 1958. La Mort et les Coutumes
    Funeraires à Madagascar. Paris: G.P.
    Maisonneuve et Larose.

Dubois, H. 1938. Monographic des Betsileo. Paris:
    Institut d'Ethnologie.

Faublee, Jacques. 1947. Recits Bara. Paris:
    Institut d'Ethnologie.

_____. 1954. La Cohesion des Sociétés Bara.
    Paris: Presses Universitaires de France.

Hertz, Robert. 1960 (1907). Death and the Right
    Hand, translated by R. and C. Needham. London:
    Cohen & West.

Kopytoff, Igor. 1971. Ancestors as Elders in
    Africa. Africa 41 (2): 129-42.

Lloyd, G.E.R. 1966. Polarity and Analogy. Cambridge
    University Press.

McLeod, Norma. 1964. The Status of Musical
    Specialists in Madagascar. Ethno-musicology 7
    (3): 278-89.

Turner, Victor. 1967. Forest of Symbols. Ithaca,
    N.Y.: Cornell University Press.

Van Gennep, Arnold. 1960 (1909). The Rites of
    Passage, translated by Monika B. Vizedom and
    Gabrielle L. Caffee. London: Routledge &
    Kegan Paul.

Wilson, Monica. 1957. Rituals of Kinship Among the
    Nyakyusa. London: Oxford University Press.

DEATH IN ISLAM: THE HAWKES BAY CASE

Akbar S. Ahmed

Abstract

The relationship between attitudes to death
and the social order is examined through a recent
case study from Pakistan.   In February 1983,
thirty-eight Shiah Muslims entered the Arabian Sea
at Hawkes Bay in response to revelations received
by one of their number. Eighteen of them died.
Various social factors which may help to explain
the incident are discussed, including tensions
arising from changing contemporary values, local
attitudes to leadership, and the kinship connectons
of the participants.   The case also raises
important issues about concepts of death,
sacrifice, and martyrdom among Shiah and Sunni
Muslims, and shows how ideas about the status of
the individual in the after-world may affect social
behavior in this one.

In this article I examine the relationship
between attitudes to death and the social order.
The anthropological literature on this subject is
not extensive (Banton 1969; Bloch & Parry 1982;
Evans-Pritchard 1937, 1965; Douglas 1970; Geertz
1969; Keyes 1981, forthcoming; Lewis 1971; Werbner
1977; Winter 1969) and information on Muslim
societies is particularly scarce.   I will raise
some of the related issues through a recent case-
study from Pakistan—the Hawkes Bay case.

Reprinted from Man 21(1986):   120-134, by
permission of the Royal Anthropology Institute of
Great Britain and Ireland.

In late February, 1983, thirty-eight people--
all Shiah--entered the Arabian sea at Hawkes Bay in
Karachi.   The women and children in the group,
about half the number, had been placed in six large
trunks.   The leader of the group, Sayyad Willayat
Hussain Shah, pointing his religious banner at the
waves, led the procession. Willayat Shah believed
that a path would open in the sea which would lead
him to Basra, from where the party would proceed to
Karbala, the holy city in Iraq. A few hours later
almost half the party had lost their lives and the
survivors emerged in varying stages of exhaustion
and consciousness.

Pakistan   was   astonished   and   agog   at   the
incident.   Religious leaders, intellectuals and
newspapers discussed the event threadbare.[1]   The
discussions revealed almost as much as those
participating in them as they did about the
incident.   Some intellectuals saw the episode as
evidences of 'insanity' (Salahudin 1983) and the
leaders of the group were described as 'mentally
unbalanced individuals with twisted and deviant
personalities, the source of death and destruction'
(Irfani 1983).   Sunnis dismissed the matter as yet
another Shiah aberration from orthodox Islam.   The
Shiahs, on the other hand, pointed to the event as
a   confirmation   of   their   faith   (Jaffery 1983;
Yusufzai 1983).   Only the Shiahs, they argued, were
capable of such extreme devotion, of such a
sacrifice.   It was, undoubtedly, a case rooted in
Shiah mythology, which preconditioned the community
to respond to, and enact, the drama. (The Shiah
lived in Chakwal Tehsil, in the Province of
Punjab.)[2]

Chakwal Tehsil

Willayat Shah's family lived in a small village, Rehna Sayyadan, about ten miles from Chakwal Tehsil in Jhelum District. Jhelum on the main Grand Trunk Road, is about seventy miles from Chakwal Tehsil. A population of about 250,000 live in the Tehsil. Chakwal and Jhelum are areas of rainfed agriculture, unlike the canal colonies, in the Punjab, of Lyallpur (now Faisalabad) and Sahiwal, with their rich irrigated lands. The population of the village itself is about 2,000, mainly consisting of Sayyads, the upper social group, and Arain, the lower. The latter are challenging the authority of the former through new channels of employment, hard work and frugality (Ahmed, A.S. 1984b). The village is somewhat isolated from the rest of Pakistan. Electricity has only recently arrived and the road to Chakwal is not yet metalled. This is one of the hottest areas in the country. Winters are short and the rainfall (about 20 inches) is unreliable. Poor harvests have pushed people off the land to look for employment outside the Tehsil. Many have joined the armed services (Jhelum District is a rich recruiting ground for the Pakistan Army) and from the 1960's the Arab states offered opportunities for employment. Willayat Shah, after his service as a junior officer in the Pakistan Air Force, left to work in Saudi Arabia. He returned to Pakistan in 1981 after a stay of four years.

Rehna Sayyadan is self-consciously religious. Its very name announces a holy lineage, that of the Sayyads, the descendants of the Holy Prophet, and means 'the abode of the Sayyads'. Many of the Shiah actors in the drama bear names derived from members of the Holy Prophets family: Abbass and Hussain for men, and Fatima for women. But there is tension in the area between Shiah and Sunni, a tension made more acute by the fact that their numbers are equally balanced. The economic subordination of the Sunni by the Shiah reinforces the tension. Conflict between Shiah and Sunni easily converts into conflict between landlord and tenant. This opposition also runs through the local administration. The local government councillor, for example, is Sunni but the village lambardar (head man) is Shiah. Even families are divided along Shiah-Sunni lines and where individuals have changed affiliation, relationships have been severely strained. (There are at least four known cases of Sunni affiliation closely related to the main actor in the drama, Naseem Fatima.) The tension is exacerbated by the current emphasis on Sunni forms of religion by the Government of Pakistan. The Shiahs, about 20 per cent of Pakistan's 90 million people, resent this emphasis. The Jamaat-e-Islami, the major orthodox Sunni political party of Pakistan, is active in the area. In the background is the larger ideological tension between the Shiahs and Sunnis in Pakistan. From 1980 onwards this tension became severe and led to clashes between the two, especially in Karachi. Beyond the south-western borders of Pakistan, a vigorous Shiah revivalism in Iran has unsettled neighbouring Sunni states allied to Pakistan, such as Saudi Arabia.

Willayat Shah was living in Saudi Arabia when Imam Khomeini returned to Iran at the head of his revolution in 1979. Being a devout Shiah, he would have been inspired by the message and success of the Imam, but Saudi Arabia was no place to express his rekindled Shiah enthusiasm. He would, however, have been dreaming dreams around the themes of the revolution: sacrifice, death, change and martyrdom. His first act on returning home was to begin the construction of a mosque.

The Hawkes Bay Case

On the 18th of February 1981, Willayat Shah had been engrossed in supervising the construction of the mosque. Late that evening Naseem Fatima, his eldest child, entered his bedroom and announced she had been visited by a revelation--basharat. She had heard the voice of a lady speaking to her through the walls of the house. The apprehensive father suggested she identify the voice. For the first few days the voice was identified as that of Bibi Roqayya, the step-sister of Imam Hussain, the grandson of the Holy Prophet, buried in Karbala.

Some hand-prints next appeared on the wall of Willayat Shah's bedroom. They were made with henna mixed with clay. A hand print has highly emotive significance among the Shiah. It is symbolic of the five holiest people in Islam: the Holy Prophet, his daughter, Hazarat Fatima, his son-in-law, Hazrat Ali, and his grandsons, Hazrat Hassan and Hazrat Imam Hussain. The news of the hand-prints spread like wildfire in the area. The impact on the village was electric. One informant described it as follows:

> for the next fifteen days or so the usual business of life came to a halt. People gave up their work, women stopped even cooking meals. Everyone gathered in the house of Willayat Hussain to see the print, to touch it, to pray and to participate in the mourning (azadari) which was constantly going on (Pervez 1983: 8).

The azadari, a recitation of devotional hymns and poems in honor of, in particular, Hazrat Hussain, was a direct consequence of the handprints. It created a highly charged and contagious atmosphere among the participants.

Sunnis, however, were cynical about the whole affair. They would remain adamant opponents of Naseem's miracles (maujza). Opinion was divided among the Shiah. Established families such as the Sayyads scoffed at Naseem and her miracles and, at first, both Willayat Shah and his daughter had their doubts. As if to dispel these doubts Imam Mahdi, or Imam-e-Ghaib, the twelfth Imam, himself appeared in the dreams of Naseem. Earlier, Bibi Roqayya had announced that the Imam rather than she would communicate with Naseem. The Imam wore white clothes and was of pleasing appearance (Ansari 1983:6). All doubts in her mind were now dispelled and he addressed her as Bibi Pak--pure lady.

The Imam, with wohom she now communicated directly, began to deliver explicit orders (amar). One commanded the expulsion of the carpenter who was working for Willayat in his house (Ansari 1983:7) and who had overcharged him by a thousand rupees, in connivance with the contractor. He was ordered never to work at a Sayyad's house again, or both would be losers in the transaction. To compensate Willayat, the Imam placed five hundred rupees in a copy of the Holy Quran and ordered the carpenter to pay the remaining five hundred. The orders increased in frequency. They soon included matters of property and marriage. The family, at least, no longer doubted the miracles. They obeyed the divine orders without question. During the revelations Naseem would demand complete privacy in her room. Her condition would change. She would quiver and tremble. Noises would sound in her head beforehand and the trauma of the revelations often caused her to faint afterwards. The orders would come to her on the days the Imams died or were made martyrs. 'The Imam', according to her father, 'had captured her mind and heart' (Ansari 1983: 8).

Local Shiah religious leaders and lecturers (<u>zakirs</u>) acknowledged Naseem and visited her regularly. Of the three most regular visitors, one Sakhawat Hussain Jaffery, was particularly favoured. Naseem claimed that she had been especially ordered by the Imam to single him out. They were often alone for long periods. Naseem began to organize <u>azadari</u> regularly. These meetings were charged with emotion and created devout ecstasy in the participants. They were held next to the local primary schools; so many people attended, with such noisy devotion, that the school had to close down. Naseem now completely dominated the life of the village. Before moving to the next phase of the case let us pause to examine the effect of the revelations on some of the main actors in the drama.

Naseem was a shy, pleasant-looking girl, with an innocent expression on her face, who had a history of fits. There was talk of her getting married. Although she had only studied up to class five, her teachers recall her passionate interest in reciting <u>nauhas</u> (poems about Karbala), many of which she composed herself. After her revelations there was a perceptible change in Naseem. She began to gain weight, wear costly dresses and use perfumes. She became noticeably gregarious and confident. In a remarkable gesture of independence, especially so for a Sayyad girl in the area, she abandoned the <u>parda</u> or veil. According to Shiah belief, any believer may become the vehicle for divine communications. Naseem turned to the dominant person in her life, her father, upon receiving communications and he interpreted them in his own light.

Willayat Shah now reasserted himself in village affairs after an absence of years. His daughter's religious experience had begun soon after his retirement from Arabia. He had an older brother to whom, because of the traditional structure of rural soceity, he was subordinate. His period in Saudi Arabia had enhanced his economic, but not his social position. Because of the miracles and revelations of his daughter, however, he gained a dominant position in the social life of the area. Sardar Bibi, Naseem's mother, was influenced by her husband and daughter and identified wholly with the latter. She was said to have been a Sunni before her marriage and this created an underlying tension in the family. In an expression of loyalty to her husband, she severed relations with her parents and brothers because they disapproved of her conversion. She unhesitatingly obeyed her daughter's revelations.

Another actor in the drama was Sakhawat Jaffery, a zakir of Chakwal. He was not a Sayyad and his father was said to be a butcher. He had risen in the social order. Willayat Shah rewarded him for his loyalty with gifts--refrigerators, televisions, fans etc. When he needed money for a new business he was presented with about 20,000 rupees. With this sum he opened a small shop selling general goods. He was given such gifts on the specific orders of the Imam to Naseem. In turn he was the only one of the three zakirs who personally testified to the authenticity of the miracles of Naseem. Naseem was regularly visited by Sakhawat Jaffery and she visited his house. In a gesture of affection, contravening social custom, Naseem named Sakhawat's male child--a few months old--Rizwan Abbass. Such names, deriving from the Holy Prophet's family, were traditionally reserved for Sayyads.

Most people were cynical about the relationship between Naseem and the zakir. Sakhawat's own wife, who had complete faith in Naseem, said people had

spread 'dirty talk' (gandi batey) about Naseem and
her husband (Ansari 1983:   4).   In spite of his
belief in the revelations, Sakhawat Jaffery did not
join the pilgrimage to Hawkes Bay. He had recently
opened his shop and explained that abrupt departure
would   ensure   its   failure.   Naseem   was
understanding: "This is not a trip for zakirs. We
want to see you prosper."

After the visions, Naseem's followers bestowed
on her the title already used by the Imam, Pak
Bibi, or pure lady.   The transformation in her
appearance and character was now complete.   She
radiated confidence. Her following spread outside
the village.   In particular, she developed an
attachment to the people of a neighbouring village,
Mureed, who were recently converted Muslims
(Sheikhs) and who wholeheartedly believed in her.
Most of them were kammis, belonging to such
occupational groups as barbers and cobblers.
Naseem, as a Sayyad, represented for them the house
of the Prophet while her father, being relatively
well off, was a potential source of financial
support.   Seventeen of the villagers of Mureed
would follow her to Hawkes Bay.

The normal life of the village was disrupted by
the   affair.   The   Shiah,   in   particular,
'wholeheartedly accepted the phenomenom' but, not
unnaturally, 'the regular routine life of the
village was paralysed'.   In particular 'women
stopped doing their household jobs' (Jaffery 1983:
10).   Some placed obstacles in Naseem's path,
teasing her family members (especially children on
their way to school), and dumping rubbish in front
of her house. Sayyads who did not believe in her
ill-treated her followers from Mureed.

Meanwhile, a series of miracles was taking
place which riveted society.   Blood was found on

the floor of Willayat Shah's bedroom.   Naseem
declared this to be the blood of Hazrat Ali Asghar,
the male child of Hazrat Hussain, martyred at
Karbala.   On another occasion visitors were locked
in a room and told that angels would bear down a
flag from heaven.   When the door was opened,
indeed, there was a flag.   On one occaion four
children disappeared, to appear again later.   But
the greatest miracle of all remained Naseem's
constant communication with the Imam.   Supplicants
would pray in front of Naseem's room, expressing
their demands in a loud voice.   The Imam would be
consulted not only on profound matters but also on
trivial ones, such as whether a guest should be
given tea or food.   Naseem, who received many of
her orders during fainting fits, would then convey
a reply on behalf of the Imam.

    There came a time, however, when Naseem's
authority was disputed.   Doubts arose first from
the failure of certain of her predictions and,
second, from the public refusal of her kin to
redistribute their property according to her
orders.   Naseem had been making extravagant
predictions regarding illness, birth and death.
Some of these came true, others did not.   In one
particular case she predicted the death of a
certain person within a specified period.   He did
not die.   In another case, the elder brother of
Willayat was asked to surrender his house for
religious purposes which he refused to do.   A
cousin also refused when asked to hand over his
property to Willayat.   In yet another case Naseem,
perhaps compensating for a Sunni mother in a Shiah
household, ordered the engagement of her cousin to
a non-Shiah to be broken; it was not.   Naseem and
Willayat responded to such rebellion with fierce
denunciation.   The rebels were branded as murtid,
those who have renounced Islam and are, therefore,
beyond the pale.   Their relatives were forbidden to

have any contact with them. In some cases parents were asked not to see their children and vice versa. While taking firm measures against those who did not believe, the followers were charged with renewed activity, calculated to re-enforce group cohesiveness. The frequency of religious meetings increased as did visits to shrines. Participation was limited to believers.

Naseem's physical condition now began to correspond with the revelations: she lost weight and her colour became dark when she was not receiving them; she glowed with health when she was. People freely equated her physical appearance with her spiritual condition.   She lost noor-- divine luminosity--in her periods of despondency and regained it when receiving revelations. For those who believed in her it was literally a question of light and darkness.   But the crisis in Naseem was reaching its peak; so was the tension in the community.

Exactly to the day, two years after the first communication began, Naseem asked her father a question on behalf of the Imam: would the believers plunge into the sea as an expression of their faith? The question was not figurative. The Imam meant it literally.   The believers were expected to walk into the sea from where they would be miraculously transported to Karbala in Iraq without worldly means.   Naseem promised that even the 124,000 prophets recognised by Muslims would be amazed at the sacrifice (Ansari 1983: 3).

Those who believed in the miracles immediately agreed to the proposition. Willayat was the first to agree: he would lead the party (Ansari 1983: 3).   There was no debate, no vacillation.   They would walk into the sea at Karachi and their faith would take them to the holy city of Karbala.   Since

the revelations began, Willayat had spent about a
half a million rupees and had disposed of almost
all his property. He now quickly diposed of what
remained to pay for the pilgrimage. The party
consisted of forty-two people, whose ages ranged
from 80 years to four months. Seventeen of them
were from Mureed and most of the remaining were
related.   Willayat, his brother and cousin,
distributed all their belongings, retaining one
pair of black clothes (symbolic of mourning) only.
They hired trucks to take them to Karachi. With
them were six large wooden and tin trunks. They
also took with them the Shiah symbols of martyrdom
at Karbala: <u>alam</u> (flag), <u>taboot</u> (picture of the
mourning procession), <u>jhola</u> (swing), and <u>shabi</u>
(picture of the holy images).

Stopping over at shrines for prayers in Lahore
and Multan, they arrived in Karachi on the third
day. Karachi was in the throes of anti-government
demonstrations and the police had imposed a curfew.
The tension in the city directly reflected the
rivalry between Shiahs and Sunnis in Pakistan. In
spite of this, the party was not stopped as they
made their way to Hawkes Bay. For them this was
another miracle (Ansari 1983:3). At Hawkes Bay the
party offered two prayers (<u>nafil</u>) and read ten
<u>Surahs</u> from the Holy Quaran, including <u>Al-Quadr</u>, an
early Meccan Surah, which states "the Night of
Destiny is better than a thousand months" (Surah
112 verse 3; Asad M. 1980). The verse was well
chosen: for the party, it was indeed the night of
destiny.

The Imam then issued final instructions to
Naseem: the women and children were to be locked
in the six trunks and the virgin girls were to sit
with her in one of them. Willayat was asked to
hold the <u>taboot</u> along with three other men.
Willayat's cousin, Mushtaq, was appointed chief

(<u>salar</u>) of the party. He was ordered to lock the trunks, push them into the sea and throw away the keys. He would then walk into the water with an <u>alam</u>. At this stage four young people from Mureed, two men and two girls, became frightened. This fear, too, 'was put into their hearts by the Imam' (Ansari 1983: 3). Naseem, therefore, willingly exempted them from the journey. The remaining thirty-eight entered the sea. Mothers saw children and children saw old parents descending into the dark waters.   But there 'were no <u>ah</u> (cries) or <u>ansoo</u> (tears)' (Ansare 1983: 4). Those in five out of the six trunks died. One of the trunks was shattered by the waves and its passengers survived. Those on foot also survived; they were thrown back on to the beach by the waves. The operation which had begun in the late hours of the night was over by the early morning when police and the press reached Hawkes Bay.   The survivors were in high spirits; there was neither regret nor remorse among them. Only a divine calm, a deep ecstasy.

The Karachi police, in a display of bureaucratic zeal, arrested the survivors.   They were charged with attempting to leave the country without visas. The official version read: 'The incharge, FIA Passport Cell, in an application filed in the court said, it was reliably learnt that one Willayat Hussain Shah, resident of Chakwal, along with his family had attempted to proceed to a foreign country "Iraq" without valid documents through illegal route i.e. Hawkes Bay beach' (<u>Dawn</u>, March 1983). The act came within the offense punishable under section 3/4 of the Passport Act of 1974. The accused were, however, soon released.

Rich Shiah, impressed by the devotion of the survivors, paid for their journey by air for a week to and from Karbala. In Iraq, influential Shiahs, equally impressed, presented them with gifts, including rare copies of the Holy Quran (Ansari 1983: 6). Naseem's promise that they would visit the Karbala without worldly means was fulfilled.

Social Change, Leadership, and Kinship in Chakwal Society

In an attempt to find a sociological explanation of the Hawkes Bay case I shall begin by putting forward a thesis based on the <u>Dubai chalo</u>, 'let us go to Dubai', theme in Pakistan society (Ahmed A.S. 1984a). Briefly, the thesis suggests that Pakistani workers, returning from the Arab lands with their pockets full of money, are no longer prepared to accept the <u>status quo</u> of the social order from which they had escaped. Those who return demand more social status and authority in society. In their own eyes they have earned the right to be respected by their long and usually hard periods abroad. But they may have little idea how exactly to go about changing society, or even whether they wish to move it 'forward' or back to older, more traditional, ways. Their new social confidence, backed by economic wealth and combined with frustration at the slow pace of change, may result in tensions and dramatic developments of which the Hawkes Bay case is an example.

Consider Willayat Shah. Belonging to the junior lineage of a Shiah family and a Sunni wife, he escaped to Arabia determined, it may be assumed, to make good on his return. After four hard years there, he returned with considerable wealth, but society had remained the same and there was no perceptible change in his social position. Willayat's immediate family were acutely aware of his predicament. His closest child and eldest daughter, fully grown and intelligent, and herself

under pressure to get married, responded to the
crisis in their lives with a series of dramatic,
divine pronouncements. In her case, social crisis
had triggered psychological reactions. The
revelations were calculated to disturb the social
equations of the village forever. Naseem dominated
not only the social but also, and more importantly
for the family, the religious life of the area.
Willayat Shah had finally arrived. Both he and
Naseem now reached out towards the better, truer
world that, for Muslims, lies beyond death.
Through their deaths they would gain an ascendancy
which would be final and unassailable. They would
triumph through the Shiah themes of death,
martyrdom and sacrifice.

For the actors in our case, society provided
the stress but failed to suggest cures. We know
that at least four individuals closely related to
the key actor, Naseem, suffered from tension due
to mixed loyalties in the Shiah-Sunni lineup: her
grandmother, her mother, her uncle and her aunt's
husband were rumoured to have been Sunni in the
past. It was known that her grandmother's family
were Sunni. By assuming the role of Shiah medium,
Naseem was socially compensating for the Sunni
connections in her family. Under such complex
pressures, religion is the most convenient straw
to clutch. The stress thus assumes a form of
illness, but the illness is both mental and
physical and 'in its expression culturally
patterned' (Fox 1973: 180). One must look for
cultural acts and symbolic forms which have local
significance, including sacrifice and martyrdom.
This case is certainly patterned by the religious
sociology of Chakwal Tehsil.

Willayat Shah compared the sacrifice of his
family to that of Karbala because 'he and his group
had been assigned a duty to save the religion and

the faith' (Pervez 1983:   22).   In an interview
given to Tariq Aziz on Pakistan television he
explained why Karachi was selected. He could have
died in a pond in the village, he said.   But the
world would not have known of their faith.   The
prediction of his daughter had indeed come true.
The world was amazed at the miracle of Hawkes Bay
and people would talk of them as martyrs forever.
Throughout the interviews he remained proud and
unrepentant.   His perception of those hours at
Hawkes Bay are revealing. He 'insisted that he had
been walking on the sea all the while like a truck
driving on flat road' (Ifrani 1983).   He felt no
fear, no regret.   Most significantly, he remained
convinced that the revelations would continue, even
after the death of Naseem, through a male member of
the family (Ansari 1983:   4).   Willayat's wife,
Sardar Bibi, reacted with a fervour equal to that
of her husband. "If the Imam tells us to sacrifice
this baby too" she said pointing to an infant she
was feeding during an interview, "I'll do it"
(Jaffery 1983:   27).

Willayat's eldest sister, Taleh Bibi, divorced
and living with her brother, lost one daughter in
the incident. She herself survived because whe was
in the trunk that did not sink. She, too, believes
the miracle will continue through a male member of
their family. In relation to the Islamic concept
of death, it is significant that she had mixed
feelings about her own survival. Although relieved
to be alive, and although she gives this as another
proof of the miracle, she is nonetheless envious of
those who died and thereby gained paradise.

Was the psychological condition of Naseem cause
or the effect of her religious experience? We know
that her peculiarities of temperament became
acceptable after the revelations. Her fits, her
rapture, her ectasy now made sense.   She was

touched by the divine. Even her acts defying
tradition in Chakwal--such as abandoning the veil
or being alone with a man--expressed her
transcendent independence. Examples of trance,
spirit possession and ecstatic behaviour have been
recorded among Muslim groups from the Turkmen
(Basilov 1984) to the Baluch (Bray 1977). It is
commonplace that highly gifted but disturbed
individuals adapt to their social environment.
Women have heard voices before, all over the world.
Joan of Arc's voices advised her to lead her nation
into fighting the English. Naseem's urged her to
lead her followers into the sea. In order to
understand the motives of those involved in this
case we need to combine an appreciation of
religious mythology with an examination of certain
sociological factors. There was more than just
jazba (emotion, ecstasy, passion) at work in
Chakwal. What did the followers think was awaiting
them at Karachi?

Both local leadership and kinship helped to
determine who would be on the beaches that night.
The importance of a leader in an Islamic community,
Shiah or Sunni, is critical. The group is judged
by its leadership (The Holy Quran, Surah 5: 109;
and Surah 7: 6-7). In different ways Willayat,
Naseem, and Sakhawat Jaffery played leading parts
in the drama, but we look in vain for a Savanarola
figure in either Willayat or Sakhawat. Leadership
was by consensus. They were all agreed upon
Naseem's special role in the drama. She led, as
much as she was led by, her father and the zakir.
The followers were responding not to one leader in
their immediate community but to the concept of
leadership in Shiah society. They were responding
to symbols centuries old and emotions perennially
kept alive in Shiah society. What is significant
is the lack of ambivalence in the majority of the
followers. Even the call for the ultimate

sacrifice evoked an unequivocal response among most of them.   Asad's interesting question, "how does power create religion?" (Asad, T. 1981: 252) may therefore be turned around.   The Hawkes Bay case provides an interesting example of how religion may create power.

Willayat Shah was a forceful person who mobilised public opinion behind his daughter.   The zakirs, especially Sakhawat Jaffery, supported him and he in turn assisted Sakhawat Jaffery financially.   Apart from assisting the zakirs, Willayat also paid sums to a variety of other people.   Among the beneficiaries were members of the traditionally lower class--mostly artisans, barbers and blacksmiths.   The seventeen people from Mureed who were prepared to walk into the sea were from this class.   In fact, four of this group backed out at the last minute and although thirteen entered the sea, only three of them died.   The people of Mureed were recent converts to Islam and, like all converts, they were eager to exhibit their religious fervour.   They looked to Willayat Shah for religious and financial support.   For them he was both a Sayyad and a man of means and they were enraptured by his daughter.   Through him and his daughter they found access to a higher social level.

Whatever the levelling effect of religion, and the loyalties it created, the Sayyads rarely allowed their genealogy to be forgotten: the rural Punjab class structure was recognizable despite the experience at Hawkes Bay.   Even in death class distinctions remained: three of the four men who held the taboot as they stepped into the waters were Sayyad, and the non-Sayyad was swept into the sea.   Later, with a strange twist of logic, Willayat explained this by suggesting that his faith was weak (Pervez 1983: 37).   His faith was

weak because he was not a Sayyad, while the three
Sayyads who survived did so because their
intentions were pure. And yet he also argued that
those Sayyads who died did so because of their
purity. Sayyads, obviously, won whether the coin
landed heads or tails. The Sayyads, of course,
provided Willayat's main support and many of them
were his relatives. Of those who walked into the
sea, twenty-five were related. For these, Willayat
was the elder of the family: father to one, brother
to another and uncle to yet others. Of the
eighteen who died, fifteen were his near relatives,
while ten of his kin survived. Religious loyalty
was here clearly buttressed by ties of kinship.

There was, however, structural resistance to
Naseem and her revelations. The Sunni dismissed
them out of hand and even the Shiah were not
unanimous in supporting her. The Sayyads, senior
in the Shiah hierarchy, ill-treated Naseem's
followers, especially the poorer ones, and teased
her family. The older, more established, Shiah
lineages felt threatened by the emergence of Naseem
since she challenged their authority. Willayat's
own brother, Ghulam Haider, suspected of having
Sunni affiliation, kept away from the entire
affair. The zakir, himself a close confidant and
beneficiary of Naseem, but worldly and wise, chose
not to accompany the party on some pretext. And at
the last moment, by the sea, four followers backed
out. But, although there was opposition and
resistance at every stage, thirty-eight people were
prepared to sacrifice their lives on the basis of
Naseem's commands and revelations. The explanation
for their behavior partly lies, I have argued, in
the forces of social change, leadership, and
kinship in Chakwal society. But there are also
other, more ideological and mythological dimensions
to consider.

Death, Sects, and Women in Muslim Society

There is no substantial difference between the core theological beliefs of Shiah and Sunni. Both believe in the central and omnipotent position of Allah; both accept the supremacy of the Holy Prophet as the messenger of Allah. The Holy Quran is revered by both as the divine message of Allah and its arguments relating to notions of death and the afterworld are accepted by both. Discussion of death is indeed central to the Holy Quran, which has many verses on the theme that 'every soul must taste of death'.

Death in Muslim society is seen as part of a natural pre-ordained, immutable order, directly linked to the actions of the living and part of a continuing process in the destiny of the individual. It becomes, therefore, a means to an end, 'the beginning of a journey' (Abd al-Qadir 1977: 6). Humans 'transfer' from this to the next world (the word for death in Urdu and Arabic, inteqal, derives from the Arabic muntaqil, to 'transfer'). The Holy Quran warns 'unto him you shall be made to return' (Surah Al-Ankabut: verse 21). On hearing of someone's death, a Muslim utters the words 'from God we come, to God we shall go'. For Muslims there is no escaping the consequences of death (Muslim 1981).

In Islam--both Shiah and Sunni--life and death are conceptualized as binary opposites. The individual is alone in that hour; all ties including those with parents and family are repudiated (Surah 82: 19). At that time all veils between man and 'the objective moral reality will be rent' (Rahman 1980: 106). Al-Akhira is opposed to al-dunya, the here and now, which may mean base pursuits. Indeed, Alam-e-Uqba, a popular book in

Urdu on death in Islam, has sections called 'Your death is better than your living' (Sialkoti n.d.: 50). Given the awesome facts of <u>al-akhira</u>, human beings must prepare for it in this life. Together, <u>al-akhira</u> and <u>dunya</u> are a unitary whole, the latter determining the nature of the former. Life after death is explicit in Islam and central to its theology. In a general sense this partly explains the attitudes to death shown both in the traditional religious war, <u>jihad</u>, and in contemporary events in the Muslim world. Those who killed Presidant Sadat in Cairo and, like Lt. Islambuli, awaited death calmly, during the trials and those who died following Imam Khomeini's call in Iran, first against the Shah and later against the Iraqis, believed they were dying for a just, an Islamic, cause. Matters are complicated when <u>jihad</u> is freely translated as a struggle against any enemy, including Muslims (Ahmed, A.S. 1983). But the problems between Shiah and Sunni lie in this world and are rooted in the history, not theology, of Islam.

Islamic history, Shiahs maintain, began to go wrong when Hazrat Ali, married to Hazrat Fatima, daughter of the Prophet, was not made the first Caliph after the death of his father-in-law. To make matters worse Hazrat Ali was assassinated. Hazrat Ali's two sons, Hazrat Hassan and Hazrat Hussain, following in their father's footsteps, opposed tyranny and upheld the puritan principles of Islam. Both were also martyred. Hazrat Hussain was martyred, facing impossible odds on a battlefield, with his family and followers, at Karbala. Among those killed at Karbala was Hazrat Hussain's six-month-old son, Hazrat Ali Asghar (who appeared to Naseem in Chakwal). The Prophet, Hazrats Fatima, Ali, Hassan and Hussain are the five key figures for Shiah theology and history. These are the <u>panj tan pak</u>, 'the pure five', of

Shiahs in Pakistan, including those in Chakwal.
Since five of them were martyred in the cause of
Islam, death, martyrdom, tears and sacrifice form
a central part of Shiah mythology (Algar 1969;
Fischer 1980; Khomeini 1981; Schimmel 1981;
Shariati 1979). Members of the Shiah community are
expected to respond with fervour (jazba) to a call
for sacrifice by the leadership.   A sense of
sectarian uniqueness, of group loyalty, faith in
the leadership, readiness for sacrifice, devout
ecstasy during divine ritual, characterise the
community.   It has been called 'the Karbala
paradigm' (Fischer 1980) and would have been
exhibited in Chakwal.

In Pakistan today, where about 20 per cent of
the population of 90 million are Shiahs, Shiah-
Sunni differences can degenerate into conflict.
This is especially so during the Muharram, the ten
days of Shiah mourning for the events at Karbala.
During this period Shiahs mourn, flagellate
themselves, organise processions symbolic of
Karbala, and recite moving poems of the tragedy at
Karbala which reduce those present to tears and
quivering rapture. Conflict with Sunnis is often
sparked as a result of overzealous Shiahs abusing
figures respected by Sunnis, such as Hazrat Umar.
It was one such riot which had paralysed Karachi
when the party from Chakwal arrived there on its
way to the Arabian Sea. Chakwal society itself is
riven with Shiah and Sunni opposition which has a
long and bitter history. Local politics, marriages
and economics are based on this opposition.
Sectarian tension and loyalties also divide
families. Some of Willayat's own nearest kin were
either secret Sunnis or suspected of being
sympathisers. These divided loyalties must have
led to severe tension both for him and his
daughter.

An appreciation of the five central figures of
the Shiahs also helps us to understand the role of
women in that community. The position of Hazrat
Fatima is central. Her popularity among the Shiah
in Chakwal may be judged by the fact that seven
women in Willayat Shah's family carry her name.
Two of these are Ghulam Fatima, or slave of Fatima.
Always a great favourite of her father, Hazrat
Fatima provides the link between her father and her
husband and between her sons and their grandfather.
The Sayyads, those claiming descent from the
Prophet, do so through Hazrat Fatima. So do the
the twelve Imams, revered by the Shiah, In
addition, Fatima's mother and the Prophet's first
wife, Hazrat Khadijah, is also an object of
reverence. Two other women feature in Shiah
mythology, but neither is a popular figure. They
are Hazrat Ayesha and Hazrat Hafsa, both wives of
the Prophet. The reason for their unpopularity is
linked to the question of Hazrat Ali's succession.
Ayesha was the daughter of Abu Bakar and Hafsa of
Umar, the two who preceded Ali as Caliph. Ayesha
is singled out as she opposed Ali actively after
her husband's death.

Thus, one of the five revered figures of the
Shiah is a woman. Among the Sunnis a similar
listing--of the Prophet and the first four
Righteous Caliphs--consists entirely of males. In
other matters, too, Shiah women are better off than
Sunnis. Shiah women, for example, often inherit
shares equal to those inherited by male kin,
whereas among educated Sunni, women receive, at
best, one half of what a male inherits. In the
rural areas they seldom inherit at all. Shiah
women also play a leading role in ritual. The
organisation of marsyas and azadari, the enactment
of the death dramas of Karbala, all involve the
active participation of women.

Of the eighteen people who died at Hawkes Bay, ten were women, a notably large number in view of the fact that only sixteen of the forty-two who set out on the pilgrimage were women. Willayat Shah lost both his mother and daughter. It may be argued that the women were uniquivocally committed to sacrifice. By locking themselves in trunks they had sealed their own fates. For them there was no coming back from the waves. Their sense of sacrifice and passion for the cause was supreme.

The attitudes of the two communities to the Hawkes Bay incident reveal their ideological positions. Sunnis, as we saw above, condemned the entire episode as 'bizarre' and dismissed it as 'insanity'. This, they argued, was mumbo-jumbo and quackery and not in keeping with the logic and rationality which is Islam. For Shiahs all the ingredients of high devotion were amply displayed. Through it they felt they had once again established their superior love for Islam. Here there was sacrifice, persecution, death and martyrdom, the Shiah paradigm. Educated Shiah, who found it awkward to explain the Hawkes Bay case, nonetheless, applauded the jazba of the group. As one journalist concluded his report: "There are millions who don't have the slightest doubt that they have demonstrated the highest degree of sacrifice by answering the call and order of the Hidden Imam" (Yasufzai 1983). The idea of sacrificing life and property for Allah exists both in Shiah and Sunni Islam and is supported in the Holy Quran. Sacrifice and its symbolism are part of Islamic religious culture. Abraham's willingness to sacrifice his son Ismail, for example, is celebrated annually throughout the Muslim world at Eid-ul-Zaha. But for the Shiahs, sacrifice holds a central place in social behaviour and sectarian mythology. Here it is necessary to distinguish between suicide--throwing away life given by God--and sacrifice, or dedication of that life to God.   Suicide is a punishable offence in Islam (Islam 1976: 267).   Sunnis, therefore, seeing the deaths at Hawkes Bay as suicide, disapproved. They saw the episode as a throwing away of valuable lives, whereas Shiahs saw it as a sacrifice which would confirm their devotion.   Willayat Shah was convinced his mission was divine and that he had proved this through a dramatic act of sacrifice. Reward, he was certain, would be paradise in the afterworld (Pervez 1983: 22).   In interviews after the event he expressed his wish to be martyred (shaheed).   There was no remorse; there was only jazba.   To a remarkable degree Shiah tradition, and the practice of death and sacrifice, coincided in this case.   For the Shiah in Chakwal, text and practice were one.

Suffering thus became as much an expression of faith as of social solidarity.   "As a religious problem, the problem of suffering is, paradoxically, not how to avoid suffering but how to suffer, how to make of physical pain, personal loss, worldly defeat, or the helpless contemplation of others' agony something bearable, something supportable, as we say, sufferable" (Geertz 1969: 19).   Suffering, martyrdom and death, the Karbala paradigm, create an emotionally receptive social environment for sacrifice.   Death in our case, therefore, became a cementing, a defining, a status-bestowing act for the community.   It consolidated the living as it hallowed the memory of the dead.

Notes

I am grateful for the interest shown in this paper by Professors Khurshid Ahmad, M. Ajmal, Z.A. Ansari, Ismail al Faruqi, E. Gellner, C. Keyes and T.N. Madan.

1. A committee was set up by Dr. M. Afzal, the Minister of Education, to examine the problem. It was chaired by Dr. Z.A. Ansari and included some of Pakistan's most eminent psychiatrists and psychologists. I represented the social scientists (Pervez 1983).

2. The organization of Punjab society into agricultural peasant groups, defined by ethnicity and occupation, is well documented (Ahmed, A.S. 1984c; Ahmed S. 1973; 1977; Alavi 1972; 1973; Balneaves 1955; Darling 1925; 1930; 1934; Eglar 1960; Ibbetson 1883; Pettigrew 1975).

3. See also Saeed 1982. In another popular book the author promises the reader, in the sub-title, 'glimpses of life beyond the grave'. One section in the book is entitled 'the depth of hell: if a stone is thrown into hell it will take seventy years to reach its bottom' (Islam 1976: 284). For discussion of djahannam, the Muslim hell, see Gibbs & Kramers 1981: 81-2. Maulana Maududi discusses the importance of death, the after-life and its relationship to man's life on earth, in a dispassionate analysis of Islamic society (Maududi 1968). See also chapter six, 'Eschatology', in Rahman 1980.

References

Abd al-Qadir, As-Sufi. 1977. Death, the
Beginning of a Journey. In Islamic Book of the
Dead, ed. Abd ar-Rahim ibn Ahmad al-Qadi.
England: Diwan Press.

Ahmed, A.S. 1983. Religion and Politics in Muslim
Society: Order and Conflict in Pakistan. New
York: Cambridge Univ. Press.

_____. 1984a. Dubai Chalo: Problems in the
Ethnic Encounter Between Middle Eastern and
South Asian Muslim Societies. Asian Aff. 15,
262-276.

_____. 1984b. Zia's Victory in the Field: the
[Arain] Work Ethic that Keeps a President in
Power. Guardian, London, 10 August.

_____. 1984c. Hazarawal: Formation and
Structure of District Ethnicity in Pakistan.
In The Prospects for Plural Societies.
American Ethnological Society.

Ahmed, S. 1973. Peasant Classes in Pakistan. In
Imperialism and Revolution in South Asia, eds.
K. Gough & H.P. Sharma. New York: Monthly
Review Press.

_____. 1977. Class and Power in a Punjabi
Village. New York: Monthly Review Press.

Alavi, H. 1972. Kinship in West Punjab Villages.
Contr. Ind. Sociol. (N.S.) 6, 1-27.

_____. 1973. Peasant Classes and Primordial
Loyalties. J. Peasant Stud. I, 23-62.

Algar, H.   1969.   Religion and State in Iran 1785–
    1906. Berkeley: Univ. of California Press.

Ansari, Z.A., et al.   1983. Urdu Notes for Study
    Based on Interviews Conducted by National
    Institute of Psychology, Islamabad.   In Hawkes
    Bay Incident,   ed. S. Pervez. Islamabad:
    National Institute of Psychology.

Asad, M.   1980.   Translated and Explained, the
    Message of the Quran.   Gibraltar: Dar-ul-
    andalus.

Asad, T. 1983. Anthropological Conceptions of
    Religion: Reflections on Geertz. Man (N.S.)
    18, 237–59.

Balneaves, E. 1955.   Waterless Moon. London:
    Lutterworth Press.

Banton, M., ed. 1973.   Anthropological Approaches
    to the Study of Religion (ASA Monogr. 3).
    London: Tavistock.

Basilov, V.N.   1984.   Honour Groups in Traditional
    Turkmenian Society.   In Islam and Tribal
    Societies, eds. A.S. Ahmed & D. Hart.   London:
    Routledge & Kegan Paul.

Bloch, M. & J. Parry, eds.   1982.   Death and the
    Regeneration of Life. New York: Cambridge
    Univ. Press.

Bray, D. 1977. The Life-History of a Brahui.
    Karachi: Royal Book Company.

Darling, M.L.   1925.   The Punjab Peasant in
    Prosperity and Debt.   London: Oxford Univ.
    Press.

_____. 1930. Rusticus Loquitur, or the Old Light and the New in the Punjab Village. London: Oxford Univ. Press.

_____. 1934. Wisdom and Waste in the Punjab Village. London: Oxford Univ. Press.

Douglas, M. ed. 1970. Witchcraft Confessions and Accusations. (ASA Monogr. 9). London: Tavistock.

Eglar, Z. 1960. A Punjabi Village in Pakistan. New York: Columbia Univ. Press.

Evans-Pritchard, E.E. 1937. Witchcraft, Oracles and Magic among the Azande. Oxford: Clarendon Press.

_____. 1965. Theories of Primitive Religion. Oxford: Clarendon Press.

Fischer, M.J.M. 1980. Iran: from Religious Dispute to Revolution. Cambridge, Mass.: Harvard Univ. Press.

Fox, R. 1973. Encounter with Anthropology. Harmondsworth: Penguin.

Geertz, C. 1969. Religion as a Cultural System. In Anthropological Approaches to the Study of Religion, ed. M. Banton. (ASA Monogr. 3.) London: Tavistock.

Gibb, H.A.R. & J.H. Kramers. 1981. Shorter Encyclopaedia of Islam. Karachi: South Asian Publishers.

Irfani, S. 1983. From Jonestown to Hawkes Bay. The Muslim, March, 4.

Islam, K.M. 1976. <u>The Spectacle of Death</u>. Lahore:
    Tablighi Kutub Khana.

Jaffery, S. 1983. Why Didn't God Take Us Too? In
    <u>The Herald</u>, Karachi, March.

Keyes, C.F. 1981. From Death to Rebirth: Northern
    Thai Conceptions of Immortality. Paper
    presented to the Annual Meeting of the
    Association for Asia Studies.

_____. In press. The Interpretive Basis of
    Depression. In <u>Culture and Depression</u>, eds.
    A. Kleinman & B.J. Good.

Khomeini, Imam. 1981. <u>Islam and Revolution</u>,
    trans. H. Algar. Berkeley: Mizan Press.

Lewis, I.M. 1971. <u>Ecstatic Religion: An
    Anthropological Study of Spirit Possession and
    Shamanism</u>. Harmondsworth: Penguin.

Maududi, M. Abu ala. 1968. <u>Islamic Tehzib Our Os
    Key Osool-o-Mobadi in Urdu</u>. Lahore: Islamic
    Publications, Shah Alam Market.

Muslim, Imam. 1981. <u>Sahih Muslim</u>, trans. Ah. H.
    Siddiqi. Lahore: Sh. M. Ashraf.

Okarvi, M.M.S. (not dated). <u>On Visiting a
    Cemetery (in Urdu)</u>. Karachi: Medina
    Publishing Co.

Pervez, S. 1983. <u>Hawkes Bay Incident: a Psycho-
    Social Case Study</u>, compiled Seema Pervez.
    Islamabad: National Institute of Psychology.

Pettigrew, J. 1975. <u>Robber Noblemen</u>. London:
    Routledge & Kegan Paul.

Rahman, F.   1980.   Major Themes of the Quran.
   Chicago: Bibliotheca Islamica.

Saeed, M.A.   1982.   What Happens After Death?,
   trans. M.H. Khan.   Delhi: Dini Book Depot, Urdu
   Bazar.

Salahuddin, G.   1983. A Glimpse of Our Insanity?
   The Herald, Karachi, March.

Schimmel, A.   1981.   Mystical Dimensions of Islam.
   Chapel Hill: Univ. of North Carolina Press.

Shariati, A.   1979.   On the Sociology of Islam,
   trans. H. Algar.   Berkeley: Mizan Press.

Sialkoti, Maulana M.S.   (not dated).   Alam-e-Uqba
   (in Urdu).   Lahore: Nomani Kutub Khana.

Smolowe, J., et al.   1984. "The Strange World of
   Cults."   January 16, Newsweek.

Werbner, R.P. ed. 1977.   Regional Cults (ASA
   Monogr. 16.) London: Tavistock.

Winter, E.R.,   1969.   Territorial Groupings and
   Religion Among the Iraqw. In Anthropological
   Approaches to the Study of Religion, ed.   M.
   Banton (ASA Monogr. 3.) London: Tavistock.

Yusufzai, R.   1983. Psychiatrists' Views of Two
   Recent Episodes.   The Muslim, March, 18.

EL CARGO DE LAS ANIMAS: MORTUARY RITUALS AND THE CARGO SYSTEM IN HIGHLAND PERU

Pierre L. Van den Berghe

Mortuary rituals practiced in the Cuzco region of Peru on All Souls Day are memorial cults. In the market town of San Jeronimo the expensive cargos for the patron saints are assumed by the mestizo elite, but the cargo de las animas does not convey much prestige. Its central feature involves ritual disinterment and reinterment of one or more of the relatives of its mayordomo. The practice appears to be unique to this town and this cargo does not clearly fulfill any of the usual functions associated with classic cargo systems elsewhere (prestige, solidarity, redistribution of wealth, egalitarian counterpoise). In general, the obligation to accept cargos in San Jeronimo is weak and ineffective, such that some of the financial responsibilities are delegated among the social network of the mayordomo. The cargo system of a class-stratified market town like San Jeronimo serves very different functions from that of an internally unstratified peasant community.

The Catholic feast of All Souls Day is the occasion in many parts of Latin America for a series of mortuary practices honoring the dead. The region of Cuzco in the Southern Andes of Peru is no exception, but local practices vary considerably and the main rituals described here are peculiar to the market town of San Jeronimo, 12 km to the southeast of the city of Cuzco on the

Reprinted with permission from Anthropological Quarterly 51 (1978): 129-136.

249

main Cuzco-Puno highway. This account is based on general field work done from July 1972 to November 1973, and more specifically, for the events surrounding the mortuary rituals, on November 1 and 2, 1972.[1]

The mortuary rituals practiced in the Cuzco region resemble 'ancestor worship' in that each family honors principally its own dead by cleaning up their graves and praying for the peace of their souls. Of course, since kinship in the Andes is traced bilaterally, among both mestizos and Indians, kin groups overlap in membership, and the cult is not based on a clear principle of filiation as is often the case in a unilineal descent society. Further, in Catholic theology, one's dead cannot be worshipped since worship is reserved for God. One prays to God for the redemption of the souls of the deceased in order to insure their release from Purgatory and accession to Heaven. One may also ask the dead to intercede with God in one's favor. These general features of All Souls Day are common to all of Catholicism, and indeed to much of Christendom.

In the Cuzco region, All Souls Day is celebrated by family groups going to the cemetery to clean up the graves of their dead relatives. Poor families, that is peasants or members of the urban working class, who bury their dead underground in simple earthen graves, weed the grave, bring a few wreaths of natural or paper flowers, and usually have a meal or at least some drinks at the tomb. They may also repaint the wooden cross, and boys with pots of black and white paint offer their services for that purpose. Richer families, especially the urban middle class, bury their dead above-ground in brick and cement buildings generally consisting of three or more layers of niches into which the coffins are sealed and in front of which one finds a commemorative plaque, with a small altar including a crucifix, candles or oil lamps, a picture of the deceased, flower vases, and the like. Middle-class families come to furbish the brass fittings of the little grave altars, to place fresh flowers on them, and generally to redecorate their graves; but the cemetery visit is generally much less of an occasion to eat and drink than it is among lower-class people.

Both rich and poor families also pray for their dead, and hire priests to recite prayers. Virtually all the clergy of the diocese are out in strength in the cemeteries to offer their services and pick up some extra income. Well-to-do families hire a priest to recite an entire mass in front of the family resting place for a fee of $2 to $5 (100 to 200 soles at the rate of U.S. $1 = 43 soles in 1972-73) while poor families ask a priest to recite two or three minutes' worth of prayers for some 10 to 25 cents (5 to 10 soles).

All Souls Day also sustains a minor seasonal industry in Cuzco. A special sweet bread in the form of decorated dolls (for girls) and horses (for boys), known as biscochuelos, is baked in all sizes and sold at the Cuzco market. Paper flowers are woven into wreaths that are likewise sold at the public market for several days before the feast.

The summary description above applies to the city of Cuzco and to small towns of the region, but the town of Jeronimo has, in addition, a series of ritual uniquely its own. San Jeronimo, a thriving market town of some 4,600 inhabitants, is a political, economic and ritual center in its own right rather than a dormitory suburb. It provides a variety of goods and services--notably fresh fruit and vegetables, and a wide range of artisan products--for the neighboring city of Cuzco, to

which many townsmen commute to work. As a district
capital and a parish, the town's economy consists
of a combination of market gardening, commerce and
artisan production, and its Sunday market is one of
the largest in the region.

San Jeronimo's population is stratified into
a mestizo elite making up about 10 to 15 per cent
of the total, a small-town Lumpenbourgeoisie, often
called cholos in the Peruvian literature,[2] and a
peripheral rural popualtion. The elite consists
mostly of professionals and semi-professionals,
salaried employees in both the public and private
sector, and a few medium-scale entrepreneurs. Its
members are all fluently bilingual in Spanish and
Quechua, are literate, and have completed their
primary education as a minimum. Often, they have
some secondary schooling as well. Almost two
thirds of the population belong to the petty
bourgeoisie; they consist of artisans, small
traders, and market gardeners, who are generally
self-employed, and combine some small-scale
horticulture with a craft or retail trade. The
adult women in this group are still predominantly
illiterate, have little or no formal education, and
are monolingual in Quechua, with only a smattering
of Spanish. The men often have some primary
education, bare literacy, and some degree of
fluency in Spanish, although Quechua is clearly
their first language. Beyond the fringes of the
town, there lives a rural population that is, on
the whole, poorer and less educated than the petty
bourgeoisie, and monolingual in Quechua. They make
up about one fourth of the population of the
District of San Jeronimo.

Until recently, the mestizo elite were running
the town council; they maintained close ties to the
departmental elite in the nearby city of Cuzco, and
took a prominent role in the religious and civic

events of San Jeronimo. Their social, economic,
educational, and political dominance has, since the
1960's, been increasingly challenged by younger
educated sons of the teachers of the town's
secondary school.

The main ceremonial activities of the town and
the most expensive cargos connected with them, are
related to the cult of the town's patron saint.
The elite still plays a leading role in assuming
these cargos. These activities concentrate on two
great annual occasions, each lasting the better
part of a week. During the feast of Corpus Christi
in June, the statue of San Jeronimo joins those of
the patron saints of thirteen other parishes in and
around Cuzco in an elaborate series of processions
through downtown Cuzco. The celebration of the
feast day of San Jeronimo on September 30 takes
place in the town, and is preceded by several days
of elaborate public displays and rituals involving
fireworks, procession, entertainment, music,
drinking, and masses, financed mostly by four main
cargo holders.

By contrast with these lavish affairs, the
rituals described here are modest and
inconspicuous. There is a _cargo de las animas_
whose incumbent is known as the _mayordomo de las
animas_. Like the other cargos in town, such as
those connected with the celebration of the feast
of the town's patron saint, the _cargo de las animas_
is passed on from year to year. Financially, it is
one of the less onerous cargos, and it does not
seem to convey much prestige. Unlike the four
cargos for the patron saint which require
expenditures into the thousands of dollars (up to
100,000 soles), which are assumed (if often
reluctantly) by members of the town's _mestizo_
elite, and which serve to establish one's claim to
elite membership, the _cargo de las animas_ is

generally assumed by people who are respectable but of modest means. It requires only a few hundred dollars (10-12,000 soles) worth of expenses, mostly for the brass band, for beverages, for the priest, for candles, and so on. This is hardly more than for a moderately stylish funeral. Mayordomos are not, to be sure, Indian peasants, but neither do they belong to the mestizo elite. Rather, they tend to belong to the petty bourgeoisie.

The central rite with which the mayordomo de las animas is entrusted is the disinterment of one or several of his relatives, the bringing of their remains back to his home for a wake similar to that which accompanies a regular first funeral, and reinterment the next day with all the usual mortuary rituals. Sometimes the skull of a favorite relative is retained in the home, and placed in a little niche in the thick adobe wall near the entrance door as a friendly protective presence to ward off evil, thieves, and other misfortunes. The skull niche becomes a little family altar where candles are burned and flower offerings placed. This particular custom of keeping a relative's skull in the house, however, is not limited to San Jeronimo or to the cargo de las animas. I have seen tutelary skulls in other towns, and even in the houses of high status professionals, such as a lawyer in the provincial capital of Urcos.

The following is a description of the ritual performed by the mayordomo de las animas in San Jeronimo on November 1 and 2, 1972. Shortly before 5 p.m. on November 1, a few male relatives of the mayordomo opened the cement vault of a tomb in the town cemetery with a pick, and took out a coffin containing the partly dessicated but still somewhat odorous remains of the mayordomo's wife who had died three years before. The lid of the coffin was opened, then closed again, and the coffin itself, which was still in fairly good condition, was replaced in the cement vault. At 5 p.m., two men entered the cemetery carrying a new and empty black coffin. Shortly thereafter, the mayordomo arrived in a state of advanced intoxication, accompanied by several inebriated male relatives. One of the mayordomo's cousins proceeded to break open another cement vault and extracted another coffin, which was also opened. It contained the bones of two persons, the mayordomo's parents, dead many years. Obviously, these bones had already been reinterred before, because the coffin was still in fairly good condition and it contained the remains of two persons.

The bones of the mayordomo's parents were then transferred from the old coffin into the new one just brought in for that purpose. A young cousin of the mayordomo carefully rearranged the bones in the new coffin, starting with the two skulls which he placed side by side at the head of the coffin, and continuing with the long bones of the limbs which he placed roughly in their correct anatomical location. Smaller bones were deposited pell-mell in the middle of the new coffin, which was then closed. The old, empty coffin was replaced in the vault. During these proceedings, which lasted a half-hour, a bottle of hard liquor was passed among the men who were all in a state best described as somber, decorous drunkenness. Around 5:30, four of the men carried the new coffin on their shoulders, and took it with a somewhat unsteady gait out of the cemetery and to the house of the mayordomo.

At the mayordomo's house, a shelter had been erected in a corner of the patio; it consisted of a canvas roof, and walls made of intertwined eucalyptus branches woven over a rough wooden framework. Within that shelter a table had been set to receive coffins, and twelve chairs had been lined up along the two long sides of the rectangular space. The men placed the coffin on the table, and two women approached it, knelt down, prayed, and began hugging the coffin and wailing in shrill voices, uttering lamentations in a mixture of Quechua and Spanish. After a brief rest, the men returned to the cemetery to fetch the other coffin containing the body of the mayordomo's wife, and brought it back to the house as well. On arrival, the second coffin was placed parallel to the first one, on the same table.

A little later, an eight-man professional brass band from the town of Anta arrived and started playing loud and rather dissonant funeral music to an assembly of a score or so of male and female relatives who settled down for the night's wake, lubricated by chicha (maize beer) and trago (alcohol), and accompanied by the men's cigarette smoking as a 'disinfectant' to protect against noxious vapors from the coffin. (Perhaps a deodorant was meant, and the eucalyptus branches served the same function.) Both men and women were moderately inebriated, but remained sober and decorous in their demeanor, quietly sitting and chatting while the band played slow-beat funeral music.

I left around 9 p.m., having been told that the wake would last all night, but on returning the next morning at 8 a.m., I was told that no one held out past midnight. By now the two coffins on the table were covered with floral wreaths and six large candles burned in front of the coffins. In a corner of the shelter, a silver embroidered black standard with a skull had been borrowed from the church. (This is normally carried by the sacristan in funeral processions.)

Around 8 a.m., the mayordomo, accompanied by the brass band, went to the parish church to make arrangements with the parish priest, and returned around 9 a.m. after playing funeral music along the street to and from church. After their return, the band rested, and its eight members were given two cases (24 bottles of 75 cl. each) of beer, tea with rum, and a thick potato soup. In the meantime, the women had been busy preparing plates of offerings with fruits, bread, cakes, beans and maize. Each dessert-size offering plate was decorated with a little paper flag.

By 10 a.m., the sacristan arrived, accompanied by two pre-adolescent boys, all three dressed in black and white church vestments. The sacristan carried the parish's silver cross used in all processions, and each boy carried a silver candlestick. Within the next 15 minutes, a procession slowly assembled and left for church. It was opened by the sacristan and the two boys carrying the cross and candlesticks, followed by the mayordomo and a dozen of his male and female relatives, each carrying two offering plates. Then came other relatives and friends of the mayordomo, followed by the two coffins carried respectively by four and two men, with the brass band closing the march and playing funeral music. Altogether, some 40 to 50 people were in the procession, not including a dozen curious children who watched from the sidelines.

When the procession arrived at the church, it was greeted by the parish priest dressed in black vestments and ornaments for a funeral mass. The two coffins were placed on a wooden platform at the foot of the main altar; the offering plates were carefully lined up in a double row at the foot of the two coffins and down the central aisle; the women sat in the front pews on the right side of the nave, while the men sat on the left (the same pattern of sex segregation is observed at most religious services in San Jeronimo). Mass was started at 10:20, with the parish priest officiating in Spanish. From their slow and confused reactions to the priest's cues in answering the prayers, it was clear that the women understood little Spanish. The sermon, based on an epistle of St. Paul, was in Quechua. After the mass, the priest sprinkled holy water on the coffins, recited the office of the dead, and blessed the mayordomo. At 10:45, the coffins were taken out of the church and left in front of the main portal while the mayordomo and his relatives went to the adjacent parish house to leave their offering plates for the priest. The offerings were formally taken by the parish treasurer (economo), and placed on a table. Before the group left the church, a Spanish announcement was made over the church loudspeaker, disclosing the name of the following year's mayordomo de las animas. (Like all cargos, this office is passed on from person to person each year, and the name of the next holder is announced a year in advance during the incumbent's ritual performance.)

Leaving the church at 10:50, the procession, accompanied by the priest and the sacristan, proceeded to the cemetery, stopping for a brief prayer at each street corner. The band continued playing all along, but all drinking had stopped from the time the procession had left the mayordomo's house, only to resume at the cemetery.

At 11, when the cortege entered the cemetery, the latter was a beehive of activity. Just outside, there was a row of some twenty women selling home-made alcoholic beverages (chicha and ponche de leche). Inside, between 200 and 300 people clumped in little groups of relatives were

bringing flowers and praying at various grave
sites. Some twenty tables were set up as altars in
front of the more substantial cement mausoleums of
the well-to-do, and several priests went from table
to table to celebrate private masses.

The mayordomo's procession went straight for
the two vaults whence the coffins had come, and
replaced them inside. The parish priest celebrated
another mass in front of the monument, accompanied
by the church organist and the brass band. After
the mass, at noon, most of the group dispersed to
drink chicha outside the cemetery gates, while a
number of men stayed behind to recement the two
vaults.

The cargo de las animas poses several
interesting problems of function and origin. No
informant in San Jeronimo could give me any account
of the origin of disinterment rituals, other than
that it was the custom (es costumbre). My
inquiries in several other towns in the Cuzco
region failed to reveal a similar practice
elsewhere, although memorial cults of the dead are
common. Orlove (1977) mentions that in the Cuzco
region, siblings sometimes take turns in
symbolically leading the souls of their parents
from the cemetery to their home on November 1,
holding a funeral feast at home, and returning the
souls to the cemetery on November 3. Widows and
relatives in San Jeronimo and elsewhere may also
set up a table covered with offerings of food,
tobacco and alcohol in their homes for symbolic use
by recently deceased spouses or kinsmen. Both of
these rituals share some elements with the rite
described here, but do not involve disinterment.
In fact, I could find no accounts of ritual
disinterment and reinterment in the ethnographic
literature of the area.[3] There is no clear or
known linkage to pre-Hispanic practices, but

reinterment, ritualized or otherwise, is not uncommon in the Christian tradition. In medieval Europe, reinterment and separate burail of body parts like the head or the heart of saintly or politically important personages was practiced; and, of course, the European and Spanish colonial practice of burial inside or near churches presented problems of overcrowding, hence the periodic digging up and reburying of remains from old graves.

At least as interesting as the problem of origin and distribution, is that of function. The literature on cargos tends to stress three functions of cargo systems (Aguirre Beltran 1967, Cancian 1965, Carrasco 1961, Nash 1958, Tax 1953, Vogt 1966, 1969, Wolf 1955). Cargos are sought because they confer prestige; they serve as a rallying point for communal solidarity vis à vis the outside world; and since they often involve considerable economic expense, they redistribute the wealth and militate against the formation of distinct social classes within local peasant communities.

The cargo de las animas in San Jeronimo seems to fulfill none of these functions to any appreciable degree. It confers little prestige to the holder, as the town's elite looks down upon the practice as heathen (pagano), primitive (salvaje), an occasion for drunkenness (se emborrachan), and wasteful (gastan su dinero). The Church officially disapproves of it, although the tolerant young parish priest who was in San Jeronimo in 1972 participated in it on the ground that it did not openly conflict with Church doctrine, and that it was better to go along with local customs rather than risk open clashes with his parishioners.

Even though the cargo has a public character,

and is publicly announced, the ritual performance
is semi-private.   Except for casual onlookers,
mostly children and visiting anthropologists, the
participants are all relatives or close friends of
the mayordomo.   Indeed, the ritual takes place on
the very day where each family is absorbed in the
cult of its own dead; this, in itself, almost
precludes general participation.   The ritual
certainly does not unite the community in a vast
collective representation of solidarity.   If
anything, All Souls Day celebrations split the town
into little family groups.   Nor does the cargo de
las animas contribute to the status of San Jeronimo
in relation to other neighboring towns.   Most
people in other towns have not heard of the custom,
and those who have generally disapprove of it.

Finally, this cargo does not significantly
redistribute wealth or serve an economic leveling
function.   San Jeronimo is clearly a class-
stratified community with two identifiable strata:
a small economic and educational elite that is
generally literate and fluent in both Spanish and
Quechua, and a large stratum of people who engage
in a mixture of small-scale agriculture, retail
trade, artisan production, and menial services,
whose women and older men are still largely
illiterate, and who are far more fluent in Quechua
than in Spanish.   Even the far more expensive
cargos connected with the celebration of the patron
saint's day have not prevented the formation of
distinct social classes, nor served as economic
equalizers.

The question is: why does the cargo de las
animas persist?   San Jeronimos reply that one
cannot decently refuse to serve as mayordomo, as
this would imply disrespect, or at least unconcern
for one's deceased relatives.   However, all rituals
connected with All Souls Day are, in a sense,

public displays for the dead. A well-kept
mausoleum and celebration of a mass serve that
purpose quite well; while among the town elite, a
mild social stigma attaches to being mayordomo de
las animas.

Indeed, the question of the persistence of
this cargo can be extended to the other cargos of
San Jeronimo, especially the four main ones
connected with the September 30 celebration of San
Jeronimo's saint's day. It is true that this main
annual fiesta is a big collective ritual of
solidarity, that it attracts many visitors from
neighboring towns, and therefore that it invites
comparisons as to which town can afford the most
lavish fiesta. The four mayordomos also compete
with each other, and are said to represent the
moiety from which they come. (A central street
divides the town into a 'left' and a 'right'
moiety, a division almost certainly traceable to
pre-Hispanic days [Zuidema 1964]. Today the
moieties seem to have only vestigial ceremonial
functions in the September 30 fiesta, and in the
rituals connected with the celebration of Corpus
Christi in the city of Cuzco.)

Acceptance of one of the main cargos is so
expensive (60 to 120,000 soles in 1972-73) that it
is virtually limited to the town's economic and
social elite. This situation is far from unique.
This is true of many Peruvian and Bolivian towns
(such as Puno and Paucartambo), and has also been
reported for Chichicastenango in Guatemala (Bunzel
1952). However, the expenses are not heavy enough
to equalize wealth in the community, and some of
them may even be indirectly recouped in the form of
advertisement and public relations. (Two at the
mayordomos in 1972 and 1973, for instance, were
respectively the owners of the town's single large,
modern restaurant, and of the single soft-drink

bottling plant.)

One must also stress that accepting an
expensive cargo, while it may help to confirm elite
status, is not a necessary condition to accede to
or maintain that status.   Indeed, in that very
elite there is much reluctance to accept cargo, and
criticism of the whole system.   Many informants
wistfully reflected to me what wonders could be
achieved for the town if the money wasted in
alcohol, fireworks, music, candles and so on could
be invested in schools, water pipes, sewage or
street pavement.   The clergy and the government
join in this chorus of disapproval, and the
archdiocese of Cuzco urges the clergy to play down
these fiestas.

The moral sanctions for the cargo system are
now so weak that people have to be cajoled into
acceptance on the basis of debts of friendship to
the incumbent.   Far from the situation reported for
some Mexican communities where cargos are so
desirable that long waiting lists are formed
(Cancian 1965, Vogt 1966), in San Jeronimo people
have to be virtually entrapped into them.   It
seems, in fact, that the main factor making for the
perpetuation of the institution is the desire to
pass on to a captive victim an unwanted onus
previously dumped on one.   Paradoxically,
friendship is used to ensnare likely candidates.
In the absence of pre-existing ties of friendship
or kinship between incumbent and future cargo
holders, the obligation to accept cargo is weak and
ineffective.

Reluctance to shoulder the responsibilities
and financial burden of cargo also expresses itelf
in the secondary institution of _jurca_ which
developed around cargo.   Soon after accepting one
of the main cargos, the _mayordomo entrante_ in turn

approaches every likely person in his broad circle of relatives, friends and business associates to assume financial responsibility for some aspect of the fiesta (e.g., to buy candles, fireworks, or cases of beer). In effect, each cargo holder delegates bits of cargo to wide circles of acquaintances who are said to be in his <u>jurca</u>, or to be <u>jurcado</u> to him. The fiesta thus becomes a communal affair to which most members of the town's upper stratum have contributed directly or indirectly.

From the above account, it is clear that the cargo system of a class-stratified market town like San Jeronimo serves very different functions from that of an internally unstratified peasant community. This is so despite the clear historical continuity between rural and urban cargo systems, and a number of common structural features. It might be tempting to predict that processes of 'modernization' or 'westernization' would lead to the gradual disappearance of cargos in urban communities. However, human inventiveness and capacity to redefine institutions often invalidate such predictions based on simple deterministic models.

Notes

1. This research was sponsored by the National
Institute of Mental Health of the United States,
and the results of the more general study of class
and ethnic relations in the Department of Cuzco
have been published (van den Berghe and Primov
1977).   I   am   especially   grateful   for   the
collaboration of George P. Primov and Gladys
Becerra de Valencia in the field work, and for the
friendship and counsel of Jorge Flores Ochoa and
Benjamin Orlove.

2. For reasons that I have given elsewhere, this
is an ambiguous term which I prefer not to use (Van
den Berghe 1974).

3. Disinterment and reinterment have, of course,
been reported in several other parts of the world,
notably in Madagascar.   Flores Ochoa (1977) also
mentioned having heard of ritual reinterment in
Ayacucho, Peru.

References

Aguirre Beltran, Gonzalo. 1967. _Regiones de refugio_. Mexico: Instituto Indigenista Interamericano.

Bunzel, Ruth. 1952. _Chichicastenango, a Guatemalan Village_. Seattle: Publications of the American Ethnological Society. Volume 12.

Cancian, Frank. 1965. _Economics and Prestige in a Maya Community_. Palo Alto, California: Stanford University Press.

Carrasco, Pedro. 1961. The Civil-Religious Hierarchy in Mesoamerican Communities. _American Anthropologist_ 63: 483-497.

Flores Ochoa, Jorge. 1977. Personal Communication.

Nash, Manning. 1958. Political Relations in Guatemala. _Social and Economic Studies_ 7: 65-75.

Orlove, Benjamin S. 1977. Personal communication.

Tax, Sol. 1953. Penny Capitalism: a Guatemalan Indian Economy. _Washington, D.C.: Smithsonian Institute of Social Anthropology_, 16.

Van den Berghe, Pierre L. 1974. The Use of Ethnic Terms in the Peruvian Social Science Literature. _International Journal of Comparative Sociology_ 15(3-4): 132-142.

Van den Berghe, Pierre L., and George P. Primov.
1977. Inequality in the Peruvian Andes.
Columbia, Mo.: University of Missouri Press.

Vogt, Evon Z. 1966. Los Zinacantecos: un Pueblo
Tzotzil de los Altos de Chiapas. Mexico:
Instituto Nacional Indigenista.

Vogt, Evon Z. 1969. Zinacantan, a Maya Community
in the Highlands of Chiapas. Cambridge,
Mass.: Harvard University Press.

Wolf, Eric Z. 1955. Types of Latin American
Peasantry: a Preliminary Discussion.
American Anthropologist 57: 452-471.

Zuidema, R.T. 1964. The Ceque System of Cuzco.
Leiden: E.J. Brill.

III. MODE OF DEATH

THE EXPERIENCE OF REPEATED AND TRAUMATIC LOSS AMONG CROW INDIAN CHILDREN: RESPONSE PATTERNS AND INTERVENTION STRATEGIES

Kathleen Ann Long

Abstract

Crow Indian children residing on the Montana Reservation appear to experience traumatic losses of family members and friends with much greater frequency than children in the population at large. Responses to these losses include interpersonal distancing, and sadness without apparent anger. Assessment and clinical intervention are considered within the sociocultural content of Indian child client and white, middle-class clinician.

The Crow Indian Reservation is located in South Central Montana and houses nearly 5000 enrolled members of the Crow Tribe. Historically, the Crows were buffalo hunters on the Great Plains. As a tribe they have always lived at peace with whites. The Crows aligned themselves with Custer to fight the Sioux at the historic Battle of the Little Big Horn, the site of which is on the present-day Crow Reservation.

At present, the major pursuits of the Crows are ranching and farming. Life on the reservation is marked by a number of serious problems including

Reprinted with permission from American Journal of Orthopsychiatry 53, no. 1 (1983): 116-126. The American Ortho-psychiatric Association, Inc.

poverty, unemployment, standard housing, and a high
rate of alcoholism.   The Crow culture now blends
modern white American notions with traditional
tribal ones in a mix that varies among individuals
and families. Traditional beliefs stress living in
harmony with nature and an acceptance of natural
events. While cooperation among tribal members is
valued, the right of each individual to act according to his own wishes is held as a major premise.
Such a background of beliefs tends to produce
nonintrusive, accepting behavior in dealing with
other persons and with natural events.   Such
behavior may be viewed by whites, who tend to have
a more action-oriented, competitive style, as
passive and resigned.

   The traditional family and kinship structure of
Crow is a feature that still appears to exert
considerable influence.   Each child is born not
only into a family but into a matrilineal clan.
These clans serve as significant social units and
provide support and caring.   Maternal aunts and
uncles are to some extent viewed as parents, while
maternal cousins are seen as brothers and sisters.
Maternal grandmothers often play a key role in
child-rearing, especially that of girls.
Traditional beliefs hold that if a woman's baby is
sickly or frail, she should, for the child's
welfare, give it away. Often the recipient is the
maternal grandmother.   Relatives of the father,
while not in the same clan as the child, are
significant. A 'clan uncle' on the father's side
often becomes a special advisor to, and one who
prays for, the child.   Paternal cousins have
traditionally been seen as the 'teasing cousins',
who serve to shape and perhaps control the growing
child's behavior through the use of jokes and
ridicule which are accepted within the context of
this special relationship.(2,5)   Thus in the
traditional view, children belong to and can be

cared for by entire groups of persons, not simply one or two biological parents. The shifting of children to caretakers other than natural parents, especially to grandparents, continues today. But the ease or degree of trauma associated with such shifts varies with the closeness of traditional familial and clan ties.

Healthcare beliefs and services among the Crows are also aspects of relevance. Traditional beliefs include the notion of illness induced by evil spirits, and this has been particularly the case with certain forms of mental illness. Tribal healers in the past consisted of three groups-- wound healers, specialists for particular ailments, and the acutual medicine men who served primarily as visionaries and advisors. Although today the distinctions among these various types of healers are blurred, the role of illnesses is still significant.

During the early 1900's, the increasing involvement of the federal goverment in the lives of the Plains Indians brought the Indian Health Service to the Crow Reservation. Modern, usually white, healthcare practitioners have been fairly well accepted by the Crows within their pragmatic approach to health care. Modern health care is viewed as particularly helpful for certain kinds of ailments, while other ailments are believed to be better dealt with using traditional approaches. It is not uncommon for Crows to seek help from both spheres for the same illness. The acceptance of modern healthcare approaches to mental health is highly variable among tribal members. A limiting factor as regards acceptance of and trust in modern healthcare providers overall is the frequent turnover of staff. Public healthservice providers on the reservation rarely remain for longer than their two-year tour of duty, so that the development of provider-patient trust is extremely difficult. Many Crows seem to limit their involvement to superficial politeness, since they know that there will be no long-term relationship with any single provider. The significance of this phenomenon for mental health care is apparent.

Loss Experience

A number of factors on the reservation combine to make the experience of significant and repeated loss a fairly common one for Crow children. The major cause of death among the Crows is accidents, primarily automobile accidents. The majority of these are related to alcohol abuse. Alcoholism is a pervasive health problem among the Crows; the death rate for alcohol-related cirrhosis is eight to nine times the rate for whites living in the Northwest. Alcoholism contributes to numerous family and social problems including child and spouse abuse, child neglect and desertion. Homicide among the Crows occurs at a rate two to three times the national average, and often follows disputes that are aggravated by alcohol intake. In general, life on the reservation is difficult, especially for young men. An unemployment rate of approximately 60%, coupled with bicultural pressures and prejudices, often causes persons to question their self-worth and their place in the world. Suicide occurs at a rate two to three times the national average and is most common in the age group 15-24 years.(2,6)

As a result of these factors children on the Crow Reservation are considerably more likely to experience the loss of parents, relatives, siblings and friends than are children in the population at large. Suicides and homicides, most common in the young adult male group, leave young children

without fathers, older brothers, and favorite
uncles.   In some instances children witness
violence leading to death, thus being doubly
traumatized. The high rate of accidental death
means that children lose parents and significant
others quickly without forewarning or preparation.
In addition, accidental tragedy often claims
several persons at once, and can result in a
child's loss of all or most of his major supportive
figures. Most children on the reservation know of
the sudden loss of significant persons through
their peers, even if they themselves have been
fourtunate enough to avoid the direct experience.
The high rate of alcoholism causes many children to
struggle with the loss of important adult figures
who abandon homes or are forced from them because
of drinking problems, or who are simply unavailable
to children because of intoxication and subsequent
debility.

The birth rate is high among the Crows, more
than two times the overall national rate. Many
children are born while their parents are
relatively young and at a time when marital ties
are unclear or unstable. Such children may be
given over to the care of grandparents, and
subsequently claimed, returned, and reclaimed by
natural mother or her relatives, and natural father
or his relatives. Thus children frequently
experience the loss of significant parenting
figures repeatedly. Since the clans and other
extended relative networks may no longer share the
geographic and interpersonal closeness that
characterized earlier periods of tribal life, the
claiming and giving-away of children can be
markedly more traumatizing now than it was in the
past.

In sum, then, the problems and pressures of
daily living on the reservation lead to adult

responses which make the consistent, supportive
parenting of children difficult to achieve. As a
result, Crow Indian youth are at substantially high
risk of exposure to repeated and traumatic loss
during childhood and adolescence.

Case Studies

The following case studies serve to typify the
kinds of loss experiences which occur among
children on the Crow Reservation.

Jonathon was brought to the mental health
office by his father, who reported that
Jonathan stole and often stayed away from
home overnight without permission.
Information from the school indicated that
the teacher saw Jonathon as a fairly good
student, but frequently withdrawn and
unhappy-looking. In the initial meeting
with the therapist, Jonathon appeared as a
quiet, anxious, but very cooperative boy,
who looked his stated nine years of age.
History revealed that Jonathon's natural
parents had separated when he was three
years old primarily because of the father's
drinking problem. After the separation
Jonathon had initially stayed with his
mother and two older brothers in South
Dakota while his father moved back to the
Crow Reservation. At age five, Jonathon
was sent to live with his father,
reportedly because he didn't behave and
didn't get along with his new stepfather.
From age five to seven, Jonathon lived with
his father, although he was frequently
cared for in the paternal grandmother's
home when his father was engaged in an
extended period of heavy drinking; these

periods apparently occurred about every two to three months. Reportedly, Jonathon, on several occasions, kept his father from freezing to death by pulling him indoors before leaving to stay with the grandmother. At age seven, Jonathon was returned briefly to his mother's care at the father's request. Upon returning to his mother's home, Jonathon learned that his two older brothers had been sent to boarding school. He never heard from or saw them again. After a few months, Jonathon's mother, unable to manage him, sent him back to his father on a bus. Jonathon subsequently moved in with his father and a new stepmother, who openly stated she did not want Jonathon in her home. The father's drinking problem continued and led to many arguments and some physical abuse between the parents.

A baby girl was born as a result of the parental union, and increasingly Jonathon was identified by the stepmother as an unwanted intruder. It was at this time that he was brought for mental health services. After six weekly sessions, Jonathon failed to come for any additional sessions, as did his father and stepmother. Efforts to contact the family proved futile. Several weeks later it was learned that Jonathon's father was drinking heavily and had left the home. Jonathon, himself, had left home and school, and had told his friends he was going to find his 'real mother.'

Joselyn was referred for mental health services by the public health nurse because of her isolative and self-destructive behavior. Joselyn was a 12-year-old diabetic who, despite adequate and repeated instruction, frequently failed to give herself required insulin injections. During the most recent hospitalization, which resulted from one such failure, she had stated repeatedly that she hoped she would die.

During the course of several sessions with Joselyn the following history was acquired. As an infant Joselyn was raised by maternal grandparents where she remained until age six. Joselyn recalled these grandparents with fondness. By the time Joselyn entered school they were too ill and debilitated to care for her. Since the location of either of her natural parents was unknown, she was sent to stay on a ranch in an isolated rural area with her three older brothers. Joselyn recalled that during her early school years she was raised primarily by a succession of brothers' wives and girlfriends, many of whom she knew only briefly. She stated that she was frequently ridiculed as a drug addict or as having a curse because of her use of insulin. There was apparently no family involvement in trying to understand her diabetes or in supporting her in self-care. Joselyn reported feeling closest to a favorite brother, one who spent time with her, taught her to ride, and gave her a colt of her own. Shortly before her tenth birthday, Joselyn witnessed the death of this brother. He was shot in a dispute over ownership of a horse.

Joselyn was seen over a period of several months although infrequently and irregularly because of the long distance

between the ranch where she continued to
live and the mental health office. During
sessions she spent a great deal of time
drawing pictures of herself on horseback.
She made moderate progress in working
through her feelings, although it was not
possible to alter her living situation.

Response Patterns

No formal prevalence data have been collected
by the Indian Health Service in relation to child
mental problems on the reservation. This clinician
found that the majority of children were referred
for help because of disruptive, and oftentimes
aggressive, behavior at home or at school.
Frequently, these children were seen to have
symptoms of underlying depression, particualrly low
self-esteem and feelings of worthlessness. Many
late school-aged and preadolescent children were
referred specifically because of substance abuse,
while many younger children were referred by the
schools because of marked developmental delays. In
many instances, developmental delays and deviations
were secondary to fetal alcohol syndrome. A
smaller number of children were seen as a result of
blatantly self-destructive behavior, such as
suicidal gestures and attempts. A few children
were referred with marked symptoms of anxiety,
usually sleep disturbances which disrupted the
household. Overall, the most common presenting
symptoms were aggressive, destructive, and
unmanageable behavior, including substance abuse
and running away.

Characteristically, children such as Jonathon
and Joselyn appeared distant, withdrawn, and
nonverbal during initial sessions with the
therapist. This behavior was not unlike that of

the majority of Crow children in their encounters with a white, middle-class therapist. However, the withdrawal was more marked and could be observed to extend to other relationships--those with family members as well as with other professionals, Crows as well as whites. Overall, these chldren tended to be passive and cooperative in sessions while revealing very little. Basic simple descriptions and responses were provided, but they gave practically no detail or elaboration, despite encouragement. After four to five sessions in which there was acceptance and little pressuring by the therapist, most children would begin to allude to events at home or school, and eventually to mention some events from the past. Deaths and losses were described without affective response. Notably the children avoided sharing or acknowledging feelings, whether these were happy, sad, or angry; this was so even when reflections and interpretations were made.

In general, the response pattern observed in Crow chldren who had experienced repeated and traumatic loss included affective flattening, interpersonal distancing, and for some children, with support, an eventual movement toward interpersonal and social realignment. Clearly the pattern had variations based particularly on circumstances surrounding loss, the recency of loss, and the existence or absence of meaningful support systems. The characteristics of the response pattern, however, tended to be present, in varying degrees, overall.

Affective flattening appears related to the prominence of denial as a defense mechanism used by the majority of children in dealing with death. Barnes noted that it is not unusual for children to use denial intermittently for many years in struggling to cope with traumatic deaths. This denial of the painful feelings associated with loss seems to expand with those Crow children who have had to deal with repeated trauma. Not only are feelings of sadness, anger, and fear denied, but in large part intense feelings of any kind are not allowed awareness and expression. This defensive response in each individual child may be exacerbated by the Crow cultural context, which emphasizes the nonintrusion of one's own opinions or strong feelings in relating to others. Thus, Crow children may receive positive reinforcement for quiet and reserved behavior, which is seen as polite.

Interpersonal distancing, seen in contact with the therapist, was generalized to include all relationships. The Crow children who were seen after experiences of repeated loss seemed to exercise measured effort in avoiding dependence on, or closeness to, other persons. The self-reliance and independent functioning of eight- and nine-year-old children were impressive. Having experienced closeness to others as a painful process, they defended well against future pain and loss. Intense and unmet needs for dependence and nurturing were managed through reaction formation, resulting in an appearance of aloofness and independence. Such a defensive response served to maintain functioning in daily life situations, and prevented despair and total disorganization in response to the severe and repeated trauma that had been endured.

Some of the traumatized children did become able to risk the reexploration of interpersonal relationships. Often, this development was dependent upon the home or community situation that could be developed for any given child. If a stable, supportive parenting figure existed or could be secured, the child was much more likely to reinvest in interpersonal relationships. The parenting figure, whether present in the home or readily available in the clan or community, provided ongoing acceptance which allowed the child to experiment with various types of behavior, and even to reject the adult without counterrejection. In addition, a consistent parenting figure who assumed some responsibility, greatly increased the likelihood that the child would attend therapy sessions regularly over a period of weeks or months.

Testing behavior, as is characteristic among deprived children, frequently occurred when a Crow child began to develop new interpersonal relationships. Certainly the need to be assured that the therapist and caretakers were consistent and reliable was intense in these children. Identity issues were combined with those of object relationships, so that children examined who they were or could be within the context of both a family and the larger community. Given, for example, the situation where a child had never known his father and had been deserted by his mother, he struggled with how or if he fit within the tribal clan system. Without support and active sponsorship he could in fact be a Crow Indian without being of the Crow social group. Children of mixed-blood parentage were particularly vulnerable to such difficulties. Despite these problems, the simple response of caring enough to ask how he or she fit within a family, a clan and the tribe overall was often a crucial first step in interpersonal investment for the child who had suffered repeated loss.

Adapting Clinical Interventions

Therapeutic work with Crow children required

modification and adaptation of standard approaches. History-taking and assessment placed greater emphasis on detailing where and with whom the child had been raised, in an effort to identify experiences that may have been perceived as loss or rejection. Since it is not uncommon for children to be shifted among relatives and foster parents, such occurrences were often not reported unless specifically asked about. This was particularly true when the child was referred, as was often the case, because of 'bad' behavior at home or school. Parents' or teachers' concerns about a child's overall happiness and sense of attachment and identity were naturally secondary to worries about immediate problems such as truancy, stealing and running away. However, in the thorough assessment of any Crow child, the significance of depression as an underlying cause of antisocial behavior required particular consideration.

Clearly it was inappropriate to consider any child's history in isolation and make assumptions from it regarding feelings of loss or deprivation. Simply knowing that a child was forced to leave a favorite grandparent's home at age five, or that he had witnessed his mother's death at age nine, was insufficient data on which to formulate a dynamic understanding. Such data did provide significant clues, but they had to be weighed and evaluated. It was most tempting to apply formulations based on the reactions of white, middle-class children to such losses, but often these were shown to be inaccurate.

In discussing regional variations in child development, Looff[4] wrote:

...the structure of adult society and the function of the family unit within this larger framework provide a context within which the growing child interprets his experiences.

Certainly this was applicable in the case of Crow children whose history revealed numerous losses. The significance of these experiences, or even their interpretation as loss, was colored by circumstance and by the explanations which the family or culture provided. A male child who was separated from his mother-only childhood home in order to live with male relatives and thus acquire appropriate male behavior, might well view this experience as an honor rather than a loss. Likewise, a girl given in a supportive fashion to a maternal aunt, a woman in the Crow language termed 'mother,' might experience little trauma, particularly if a close clan structure allowed her frequent contact with her original parent. The very fact that the Crow language and kinship structure allow for numerous mothers, fathers, sisters and brothers (identified in white culture as maternal aunts, uncles and cousins), leads to different interpretations of family, relationship and identity.

For some Crow children this larger family notion allowed family-to-family transfers to occur with relative ease. Such interfamily transfers appeared most likely to be nontraumatizing when the following factors were present: the child and biological parents held traditional beliefs about the clan and were a close-knit part of the matrilineal clan; the child was transferred to culturally 'correct' relatives (usually maternal grandmother's or maternal aunt's family); the transfer family was emotionally and geographically close to the original parent or parents; and the child did not perceive the transfer as a response to bad or troublesome behavior. The age of the child at the time of transfer and the number of such transfers that occurred seemed, somewhat surprisingly, less significant to the child's well-being than the presence of the above factors.

Certainly the fact that Crow children live in a context where the transfer of children among the larger clan family is fairly common, and is thus a shared experience among peers and siblings, contributes to their perception of the event in a fashion much different than that of white, middle-class children. Further, such frequency of transfer and the larger family concept often created confusion for the white, middle-class therapist when she requested a child to draw or describe his parents or his family.

Despite the presence of mitigating factors in the social fabric, there clearly were children who were traumatized by separations, deaths and other losses. Often, children were suddenly left alone because of a caretaker's death, or they were abandoned or abused as a result of adult alcoholism. Further, many children labeled as bad, uncontrollable, or otherwise undesirable were 'dumped' from one unwilling family to another. These situations differed markedly from the more positive transfers from one caring family to another.

As described earlier, circumstances on the Crow Reservation make it likely that a large proportion of children will experience and be hurt by losses. In fact the very endemic quality of such loss experiences appeared to make it difficult for the child, the family, and the mental health clinician to recognize and appreciate the degree of fear and sadness involved. In describing the endemic depression of persons who live in poverty-stricken black subcultures, Wortman[7] observed that:

...they did not know they were depressed
and ill; depression is a sneaky problem and
catches people of all groups unaware.

Such was often the case among depressed Crow
children as viewed by themselves and their
families. Their withdrawn, distant behavior was
not seen as very different from that of their
peers, and their life histories of abandonment,
separation, or neglect were fairly common.

Developing a therapeutic contract with the Crow
child and attempting to facilitate the work of
therapy presented a number of unique challenges.
The most common response seen in children brought
for therapy was that of passive resistance. Often,
they were brought because they were viewed by
adults as 'bad,' and thus a defensive, stubborn
posture was adopted in preparation for the
condemnation and blame they expected from the
therapist. This, coupled with a strong need to
deny dependency needs and the feelings associated
with loss and trauma, made for numerous quiet and
inactive early sessions. Lack of responsiveness
appeared related to both cultural and intrapsychic
aspects; often it was difficult to differentiate
the two.   The Crow culture emphasizes self-
reliance, individual independence, and a 'keeping
to oneself.'   Thus the sharing of significant
events and feelings with a relative stranger, and
especially a non-Indian stranger, would tend to be
viewed in the culture as inappropriate, even
embarrassing social behavior.   In addition,
children who had experienced repeated losses needed
to defend against interpersonal closeness by
avoidance and excessive repression. The cultural
norms and the intrapsychic mechanisms tended to
reinforce each other. Even as some of the initial
resistance decreased in the course of nonjudgmental
and relatively unstructured sessions, it became

evident that the expression and working through of feelings would be exceedingly difficult.   Crow children are taught, directly or through their social experiences, not to impose their thoughts or their sentiments on others.   One does not correct others or indicate that the other's perceptions are incorrect.   Tolerance of others is highly valued, and is practiced through silence and nonintrusive behavior.

During the first two or three sessions an effort to promote beginning trust was made through nonjudgmental interpretation, assurance regarding appropriate confidentiality, and a balance of reasonable limits and accommodation.   Following this, an effort was made to establish goals for therapy sessions in conjuction with the child.   If the child was extremely withdrawn, the therapist supplied a choice of goals, and the child was asked simply to agree or disagree, even if only by nodding.   An attempt was made to blend reality-oriented, concrete goals, such as learning to play checkers, with those focused more on self-expression and insight development, such as role-playing or drawing specific circumstances.   As with therapy in other social contexts of deprivation and crisis orientation, work with the Crow children had to be telescoped.   Rarely were children brought for sessions after some resolution of presenting 'bad' behavior was achieved.   Thus few children were seen for more than eight to ten sessions and often these were sporadically spaced.

Time-frame issues became significant within the cross-cultural context.   The white notion of clock time is not accepted by many Crows, who view it as arbitrary and unnecessary and who prefer to do things more naturally, giving to each event or experience whatever amount of time is needed. For the white therapist, used to an appointment

schedule and with limited hours available for
service provision, this approach to time presented
problems. An accommodation of sorts was reached by
seeing children or parents if they arrived any time
during their appointment hour and continuing until
either the end of the assigned hour or until the
next client arrived for the appointment, whichever
occurred later. In those cases where a child or
parent could be seen only briefly, an effort was
made to schedule another appointment as soon as
possible. Explanation was made regarding the
realistic constraints of the appointment procedure
with every effort to be nonjudgmental regarding the
child's or family's method of dealing with time.

As the child became engaged in the therapeutic
process, an attempt was made to evaluate the
child's emotional status vis-à-vis Kubler-Ross's
forumulations of grieving.[3] This was particularly
appropriate when it was clear that the child had
suffered a significant recent loss or a series of
unresolved losses. Paintings and drawings were
often particularly useful in understanding a
child's feelings. Most children were comfortable
with these activities since artistic endeavors are
values in the Crow culture. While one is not
encouraged within the culture to be verbally
expressive, the expression of self in arts and
crafts is acceptable, so long as one does not
become individually prideful. Crow children tended
to draw outdoor scenes, plants, and animals more
readily than pictures of people or houses. In
doing so, they seemed to reflect their greater
experience with the outdoors, as well as the
symbolic value their culture places on many animals
and natural events. It was possible to gain
insight about a child's feelings related to self
and significant others by listening to the child's
stories about rocks and animals. A nine-year-old
girl, separated from her family by a court order

because of neglect, spent many sessions drawing a bird "...all alone above trees, not able to find a nest." Another very withdrawn child first demonstrated feelings of closeness by drawing two horses, instead of the usual one, indicating to the therapist, "...and that one's for you. You can ride with me." Thus, many children who spoke very little throughout the therapy process revealed a great deal through their coloring or painting. Over time it was possible to offer tentative interpretations or insights regarding the pictures and have these commented on by the child. One child, for example, repeatedly drew his alcoholic father as asleep while he, the child, was caught in some dangerous situation. Eventually the boy's fear and sense of abandonment were explored. Children hesitant to draw or paint could often be encouraged by the therapist's casual initiation of drawing during the session and by her continuing to draw or paint with the child. The exchange of 'good-bye' pictures depicting various aspects or events in the therapy process was often a useful adjunct to the termination process.

In contrasting the loss responses of Crow children with those described by Kubler-Ross,[3] some variations were noted. Most of the Crow children who had been traumatized by repeated losses seemed to defend themselves by maintaining a state of feeling denial and interpersonal isolation. In its extreme, this state produced an apathetic child devoid of desire or capacity for interpersonal warmth. Those children able, with support, to work through their defensive denial tended to express relatively little anger during the process. One wonders if a cultural set that emphasizes acceptance of all natural processes and resignation to one's fate had an influence in this area. White children, especially those of the middleclass, tend by virtue of their culture to see nature as a force to be controlled and they are urged to be masters of their own fate. Thus, when faced with a death or separation, which they cannot control, anger seems an appropriate response. For Crow children, sadness may be the more prominent feature. Having accepted the process of loss, which they see all around them as a natural order, they appear to be left more lonely, deprived and needy than angry. The depth of such feelings in the Crow children seen was poignantly expressed in their drawings and paintings, although they rarely had words, especially English ones, for their grief.

The therapy focus, once a child moved to acknowledgment of his or her sadness, was simply one of support. Reassurance was needed regarding the appropriateness of sad feelings and the expression thereof. Many of the children seen had never had either time or the interpersonal support necessary for grief work. Some children were able in therapy to reach a point of accepting both their losses and the feelings associated with them. It was then possible to explore a renewal of interpersonal closeness. This often took the form initially of the child's closeness and warmth with the therapist, for example, allowing and seeking physical touch and bringing small gifts. Therapy efforts were focused on transferring this desire for interpersonal relationship to family and community members who could sustain it after the therapy relationship ended. In this regard clan members and other relatives, as well as informal community leaders, were quite helpful particularly when a child was in a relatively non-nurturing home situation.

Conclusion

Mental health work with children on the Crow Indian Reservation revealed a situation where repeated and traumatic losses are fairly common childhood experiences. The resourcefulness of children in coping with such trauma was impressive; yet, at times their coping style was also restrictive and emotionally damaging. Learning about the circumstances and beliefs of the Crow child, over time, assisted the therapist in better understanding response patterns and behavior. Adaptation in therapeutic approaches were necessary in order to provide meaningful help for Crow children, many of whom existed in a world somewhere between a traditional Indian sphere and a modern, white technology. Perhaps the greatest challenge was in the development of a helping relationship that spanned age, cultural and experiential differences. Where such a relationship developed, one had to credit the generous, enduring spirit of the Crow child no less than the patience and persistence of the therapist.

References

1. Barnes, M. 1978. The Reactions of Children and Adolescents to the Death of a Parent or Sibling. In The Child and Death, ed., O. Sahler. St. Louis: C.V. Mosby.

2. Hardin, R. 1981. The Crow Indian People: Health Care. Videotaped lecture, Montana State University School of Nursing. Billings, Montana.

3. Kubler-Ross, E. 1969. On Death and Dying. New York: MacMillan.

4. Loof, D. 1979. Sociocultural Factors in Etiology. In Basic Handbook of Child Psychiatry. ed. J. Noshpitz. New York: Basic Books.

5. Medicine Crow, J. 1939. The Effects of European Cultural Contracts upon the Economic, Social and Religious Life of the Crow Indians. Unpublished Master's thesis, University of Southern California, Los Angeles.

6. U.S. Public Health Service. Community Health Statistics, 1970-79. Unpublished reports. Indian Health Service, Crow Agency, Montana.

7. Wortman, R. 1981. Depression, Danger, Dependency, Denial: Work with Poor, Black, Single Parents. American Journal of Orthopsychiatry 51(4): 662-671.

"HE DIED TOO QUICK!"
THE PROCESS OF DYING IN A HUTTERIAN COLONY

Peter H. Stephenson

As a hematologist percussed the right side of his twenty-nine-year-old patient's chest, his discovery of dullness and the recurrent pleural effusion it signalled brought the realization that a remission had come to an abrupt end. "Oh, shit," he muttered. Then realizing what he had said, he added hastily, "Oh excuse me, Bill." "That's all right," the young man replied, "It's nice to know you care."[1] [pp. 582-583]

This statement exemplifies the isolation which dying persons experience in what might be called our 'thanataphobic' culture. Glaser and Strauss studied the behavior of nurses and found that the closer patients were to death, the less time was spent with them even though these seriously ill persons were located closer to the nursing station.[2] Although dying persons fear abandonment [pp. 961-1128],[3] avoidance of them by family, friends, and even health professionals is too commonplace. Because dying patients are individual human beings with varying needs, in Cassem's words, "there can be no one 'best' way to die" [p. 582].[1] Nonetheless, some values appear to cluster about our conception of death, and these, when taken together, may constitute our death ideal.

Reprinted from Omega, 14(2), (1983-84): 127-134, with permission from the author and Baywood Publishing Company.

Perhaps the most important value which we
express in regard to death is freedom from pain.
Saunders found among cancer patients in St.
Joseph's Hospital (London), that pain was one of
their greatest three fears (the other two were
abandonment and shortness of breath).[3] Additionally, Weisman and Hackett have described what they
call 'appropriate death' which may be taken to
represent a coherent statement by medical practitioners of what constitutes a 'good' death.   As
such it is an indicator of our values.[4]   Among
Weisman's conditions for 'appropriate death' is the
proviso that the person be relatively pain-free.[5]
The difficulties we have in coping with terminally
ill patients are profound, and they stem from many
conflicts, not the least of which is the basic
conflict between the desire to alleviate pain and
the knowledge that only death--the avowed enemy of
every health-care professional--can ultimately
release the terminal patient from pain.   Thus we
encounter the notion that persons in pain should
ideally not suffer for long.   The phrase, "It was
sad, but really a blessing in disguise," has so
often been used that we can all recognize it along
with its counterparts: "It was really a good
thing, he suffered so," and "It was a mercy."   The
ideal death for us is as painless as possible,
which also implies that dying should take place
quickly.   The ideal death also does not result from
disease but is the product of so-called 'natural
causes,' and occurs during sleep.   We are presented
with a portrait of isolated persons often gripped
by profound fears, attended by others (strangers
rather than family) who hope that death comes
swiftly and painlessly, yet whose efforts often
prolong life and with it, sometimes, agony.

Some Basic Hutterian Values And
Behavior Related To Dying

This portrait contrasts markedly with the process of dying among the Hutterian Brethren of the prairies. For the Hutterites the ideal death is a prolonged affair. During the period of dying a person is virtually never alone, for everyone is anxious to see 'the fortunate' one. Hutterites do not distinguish between 'natural causes' and disease categories because 'all deaths are willed by God.' Eaton reports that Hutterites show little fear of death and actually embrace it as their final reward for a life filled with tribulation and pain [6]. One Hutterite, in conversation with John Hostetler, summarized Hutterian values as follows:

> We prefer slow deaths, not sudden deaths. We want to have plenty of time to consider eternity and to confess and make everything right. We don't like to see a grownup go suddenly.[7] [p. 248]

When severe illness strikes and a person becomes aware that he or she is dying, word is sent to relatives and friends, who converge on the colony where the person resides, often travelling from several hundred miles away. Small children and adults are brought to see the dying person, who talks with them. Often the subject matter of conversation is religious, and the 'paradise of eternal life' is stressed. Thus the visitors and the dying person mutually socialize each other into an awareness of mortality and toward its graceful acceptance. Hutterites have also preserved the bedside accounts of the deaths of some of their ancestors, whose last words are often put to verse and sung [see ref. 8, p. 44; 9].

The degree to which the dying person becomes the

focus of activity is stunning.   The dying person
may request favorite hymns to be sung, food to be
prepared, or a particular person's presence.
Indeed, Hostetler reports an instance in which a
terminally ill person was sung to day and night by
members of several colonies in rotation until 'the
steadfast soul was ushered into the banquet of the
redeemed'[7] [p. 172].   The dying Hutterite adult is
also aware that those visitors who now attend him
or her will remain for the wake which follows.
Special funeral buns are being cooked and a coffin
will be made later by a life-long friend.   Funerals
are major social events, and, as every Hutterite
knows, courting takes place at them.   Perhaps the
dying Hutterite's children or grandchildren will
meet their wives and husbands at the funeral.

The only exception to the ideal of a long death
period (several weeks at least) is the death of a
child.   Following the death of a seven-year-old
girl by scalding, it was said, "She will sure be a
beautiful angel," and a mature father noted, "When
these little ones die we know they are in heaven,
but we never know what will happen to them if they
grow up.   I sure wish I would have died when I was
a kid"[p. 249].[7]

Hutterian values and behavior surrounding death
appear to reverse our own.   Hutterites prize the
deaths of children while we abhor them and they
regard a long death period as desirable while we
regard it as unfortunate, particularly if it is
painful.   Hutterites regard the ability to keep
faith even in pain as the hallmark of a true
Christian martyr.   One who has lived with much pain
is regarded as special.   I can recall commenting on
the arthritis of one man's wife and he replied,
"Yes, but she'll sure walk fine in heaven!"

Some of the relative equanimity with which

Hutterites greet death stems from their practice of adult baptism (<u>beigiessungstaufe</u>), which they term 'a dying of the old man and a putting on of the new.' Hutterites baptize only adults, who become accountable to God for their acts after they are reborn in baptism. After baptism one joins 'the body of Christ' (<u>corpus christi</u>), participates fully in religious ritual (the Lord's supper) and is allowed to marry. Children's misdeeds are already forgiven through Christ's suffering, and so children automatically go to heaven. Adults, during their death-bed period, are essentially supposed to 'relive' their lives, to forgive others and to be forgiven. Since the baptized adult has already died and been reborn in ritual once before, it is clearly implied that his or her final death is nothing more than a birth to eternal life. This is expressed in the funeral hymn itself. All assembled intone the lines:

> Each man and woman surely dies,
> For we know all flesh is hay.
> First this body must decay
> If it ever is to rise
> To the glory that awaits
> All the good at heaven's gates.[10]

The dying person must slowly pass into eternity because he or she has a moral obligation to self and others to die socially before actually physically expiring. Old quarrels, grudges, mistakes, etc., must be acquitted, and in this respect a person's death corresponds to baptism. At that earlier ritual or rebirth the person died to the life of the child--a life of evil--and took up responsibility. At the deathbed the same time, writ large, must occur: a life must be shed.

Paul's Death: A Case History

Through Christ I live,
Death is my goal.
To him I give
My joyful soul.   (from a Hutterian hymn)

During the autumn of 1975, Paul Stahl, a forty-eight-year-old Hutterite man whom I know quite well, died from lymphosarcoma [see 11].   He was kept in the hospital in Calgary for nearly two weeks and finally taken by ambulance to his home colony, about forty-five miles outside the city. He arrived in the evening but died at approximately 4:00 A.M.   The reaction of several of his kin, in particular one brother, was astonishingly atypical of Hutterians when confronted with death.   This death was regarded as sudden despite the intervening period of two weeks after his initial collapse, partly because he was not at home during this period and partly because neither he nor his relatives were appraised of the mortal quality of his illness at the outset.   The result was that all of the grief-work normally vitiated through the anticipatory procedures described earlier in this paper could not be accomplished.   Paul's brother John grieved in a manner inconsistent with the ideal.   He showed anger, sullenness, and despair. Once he wept openly and uncontrollably, although briefly.   Usually the public sobs of the bereaved are highly stylized, occur only at graveside, are given only by women (from oldest to youngest in sequence), and are meant to represent the grief of the living for their own sad plight.

Whatever had needed to be said between these brothers had been left unsaid.   Over 500 people came to Paul's funeral.[*]   The following are excerpts from my fieldnotes dated Sunday, October 26, 1976.

There were over twenty-five people in the apartment. John sitting with one twin (grand-children) on each knee. David (Stahl) brought me a beer and a girl brought juice for several of the men...quite abruptly a large contingent of visitors from Lethbridge left...all visitors... they shook hands with the Stahls, Dave and John, and left quickly and quietly. John's comments were, "He died too quick, too quick...he was so alive." "Well I've seen worse cases...men who went out in the morning to work and who never came back!" "But, he just died too quick!"

(later)

We walked to my car...and shook hands... myself, John, and one of his younger sons. On the way, John pointed to the cemetery on top of the hill...silhouetted against the sky, in the snow, one could see a fresh grave dug in the frozen ground. He turned to me with a flushed face and said to me that "discrimination is a part of ignorance, maybe your work will help that. You wouldn't believe the questions people ask about us...do the Hutterites have cemeteries? They even say we feed them to the pigs!" To communicate his grief he would even let out such a horrible suggestion as that!

John was more depressed than other Hutterites following more 'conventional' deaths. His grief was almost palpable and lasted for months. He was a sensitive man, so his grief reaction would perhaps have been more obvious than that of another even had his brother died more appropriately.

However, his reaction was not the only one I witnessed. Several others from this family also showed clear signs of anxiety; not eating or sleeping well. The entire colony seemed somewhat confused, but kin were especially upset by this death. Paul was one of the most important men in the colony and would have been a likely candidate for an important administrative post in the new 'daughter colony' which was being constructed. Non-kin did not react as strongly to Paul's untimely death, and so a slight schism between the two kin groups in this colony became manifest. This division would not have been obvious had Paul been able to sustain a prolonged deathbed.

Generally Hutterite colonies divide in half when their populations double [see ref. 12, pp. 118-161]. Ultimately, when this colony divided, Paul's kin-group moved away to the new colony. I think that the constituencies of the parties in this division were partly precipitated by Paul having died 'too quick.'** The choice of the word 'quick' here is interesting, especially followed by 'he was so alive.' This conversation was in English, but 'quick' in the sense of 'alive' (leben) means much the same thing in both German and English. When Paul died he was still too much alive -- he was still among the 'quick' and not yet with 'the dead.' He did not have time to put his social persona to rest. As a result, more grief was shown than is normal in Hutterite life. Since close kin demonstrated this grief while non-kin did not, a gap was exposed between the kin groups in this colony which could not be closed, and which ideally should not have been there.

Some Recommendations For Treating Hutterians with Terminal Illnesses

The recognition of cultural variation in the

practice of medicine is widely espoused, yet specific recommendations are only rarely made. The following suggestions are meant to be broad enough to apply to Hutterian patients in general but specific enough to refer in application to discrete cases.

1.   When Hutterian patients are diagnosed as terminally ill they should be returned to their home colonies as speedily as possible following some stabilization of their conditions.

2.   When possible, visitation should be allowed or even extended. I have visited Hutterian patients hospitalized where 'visitor's hours' were only for two hours during the evening and limited to three persons. Given their distance from home and the time necessary to travel to them, they received almost no visitors, and their isolation was almost total. For a Hutterite who has lived totally submerged in his or her gemeinde, an hour-long visit with several people is completely inadequate. The fear of isolation experienced by terminally ill patients in our society is quite profoundly compounded for Hutterites.

3.   When children die in our society our emotional reactions are very strong, yet Hutterians regard the deaths of children as 'a blessing.' If this is recognized by health-care workers, the subdued responses to childhood deaths which the Hutterites sometimes demonstrate will not be misinterpreted as shock or lack of affect. This does not mean that all Hutterites gladly accept the deaths of

their children.   They are supposed to,
but the conflict of the ideal value with
emotional sense of loss sometimes leads
to depression of a peculiar kind.   The
mother and father may be depressed
because their feelings are not attuned to
the values, and a sense of unworthiness
may pervade them.   This form of
depression is termed 'Anfechtung'
(temptation by the devil) by the
Brethren. In either case, simple lack of
affect is not an appropriate reading of
the behavior.

4.   Should a psychiatrist have to deal with
a Hutterite suffering from depression
following what for ourselves would
constitute an 'appropriate death,' he or
she should treat the patient as any other
patient whose loved one has died a sudden
death where anticipating grief-work had
not occurred.   Assuming these cases to
be 'abnormal grief reactions' and
pursuing a therapy where the relationship
between the deceased and the patient is
examined would be ill-advised--that
relationship has already been hyper-
cathected and at least initially should
be avoided.

5.   Outpatient care of Hutterians who can be
put on maintenance schedules wherever
possible is probably a wise policy.   The
use of 'visiting nurse' procedures may
assist health planners in this situation.

ACKNOWLEDGMENTS

The author thanks the council for their support and Skip Koolage and Margie Rodman for their comments on an earlier draft presented at the Canadian Ethnology Society meetings, February 1980, in Montreal. Most especially, this paper is dedicated to Ira Goldhar (1947-1983).

Notes

*The name Paul and those of his brothers in the excerpts which follow are all fictitious.

**A number of other incidents involving the two groups also developed shortly after this including a <u>pshrien</u>, 'evil-eye' suspicion which crossed kin lines. [See ref. 10, pp. 250-261 for a discussion of 'evil-eye' beliefs among the Hutterites.]

References

1. Cassem, N.H. 1970. Treating the Person Confronting Death.   In The Harvard Guide to Modern Psychiatry, ed. A.M. Nicholi, Jr. Harvard-Belknap Press, Cambridge, 1970.

2. Glaser, B.G. and A.L. Strauss. 1965. Awareness of Dying, Chicago: Aldine.

3. Saunders, C. 1959.   Care of the Dying: The Problem of Euthanasia. Nursing Times 55, 960-1130.

4. Weisman, A.D. and T.P. Hackett. 1961. Predilection to Death: Death and Dying as a Psychiatric Problem.   Psychosomatic Medicine 23, 232-256.

5. Weisman, A.D. 1972. On Dying and Denying. New York: Behavioral Publications.

6. Eaton, J.W. 1964. The Art of Aging and Dying. Gerontologist 4, 94-101.

7.   Hostetler,   J.A.   1974.   Hutterite   Society. Baltimore Maryland: Johns Hopkins University Press.

8.   Estep,   W.R.   1963.   The   Anabaptist   Story. Nashville: Broodman Press.

9. Stephenson, P.H. 1978.   Like a Violet Unseen: The Apotheosis of Absence in Hutterite Life. Canadian Review of Sociology and Anthropology 15:4, 433-442.

10. Holzach, M. 1979. The Christian Communists of Canada. Geo, 1, 126-154.

11. Stephenson, P.H. 1981. The View from Rattenburg-on-the-Inn and the Ethnography of Intuition. In _Proceedings of the Canadian Ethnology Society-1979_, Doyle G. Hatt and Marie-Francoise Guedon (eds.), National Museum of Canada, Ottawa, pp. 183-189.

12. _____. 1978. A Dying of the Old Man and a Putting On of the New: The Cybernetics of Ritual Metanoia in the Life of the Hutterian Commune, Ph.D. dissertation, University of Toronto, Microfilm: National Library of Canada, Ottawa.

13. _____. 1979. Hutterite Belief in Evil-Eye: Beyond Paranoia and Towards a General Theory of Invidia _Culture, Medicine and Psychiatry_ 3, 247-265.

"I'M NOT DEAD YET!" AGING AND DEATH: PROCESS AND EXPERIENCE IN KALIAI

Dorothy Ayers Counts and David R. Counts

Introduction

In North America old people are frequently stereotyped as being infirm, senile, childlike, and worthless (Berezin 1978: 542). This stereotype is exacerbated by the loss of self-respect that frequently accompanies retirement and by the fact that the most pervasive experience shared by the North American elderly seems to be loss--of physical function, of social contact as friends and spouse die, and of self-esteem as people exchange the satisfaction of useful occupation for uselessness and dependency. As a result, cultural gerontophobia--the irrational fear and/or hatred of old age and the elderly both by society and by the old people themselves--is prevalent. This fear exists in spite of the fact that most people age comfortably and in good health (ibid.)

The above stereotype illustrates one widespread misunderstanding about old age. Another is the notion that agedness, frequently undefined and therefore usually assumed to mean decrepitude, begins much earlier among 'primitives' than it does among the people of the industrialized world (see for example Cowgill and Holmes 1972: 8).

Reprinted from Aging and Its Transformations: Moving Towards Death in Pacific Societies with permission of University Press of America: New York, 1985, pp. 131-155.

307

Despite their alleged entry into the ranks of the elderly at an early chronological age, people in non-industrialized societies do not, as a general rule, seem to suffer from the fear of old age that is said to characterize our society. Rather, cross-cultural studies conclude that loss of prestige and esteem by the elderly and negative images of aging are the by-products of urbanization, industrialization, and modernization (Cowgill and Holmes 1972: 322; Fry 1980a: 4-5). In pre-industrial societies old people often control useful knowledge and hold positions of political and economic power. As a result their status is high and they are respected or feared (Swain 1979).

This is, indeed, a strange situation. Does modernization really result in a state of affairs in which North Americans hate and fear the same condition and category of people who are respected and esteemed in non-industrialized societies? Is a seventy-year-old North American really at the same physical and social stage as a fifty-year-old Melanesian? The difficulty is that the terms 'old person' or 'elder'--or words that have been translated that way--have not been carefully defined so that there is distressingly little content to statements such as, "Among the Bugabuga, people are old at forty." Words are taken out of context, the content of the condition 'old' is not defined, and no distinction if drawn between being old, however it is defined, and being decrepit, defunct, or socially disaffiliated. Watson and Maxwell note (1977: 6) that much of this confusion is due to the fact that little attention has been directed to the sociocultural context of aging. In this chapter we direct our attention to aging, old age, and dying as they are perceived by the Lusi-speaking Kaliai people of Northwest New Britain,

Papua New Guinea. Specifically, we examine the
criteria that the Lusi use to define age
categories; we explore the expectations that the
Lusi share with regard to the aging process and the
role of the elderly; and we demonstrate that old
age and death are not necessarily fixed categories.
Indeed, their boundaries are mutable and their
attributes are complex aggregates of physical
characteristics and social relationships that are
open to interpretation and manipulation.
Consequently, it may be unclear how others should
treat an older person, and people may disagree as
to whether an individual has begun the process of
dying.   The placement of a person in the
appropriate category may become a strategic act
subject to negotiation.

There are about 1000 speakers of Lusi living
along the northwest coast of West New Britain.
Their social organization is ideally patrilineal,
virilocal, and egalitarian. Their maroni
(traditional leaders) are men whose economic and
social prowess allows them to receive community
recognition.   In recent years the Kaliai have
elected to public office younger men whose
experience and education equips them to deal with
the political realities of modern Papua New Guinea.

Most of the data for this paper were collected
in Kandoka village, the largest Kaliai village and
the second largest community in the Gloucester-
Kandrian area of West New Britain Province. During
the nearly two decades since 1966, we have made
four field trips and spent about two and one-half
years in northwest New Britain, mainly in Kandoka.
There are many advantages to long-term field
research in a single community (see Foster et al.
1979 for a discussion of these advantages). This
is particularly true if the topic of study is aging
and dying. First, aging is an experience of change

that is best understood if it is shared, and this
sharing can only occur over the passage of time.
During the past nineteen years we have aged along
with our friends and consultants. We have shared
and compared this experience with them and we, too,
have been reclassified as 'elders'.

Second, people may revise their explanations of
socially traumatic events, such as death, as the
full effects of such an occurrence become apparent
and circumstances change with the passage of time.
Long-term participation in the village has enabled
us to observe the process whereby facts and
explanations are adjusted to be consistent with
current cultural reality.

Life, Humanity and the Spirit World

The Lusi do not oppose life and death in the
same way that English speakers do. They have no
generic term for 'life'. They oppose existence (i
moro, 'it is') and a condition they call mate, a
word that may be translated 'dead', 'unconscious'
or 'ruined'. The world experienced by the Lusi is
full of beings that move, grow, and interact with
others in the environment--or at least they have
the potential to do so. These beings may take the
shape of natural formations such as mountains or
stones, or they may appear to be insects, animals,
plants or human beings; or they may have no
constant form at all. The relevant question to ask
about something, therefore, is not, "Is it alive?"
but "Is it what it appears to be?" There is no
empirical test for stones or mountains. Their
identity is known through myth, and those that have
a history--those that once were pigs, or culture
heroes, or malevolent spirits--are identified and
their stories told. Occasionally, one of these may
identify itself by its actions. If, for example,

someone moves a spirit-stone from its resting place
to a new spot, say in a village, it may very well
remove itself back to its chosen resting place
under cover of darkness. Such things are best left
alone.

It is not always possible to know with certainty
whether a thing is as it seems. Kaliai legend is
replete with instances of people mistaking an <u>antu</u>
(spirit being) for the animal or human it appears
to be. Indeed, the spirit being may consider
itself to be a true resident of the substantial
world while <u>iavava</u> (humans) are only 'those who
frighten parrots' (see Counts 1980a for a
discussion of the Kaliai myth "Akro and Gagandewa"
which explores the concept of a relative reality).
Nevertheless, there are clues that aid the Kaliai
in their attempts to make positive identification.

Spirit beings do not leave the same signs as do
corporeal beings. Ghosts and spirit-pigs leave no
tracks, and the songs of spirit-birds sound like
human speech instead of bird song. Furthermore, a
real animal--a bird or pig for instance--can be
killed and the hunter can find its dead body. In
contrast, a hunter may spear or shoot a spirit-
creature at point-blank range and it will likely
melt into the brush and disappear. This does not
mean that spirit beings are immortal (a concept
that should be distinguished from the notion of
life after death, as Rivers noted [1926 in Slobodin
1978: 216]), for they do die and they can be
killed. However, they do not stay dead, and they
seldom allow humans to find and eat them. When a
spirit being is eaten, the consumer always suffers:
<u>caveat esor</u>!

Human beings, as opposed to animals, are defined
by the presence of a spiritual component that has
two aspects: <u>-tautau</u> (spiritual essence) and-

312 Aging and Death

anunu (shadow or image) (in chapter 11, Scaletta discusses similar concepts regarding components of the human spirit among the Kabana of Bariai). The complexity of the notion of spiritual being that is embodied in these terms, used interchangeably by people who are discussing ghosts or spirits, illustrated by the several meanings of these Lusi words. The term -anunu also means 'dream' (anunuqu, my dream) and 'reflection', while -tautau incorporates the notion of essence and self. The edible meat of a coconut is nui aitautau, the fleshy part of a woman's breast is aituru aitautau, and our consultants say the portion of something that is called aitautau is its 'true' or essential part. The term aitau also means 'himself' 'herself', 'itself' as in aitau iraui (he struck himself) while taugau may be glossed 'myself' (taugau ngaraugau, 'I struck myself'). No animals have this spiritual component, while it is a part of all living humans, including the fetus and the mentally incapacitated. Either aspect may leave the body of one who is ill, and either the 'spiritual essence' or the 'image' of a dying individual may be seen by others as far as several miles from the still-breathing person. When death occurs both aspects permanently leave the corpse. People disagree about what happens then. From comments that our consultants made in 1966 and 1967, we conclude that many Lusi once believed that one or both aspects of the spiritual component of the deceased person remained near the body until it decomposed (Counts and Counts 1974). In 1981, after fifteen additional years of Roman Catholic influence, the same persons that we talked with in 1966 firmly maintained that the sol (soul)[1] goes immediately to its spirit home. The only circumstance under which the 'soul' might remain near the grave, people now say, would be if the surviving kin failed to pay to have a final Mass said for the deceased. However, death is a social process as well as a physical event, and the Kaliai consider death to be reversible. The spiritual component(s) of an individual may leave and return to the body many times before abandoning it forever.

The Aging Process

The Lusi recognize a number of named stages in the development of the life cycle: <u>maseknga</u> (newborn); <u>kekele</u> (child); <u>iriao</u> (youth) and <u>tamine vilala</u> (maiden); <u>taming/tomone uainga</u> (married woman/man); <u>tanta pao</u> (new person or parent of dependent child(ren)); <u>tamparonga/taparonga</u> (elder or senior female/male); <u>tanta taurai</u> (decrepit person).[2]

The criteria for location in the life cycle are egocentric and physiological when the individual is young. For instance, an infant ceases to be 'newborn' when its skin darkens and it becomes plump. Childhood lasts until the individual approaches puberty. A girl becomes a 'maiden' when her breasts 'fall' and she begins to menstruate, but there is no agreed upon point of transition when a boy become a 'youth'. An initiated but sexually immature boy is not a 'youth' until he demonstrates the secondary characteristics of sexual maturity. After a person reaches puberty, the criteria for movement through developmental stages cease to focus on the individual's physical development and concentrate instead on social events in that person's life and on his relationship with others. As most married people are parents of their own and/or adopted children, and most parents are married, the terms 'married woman/man' and 'parent of dependent children' are usually used interchangeably.

The years that a person spends as a young spouse
and parent are the years of peak sexual activity,
and it is during this time that the behavioral
dimorphism of the sexes is most extreme.   All
statements by consultants--female and male--
confirm that the Lusi perceive gender role behavior
to be inseparable from genital sex.   Unlike some
other New Guinea people (see Strathern 1972:   161;
Poole 1981:   125; Herdt 1981:   208, 216) the Lusi
consider gender to be fixed in the womb.   People
responded with puzzlement to the suggestion that a
woman or man might wish to engage in activities
inappropriate to the individual's genital sex.
They commented that while foreigners or whites
might do such things, Lusi do not.   One man
responded by recounting the tale of a person whose
genitals and gender role behavior changed from male
to female as the result of his encounter with a
spirit-creature in the bush.   In fact, dressing and
acting like a member of the opposite sex is a way
of clowning that is usually done on ritual
occasions.   Informants readily delineated the tasks
and behavior appropriate to each gender,   and
attributed failure to perform these tasks to the
irresponsibility of youth, the poor training given
by parents, inexcusable laziness, excessive
preoccupation with sexual affairs, or to
enchantment.

During the parenting years the ultimate
responsibility for the completion of certain tasks
lies unequivocally with either mother or father
(see Gutmann 1975).   These are also the years when
an individual's behavior sets in motion the process
of deterioration that accompanies aging, for the
Lusi consider sexual activity and childbirth to
hasten this process in both women and men.   The
association of sexuality with diminished strength,
illness, and aging is common in Papua New Guinea
(see Kelly 1976; Meggitt 1964; Jorgensen chapter

10), but the Lusi do not seem to fear sexual contamination with the wholehearted dread that characterizes some other New Britain peoples (see Chowning and Goodale 1971; Chowning 1980; Goodale 1980 and 1981). Sexual activity is potentially debilitating for women as well as men. As do the Kafe (Faithorn 1975), the Lusi consider male sexual fluids, as well as those of women, to be contaminating. The odors of sexual fluids and menstrual blood may cause weakness, illness, and death to vulnerable people: the very young, the very old, the sick, and the newly initiated; and seminal fluid, if ingested in mother's milk, may cause an infant to become ill (see Counts 1984). Fear of female contamination was one basis of the custom requiring initiated boys and men to sleep in the men's house rather than in houses with women. 'Senior' men say that their fathers urged them to space their sexual encounters with women several days apart. They were warned that men who engaged in frequent intercourse would become sickly, thin and desiccated, and would age prematurely.

The effects of sexual activity on women are explicitly described in the Kaliai myth "Akro and Gagandewa". In the story, Gagandewa's mother suspects that her daughter is secretly married because of the physical changes in the girl. She says:

> Gagandewa, the look that you have is not that of a virgin but that of a married woman. Your eyes have lost their lustre. Your skin is no longer bright and smooth with oils as it was. You have the dull eye and the long neck and the dry, dirty skin of a married woman (Counts 1980a: 38).

Gagandewa is pregnant and, in fact, frequent sexual

intercourse is debilitating to women <u>because</u> it is likely to lead to pregnancy. A woman who is too frequently pregnant is likely to be weak and sickly, and to age prematurely because of the physical strains of pregnancy and childbirth, and the hard work involved in caring for several small children. On the other hand, women should not be childless, for the expulsion of the mixture of old blood and sexual fluids present in a woman's abdomen and its replacement by new new blood after childbirth is essential for her good health. Ideally a woman should achieve a balance between too many children and none at all, for either extreme renders her vulnerable to disease and premature aging.

The Old

People are not classified as 'senior' because of their chronological age; most people do not know how old they are. They are, however, acutely aware of their relative age, of the category and activities appropriate to their contemporaries, and of the progress through the life cycle of their kin in adjacent generations. It is the changing status of these people--parents and children--that defines an individual as an 'elder', for this status is a relational one. Specifically, a person becomes an 'elder' when his parents are dead or socially defunct and when his children marry and he becomes a <u>tuvu</u>--'grandparent' (this reciprocal term may be glossed either 'ancestor' or 'grandparent/grandchild'). These changes are expected to occur coincidentally. Kaliai note that by the time a person is a grandparent his own parents are likely either to be dead or decrepit and dependent. The Lusi terms for 'elder' or 'senior', <u>tamparonga</u> for a woman and <u>taparonga</u> for a man, are terms of respect and are commonly used by younger people as

terms of address and reference.   Although no one
expects that the achievement of 'senior' status is,
in itself, enough to make a foolish person wise,
'elders' are generally expected to be the stable,
responsible members of the community.   Use of the
term 'elder' in address or reference is, in fact,
usually restricted to those who are respected.   As
long as 'elders' are active they are ultimately
accountable for the behavior of their children,
even those who are married, and the other younger
members of their kin group.   A married woman may go
home to her mother (this is how the Kaliai phrase
it), and a man can look to his father to help him
obtain a bride, initiate his children, and pay
compensation if he is on the wrong side of a
quarrel.   Two examples from the life of Nathan,[3]
whose biography is sketched below, will provide
examples of ideal 'elder' behavior.

1.   In 1975, Victor and his parents were
declared in village meeting to be culpable in the
suicide of a teen-age girl (see Counts 1980b for
details).   Although Albert, Victor's father, was
probably in his early fifties, the ultimate
responsibility for both his and his son's behavior
was shouldered by the 'elder' of their kambu
'patrikin group'.   Nathan, classificatory father to
Albert and the acknowledged leader of their group,
not only insisted that Albert make more generous
compensation than demanded, but provided much of
the wealth to make the payment.

2.   In 1981, a group of young men got into a
village brawl in support of their relative Paul,
Nathan's unmarried son.   The men were each fined
fifty kina for their part in the disturbance.[4]
Nathan paid the fines for all of them.

There is ambiguity in 'senior' status.   The
Kaliai share with other New Guinea people the

notion that the reproduction of human life and society has a cost (for example see Gell 1975; Kelly 1976; Goodale 1980 and 1981).   The waxing strength and knowledge of the younger generation is accomplished at the expense of the waning capability and mental acuity of their parents. People specifically attribute the weakness and senility of the very old to the fact that their vitality has been expended into their children. Older consultants warn that if a man marries before he is old enough to grow a full beard his strength will go into his children and he will never achieve his own potential growth and abilities.   They also say that if the first-born child of a marriage is a girl, both parents will age prematurely (girls are thought to develop more rapidly than do boys). The birth of a person's first grandchild is especially significant, for it marks the beginning of the decline into old age.   It is not long thereafter, people say, that a person's strength and keenness of thought begin to diminish: in Tok Pisin, <u>bai ol gutpela tingting i aut i lus</u> (the ability to think well is lost).

The years spent as an 'elder' are the prime years of life. Physical strength decreases, but this loss is offset by the norm that no 'elder' should do a strenuous task if there is a younger person available. The 'senior' years are a time of <u>-gava-</u> (ease) when a person can rest from hard labor but still be active, vital, and respected. Younger people are expected to honor 'elders', and both women and men readily make their opinions known in public meeting. These are the years when a woman is no longer burdened by pregnancy and the care of young infants. She directs her daughters and daughters-in-law in the preparation of feast foods, the care of pigs, and the production of pandanus mats that constitute the ceremonially distributed woman's wealth. However, embedded in the enjoyment of heightened authority, respect, and responsibility is the knowledge that one's prestige and faculties will soon decline and the fear that the knowledge possessed by the individual may be lost, not only to him but to society as well. The 'elder', therefore, has the duty to pass on knowledge, especially secret knowledge, to others so that it will not die with him. He is also obliged to begin deferring to the judgment of younger kin so that when the 'senior's' strength and abilities are spent others will be trained to take his place or, as the Lusi express it, -kisi aimuli (to take his bed). Our consultants observed that persons who exercise authority invariably make enemies and risk being the victims of sorcery. This is the cost of leadership that an 'elder' must pay, but when a person's grandchildren are born the hazards of sorcery begin to seem oppressive and he starts to think with longing of a peaceful old age. He begins, therefore, to withdraw from those activities that are likely to offend others and create rivals. So it is when a person is an 'elder' and at the peak of his powers and influence that he is likely to begin the long process of withdrawal from active social life.

Once a person is classified as being taparonga/tamparonga (senior male/female), people begin to look for and note the physical changes characteristic of old age. These include failing eyesight, dry slack skin, white hair, loss of teeth, and mental decline including forgetfulness, inability to concentrate for long periods of time, and the condition called vuovuo (childishness, senility, or mental incapacity)—a term used to describe both the very young and the very old.

Under normal circumstances the fact that little girls learn, grow, and mature faster than little boys does not mean that women age more rapidly than

men. Instead, tall, skinny people are said to show
the signs of old age sooner than do heavy-set
people who retain the full-fleshed, plump liquidity
that the Lusi associate with youth.   There is no
special terminology for menopause, nor is the end
of menstruation   necessarily   associated   with
physical decline or with the unpleasant symptoms-
hot flashes, irritability, emotional instability-
reported by many North Americans. Postmenopausal
women say that they welcomed the end of the burdens
of pregnancy and childbirth. However, the end of
fertility does not mean that they will no longer
mother children, for adults who are well into their
sixties and even their seventies adopt and care for
grandchildren, nieces and nephews, and other young
relatives.   As with the women of other Pacific
societies, the concern of Kaliai women for young
children continues through the life cycle despite
their loss of reproductive capacity (for a
discussion of the stress that post-reproductive
white New Zealand women place on their roles as
mothers see Dominy chapter 3).

    The end of fertility and the achievement of
'elder' status also does not necessarily signal the
end of sexual activity (also see Lepowsky, chapter
8). This seems to be entirely idiosyncratic. As
one informant commented, "Some old people itch for
sex.   Others don't." Adults of all ages have
sexual affairs, and widows and widowers may
remarry, even though they are well into the
'senior' stage of life and are not strong enough to
clear, plant and maintain gardens without the
assistance of their adult children. People do not
feel that it is shameful for a grandmother to
continue bearing children, as Chowning reports for
the neighboring Kove (1981:   18) or for a male
'elder' to father infants. In 1981 they spoke with
amusement of a bent old man from a neighboring
village who had married a young wife and fathered

several children. They were less amused by the antics of a married grandmother, nicknamed 'Frog' because she hopped from one lover to another, who had an affair with a young man the age of her son. Her behavior was scandalous, especially because she was not discreet and she did not limit her lovers to men her own age (the Vanatinai have a similar opinion of lovers whose ages are widely separated; see Lepowsky, chapter 8).

The simplest Lusi term that may be glossed as 'old' is moho. People as well as things become moho (old) and worn out, and occasionally a person will refer to his age in this way. Far more frequently the Lusi describe their age/condition by the terms that are best glossed as 'elder' or 'senior' (taparonga/tamparonga) or 'decrepit' (taurai). As already noted, one achieves the status of 'elder' following the marriage of a first child, the birth of the first grandchild, and/or the death of one's parents. This status may continue for as long as an individual is active and responsible, even long after the death of one's spouse and without respect to gender or the continued maintenance of a domestic household. The status depends upon the individual's activity level and, as with Donna who is mentioned below, it may be lost by a person's failure to act. While most Lusi are sympathetic with persons who are incapacitated by chronic illness, they express impatience with people who retire from active life and become dependent solely because of their advanced years. Their attitude toward maintaining physical ability and independence is aptly summarized by the phrase 'use it or lose it,' a sentiment applied to lazy people and sedentary town workers as well as the aged.

The transition to the status taurai (decrepit person) is a gradual progression along a continuum of degrees of physical ability and social interaction. These include mental acuity; physical strength; independence, especially the ability to garden and to meet one's own basic needs; and social activity including effective participation in ceremonial exchanges. Because there is no marked boundary between 'elder' and 'decrepit person', the way in which a person is classified depends largely on the way in which he presents himself to others and the manner in which he permits others to treat him. Some biographies will illustrate the differences in presentation of self (Goffman 1959) that distinguish 'elders' from 'decrepit persons'.

<u>Nathan</u>

Nathan, who was in his late sixties in 1981, is an exemplary case of an active 'elder'. He retired from his career as a policeman and returned to his natal village in 1963 after an absence of twenty-five years. Though widowed shortly after his return from the police, and burdened with the care of a number of young children, Nathan neither remarried nor entrusted the care of his children to anyone else.

Today, with most of his children married and seven times a grandfather, he sleeps in his men's house. He remains an active gardener and is the undisputed leader of his segment of the village. As leader he is responsible for his own children, for those of his deceased elder brother, and for the children of another, more distant, deceased kinsman. All these relatives, taken together, constitute his <u>kambukambu</u> (extended patrikin group). His activities in any given week are varied. He is joint owner and sometimes storekeeper in a trade-store venture with two of his married sons who are resident in the village.

He keeps the key to the cashbox and he controls the
money from the store. Nathan acts as overseer of
his sons' cash-crop activity and he has insisted on
a policy of separation of their holdings in order
to lessen the possibility of conflict between them.
He is frequently absent from the village for
several days at a time when he goes with his sons
and their families to tend distant gardens as part
of his policy of maintaining, by continued use,
clear title to unoccupied land. His authority is
usually undisputed, and he is sufficiently
confident in the support of his followers to have
publicly faced down one of them whom he suspected
of practicing sorcery. When someone commented on
his sons' good reputation in the village, Nathan's
immediate response was, "Of course! I still hold
them in my hands!"

Nonetheless, his age also allows Nathan to
present himself as weak and dependent when he
considers it advantageous to do so. Fearful of the
ramification should he fail to stop a brewing fight
between Peter, one of his sons, and a village
leader, he begged that the fight be avoided and the
dispute left to the law to settle. Using the
keening cry and tears of the very old he clutched
at his angry son, alluding to himself as helpless,
near death, and desirous of peace. His stratagem
was successful and his son withdrew from the fight.

The recognition of Nathan's authority is not
limited to his own followers. For example, another
respected village elder and the adoptive father of
one of Nathan's grandchildren declined to sponsor
an initiation rite for the child. He reasoned that
Nathan was the appropriate one to make such a
decision and that it would be presumptuous of him
to intrude, even in rites for his own daughter.
Although Nathan continues to be in control of his
affairs, he has begun to share his knowledge with

his younger kin and to defer to the judgment of his older sons. For example:

(1)   He spent several weeks taking all of his children on a trek through the bush to the boundaries of the tract of land owned by his 'patrikin group'.   Eventually, he reasoned, population pressures will lead to dispute over unoccupied land, and he wanted his descendants to be clear about the exact location and boundaries of the land to which they hold title so that they will be able to protect their heritage.

(2)   He sponsored <u>naveu</u>, a ceremonial visitation of spirits, that had not been performed in its fully elaborated form for at least twenty years, so that the procedures, songs, and stories associated with the ceremony would not be lost when he died.

(3)   In a public controversy arising out of the polygynous marriage of his oldest son, Nathan refrained from interfering or expressing his opinion in a village meeting.   He practiced restraint because he regarded his son as fully adult and responsible for settling his own affairs.

<u>Sarah</u>

Sarah, a woman in her mid-sixties in 1981, has been since 1975 the widow of Nathans' older brother. She remains an active, involved member of the community and is often cited by others as an exemplar of the active elderly woman in contrast to Donna, a similarly widowed age-mate who, though healthy, has permitted herself to become an utterly dependent person. As is true of other widows, Sarah no longer maintains her own household. Instead she resides as part of the household of a married son, usually sleeping in the cooking house attached to the main dwelling. Although she is part of her son's household, she is not dependent on him, for her labor continues unabated.

In addition to gardening, harvesting, and food preparation, Sarah often frees her daughter-in-law by caring for her grandchildren. She also serves her own and neighboring villages as a healer. Sarah is highly respected for her knowledge and regularly directs the activities of her daughters and daughters-in-law in feast preparation, food distribution, and the production of pandanus mats and shell money. Her authority and the respect that she commands take on special significance because she is living in the village of her former husband. As a small girl she came as a bride from an interior village whose residents speak a language unrelated to Lusi. She makes regular trips back to her natal village to provide healing expertise, food, and care for ailing elderly kinsmen there. A cheerful and pleasant woman, Sarah has acquired a host of nicknames. Among them are 'Ricebag' from the discarded ricebag that she carries in lieu of the traditional fiber basket and 'Cookie' from the last food request of her dying husband. She accepts her nicknames with good humor and frequently engages in joking repartee with all and sundry about what they may or may not call her.

Sally

Sally, who was in her late fifties or early sixties at the time of our 1981 visit, was the only child of one 'village leader' and the wife of another. It is not surprising, therefore, that she has a life-long reputation as a strong-minded and independent woman. She was actively involved in the negotiations leading to her children's marriages and, during one stormy disagreement with her first-born's prospective father-in-law, she publicly shamed the man so that he tore down his men's house to demonstrate his anger and humiliation. In the early 1970's, Sally began suffering severe headaches and continuous eye infections, and by 1981 she was totally blind. Over the years, Jake, Sally's husband, became increasingly distressed by what he saw as the accelerating level of dissension, violence, and sorcery in the village. When thoughtless children teased Sally about her blindness, he declared this to be the culminating display of the deterioration of public morals and moved with his followers, establishing a new hamlet at an uninhabited point about two miles away. Today Sally and Jake live in this small hamlet with two of their married children and their families, her mother, Jake's brother, and a number of other kinsmen and friends. Sally and Jake have adopted a grandson to be a companion to Jake, and the young daughter of a distant kinsman to be Sally's helper. This girl leads Sally to the toilet area, carries water and firewood, helps Jake in the household's small garden plot, and cooks for her adopted parents. Even though she is blind, physically dependent, and frequently ill with painful headaches, Sally continues to be active. She still weaves fine coconut-leaf baskets and she participates in ceremonial exchanges. She has publicly challenged a notorious local sorcerer who, she claims, is in her debt and has not distributed to her the wealth she considers to be her due. In 1981 she attended an important ceremony that was to culminate in the feeding and release of dangerous ancestor spirits. Ordinarily, women must flee the village when the spirits are fed but, because of her age and infirmity, the men classified Sally as a 'decrepit one' and invited her to remain in the village. She firmly refused the offer and left to feast and laugh with the other women, as she had always done.

Koroi

Koroi was the oldest man in Kandoka village in 1981, and one of the oldest Kaliai then living. We placed his age at between eighty and eighty-five, for he had clear memories of the coming of the Germans and the first establishment of indirect rule shortly after the turn of the century.

In the years since our research began in Kaliai, Koroi had become increasingly enfeebled, and restricted to painful walking with the aid of a stick, so that he seldom left the village. Most of Koroi's days were spent in the immediate vicinity of the men's house where he slept despite the fact that his wife was still living and maintained a household. Koroi's daily round seldom gave a hint of his former status as the acknowledged 'leader' of Kandoka. He babysat his grandchildren and great-grandchildren, did household chores around his men's house--including keeping the ground in front of it swept clear of debris--and sat reminiscing with other old men. When, on occasion, he attempted to act as director of ritual events in which his sons were involved, he was gently pushed aside and ignored, though he was welcome to attend as a spectator.

Not only did Koroi suffer from physical disability, but he was generally regarded as failing in mental acuity as well. He was said, therefore, to be <u>vuovuo</u> (childlike or senile), and he described himself as <u>taurai</u> (decrepit). Though he usually accepted this characterization pas- sively, he sometimes struggled against it. When one of his daughter's children was to be initiated and the men of the village were preparing the shell money for distribution, he heard of it and painfully made his way to where the people were gathered. Seeing his daughter, he began to upbraid her:

> Why didn't you tell me what you were doing?
> I'm not dead yet, so that you can forget to
> tell me about this kind of work. I'm still
> your father. If you had finished this and then
> I had heard about it, it would have made me
> cry. Why can't you tell your own father about
> your work?

He had come with eleven fathoms of shell money to make his own contribution, but thinking about how mistreated he had been he became distracted and, instead of giving the money to the organizers, his speech drifted off into complaints about his children. He was always cold, he said, and although he had cared for them when they were young and helpless none of them thought to bring him sugar for a hot drink. Some people in the crowd began to snicker, while others tried to remind him that he came to give shell money and not to get sugar. Finally, one of his relatives gently took the shell money from him and led him, still complaining, back to his house.

During 1981, Koroi's sons began to acknowledge by public ritual their father's retirement from active life. They held the first stage of Koroi's ololo (mortuary ceremony). Their explanation was that they were doing it ". . . so that he can see, before he dies, how much we honor him." The final mortuary ceremonies were completed during the summer of 1982 with a reported distribution of hundreds of fathoms of shell money, cash, pandanus mats, clay pots, wooden bowls, and forty pigs (Scaletts, personal communication). With the completion of his mortuary rites, Koroi was socially dead. His sons had brought to a conclusion the complex of debts, obligations,

credits, and social ties that were begun for Koroi
by his father and grandfather and upon which he
built his reputation as a 'leader'. He no longer
had any business; it was finished.   The final
'mortuary ceremony' marked the culmination of
Koroi's life; his physical death would be
'something nothing' and would be marked by only
minimal funerary rites.   There would be no public
mourning, only the private grief of his family.
The completion of Koroi's 'mortuary ceremony' also
enabled his sons to become 'leaders' in their own
right.   They had increased their reputations and
validated their claims to leadership by their
sponsorship of the ceremony for Koroi, an
accomplishment normally denied to men until well
after the death of their fathers.[5]

Mary

Mary died in 1976 in her late sixties or early
seventies.   Like Sarah, Mary had long been a widow
but, unlike Sarah, her physical infirmities had
made her a dependent person unable to contribute
in any way to those who supported her during her
declining years.   Stricken by blindness more than
ten years before her death, Mary, like Sally,
required assistance in almost everything that she
did.   Someone had to lead her to a place where she
could relieve herself and to provide and prepare
all of her food, drink, and firewood.

Unlike Sally, Mary did not cling to the status
of active 'elder'.   Instead, Mary's days were spent
huddled in a little cooking house, near but
separate from the household of her stepson, and she
could be heard at all hours of the day or night
keening that she had no water to drink, no food to
eat, or no one to help rekindle her fire.
Technically, Mary's care was the responsibility of
her stepchildren, but both of them had large

families of dependent children. On the one hand, Mary's stepchildren could pass her care into the hands of their children, which they did. On the other hand, the fact that both of her stepchildren were responsible for large families contributed to their resentment of the added burden of caring for someone to whom they were but tenuously related. In the final analysis, there was no one person who was directly responsible for Mary, and this ambiguity contributed to her tragic death. Alone in the village on a day when nearly everyone was gone to their gardens, Mary tried to rekindle her fire. Apparently she fainted and fell into the burning embers. She lay there undiscovered for hours until the villagers began returning in the late afternoon. She died a few days later of her injuries. Although no one was charged with culpable neglect in Mary's death, some in the village harbored ill-feeling in the matter for several years, and her fate is pointed to as an example of the tragedy facing the aged who do not have their own children to care for them.

Discussion

There is no clear line separating the 'elder' from the 'decrepit person'. Rather, there is a continuum of characteristics and behaviors defining each status. An aging Kaliai may well decide that it is disadvantagous to be assigned to a particular age category and may, therefore, attempt to negotiate his status. In this case a person may choose to emphasize one or more of a set of qualities and de-emphasize others in his presentation of self. Physical condition and appearance are components in the assignment of one's age category, but they are not definitive ones. Sarah's appearance, for example, is that of an old woman. Her skin is wrinkled, her eyesight is poor, and she is nearly toothless. Nevertheless, her demeanor and life style are consistent with the status of 'elder', and that is how she presents herself. Although an 'elder's' physical condition may deteriorate and he may become increasingly dependent on his children, he is not normally regarded as decrepit until he meets some or all of the other characteristics associated with the decrepit person. Indeed, ther term taurai (decrepit person) is usually restricted to those who are too ill, weak, or senile by reason of age to bear the responsibilities of normal social life. Persons who are physically helpless while still of an appropriate age to think of themselves as merely elderly will resist both the application of the term and the questionable privileges that go with it, as Sally did. Contrarily, the term may be self-applied by a person to whom it would otherwise be inappropriate, as was Nathan's case.

Let us consider the strategies used by Nathan and Sally and the reasons for their behavior. Why did Sally reject 'decrepit' status, and what did she achieve by her rejection? Although we did not discuss with Sally the reasons for her decision, there are several factors that we think are relevant. First, Sally's physical condition is appropriate for a 'decrepit person'. She is wrinkled, grey-haired, many of her teeth are missing, her health is poor, and she is blind and totally dependent on others to meet her bodily needs. Second, the status of 'decrepit person' was imposed on her by others. Considering her physical condition, if she had accepted placement in that category, it would likely have been permanent. Third, a 'decrepit person' is no longer an effective social being. He is not expected to participate in a meaningful way in ceremonial exchanges. He is, in Leenhardt's terms, treated as though he were already defunct (1979:   33-34).

Therefore, those who otherwise would include him in their wealth distribution may ignore his demands for consideration. If Sally had accepted the appellation 'decrepit person' her rightful claims for reciprocity probably would have been rejected. Finally, the men's invitation to Sally to remain in the village for the feeding of the spirits was not an honor, nor would she thereby have assumed the attributes of, or have been given the privileges of, a man. Rather, she would have lost her status as a socially significant woman and a person to be reckoned with. Sally had nothing to gain and everything to lose by presenting herself, or by permitting others to classify her, as a 'decrepit person'. She, therefore, successfully attempted to negotiate her status as an active and still socially vital 'elder'.

In contrast, Nathan described himself as old and helpless--as a <u>taurai</u>--and temporarily placed himself in that status in order to accomplish a specific goal: to divert his son from a fight. Although his appearance--thin to the point of emaciation, wrinkled, white-haired, toothless, and partially blind--is that of a very old man, Nathan's mental acuity and his ability to control his own affairs preclude his being classified by others as 'decrepit'. Under normal circumstances Nathan would not present himself this way, but he was faced with a crisis situation. He, therefore, proceeded to negotiate for himself a status that he intended to hold only temporarily and for a specific purpose. Later Nathan explained to us that he had feared that the fight might result in serious injury or death, and he knew that he lacked the physical strength to restrain his angry son. So he resorted to the keening and tears of a 'decrepit person' in order to shame Peter into obedience. Nathan's behavior was a conscious ploy and it worked, for one does not easily ignore the

public begging and weeping of an aged and helpless
parent. Nathan was not concerned that his self-
imposed status would be permanent and, in fact, the
next morning he resumed his roles as manager of his
trade-store operation and supervisor of his sons.

The five people whose biographies we have
sketched above provide for us a continuum of the
roles of old age as they exist among the Lusi of
Kaliai. Sarah is an 'elder' who has no occasion
to place herself or to be placed in the 'decrepit'
category. Nathan is a 'senior' man who presented
himself as a helpless and dependent old person as
a strategic ploy. Sally is an 'elder' who resisted
the attempts of others to categorize her as
'decrepit'. Mary and Koroi were categorized as
'decrepit' and were treated as though they were
already defunct. A 'decrepit one' is a person who
has begun the process of dying. This is clearly
seen in the behavior of Koroi's children and in his
response to them.

1. Koroi's sons sponsored his mortuary ceremony
before his physical death had taken place.

2. His daughter neglected to include him in the
planning for her son's initiation--in the gathering
and distribution of shell money, the principal
activity through which leadership is expressed.

3. Koroi was ambivalent about being placed in
this category, and was unsuccessful in his effort
to negotiate his status. He seemed to accept being
categorized as a 'decrepit one' when he danced with
the masked figures who came to celebrate his death,
but he rejected it when he protested his daughter's
neglect: "I'm not dead yet!"

It is possible that the placement of Koroi in
the status of 'decrepit person' was a strategic act

by his sons who wished to honor him and at the same time to advance their own careers by their sponsorship of Koroi's mortuary cycle. It is certain that Koroi had little room for negotiation. His physical dependency, his lack of mental acuity, and his inability to engage in meaningful participation in ceremonial affairs were characteristic of a 'decrepit person' and placed him squarely within that category.

Mary, too, was regarded as defunct. Unable to care for herself, she was presumed also to be incapable of expressing her wants and needs accurately. Her kin regarded the care they gave her to be adequate. They ignored her plaintive cries for food, water, or firewood not because they were mean, but because they thought that they, not she, were the best judges of her needs. In this regard their behavior toward her was analogous to that of a parent toward an irresponsible child. The analogy of responsible people behaving toward a 'decrepit person' as they would toward a very young child is appropriate, for the condition of being vuovuo (mentally incapacitated), frequently an affliction of the very old, is specifically likened by the Lusi to the condition of a child before it is iavava (fully human). We should stress that vuovuo is not adequately translated by the English term 'senile', which has principal reference to the loss of mental acuity as a result of old age. Rather, vuovuo means inability to reason, lack of sound judgment often combined with physical dependency. Hence the term is also used to describe the condition of very young children until they are capable of rational thought. One 'elder' commented that he thought of being vuovuo as being analogous to having a hole between one's shoulder blades where the thoughts ran out. He anticipated this would happen in his own case, he explained, because "my knowledge has gone to my children. My strength is finished."

'Decrepit' or defunct persons are also like
children in the lack of formality with which their
deaths are treated. The physical death of such
aged persons is, after all, merely the completion
of a process begun long before. The point to be
made here is that, as in the death of a young
child, there is seldom any attempt to assign
culpability for the death of a very old person, and
that the passing of such persons is usually a
matter of concern and grief only to their close
kin.

A final point about being 'decrepit', a point
only suggested in the biographical sketches, is the
declining significance of the behavioral expressions of gender that mark the years of active
adulthood. As we noted earlier, the expression of
gender dimorphism are most strongly marked during
the years of parenting. As parenting responsibil-
lities decline with age, so also do the behavioral
markers of gender until, in old age, even those
most strongly entrenched may disappear. Koroi's
use of a broom to sweep the area around his men's
house--a task usually done by women--and the
tolerance of 'decrepit' women at otherwise
exclusively male ceremonial events illustrate the
fading of rigid gender roles in advanced age. But
we must stress that such 'decrepit' men and women
do not comprise a neutral or third gender category,
and their gender location is not reversed.

Death

It is rare for people in Kaliai to die of old
age. Death much more commonly strikes people when
they are active and vigorous than when they are old
and feeble. The Kaliai, therefore, do not usually

see death as a natural event. Instead, the friends and relatives of the deceased almost always look for a culpable agent--usually a sorcerer (see Counts 1976-77; Counts 1980b; Counts and Counts 1983-84 for detailed discussions of Kaliai responses to death).

Lofland argues that in premodern society the dying period, the time 'between admission to the dying category' and the actual occurrence of death, will typically be brief (1978: 18). Lofland suggests several reasons for this brevity. First, premodern societies commonly have a low level of medical technology. This delays diagnosis of terminal illness and prevents people from interfering with the dying process. Second, premodern people usually have 'a simple definition of death.' When a person enters the dying category, the customary response is for him to commit suicide, or for his kin to kill him or to respond to his condition with 'fatalistic passivity' (Lofland 1978: 18). This response hastens, or at least does not slow, the process of dying and ensures that, typically, the time that a person spends dying will be short. Analysis of the dying process in Kaliai suggests that Lofland's scenario requires modification.

Lofland does not define what is meant by 'brief duration dying' (1978: 18) but opposes it to the 'prolonged' state artificially maintained by the medical technology available in modern hospitals. Lofland has, however, failed to take into account indigenous definitions of dying and the fact that the length of time a person spends in the dying category depends on the readiness of the people in any given society to diagnose an illness as terminal. The people of Kaliai, for example, are prepared to diagnose as potentially fatal any fever or internal pain or illness that does not respond

readily to treatment, either by traditional healers
or the personnel at the medical clinic (see also
Scaletta, chapter 11, for an extended example from
the Kaliai's near neighbors, the Kabana of Bariai).
We know of people who were in the process of dying
for a period of up to three months. Some of these
recovered; others did not. In all cases of which
we are aware, the dying person himself made the
decision that his illness was terminal. His
subsequent activities--moving onto the beach under
a tent or temporary shelter, sending for friends
and kin to come to say farewell and settle accounts
--and the response of his relatives made the dying
person's condition a matter of public knowledge and
community   concern.   Contrary   to   Lofland's
generalization that premodern people have a simple
definition of death, this is not the case with the
Kaliai. The Lusi word that is usually translated
as death, mate, may in fact be glossed in several
ways: to be ruined, fatally injured, or terminally
ill (ngamatene, 'I'm dying'); to be unconscious or
partially dead (isoli matenga, 'he's half dead');
to be 'really dead' (imate gasili) or 'completely
dead' (imate kuvu). A person who is mate may
return to life any time after he begins the process
(imate suvu, 'he dies and returns'), including
after he is 'really' and 'completely' dead.

   People know that dying is almost complete if any
one of a number of the following are present: the
dying person's breath smells of death (aiwari
masmasi, 'his salty/sweet smell', 'his death
smell'); if he stares without blinking or shame at
another person's face; if he is restless and asks
to be alternatively lifted and laid down; and if he
loses control of his bladder or bowels. Dying is
complete when a person stops breathing; when his
heart ceases to beat; when his eyes and mouth hang
open. The spiritual component usually leaves the
body through the eyes or mouth or, if both are

closed, by the anus. Burial of adults usually occurs from twenty-four to thirty-six hours after death is judged to be complete. Infants and uninitiated children are often interred more quickly, for there are fewer people in a young child's social network to come to the funeral. The corpse is usually uncovered for public view until it begins to bloat, at which time it is wrapped in pandanus mats and hidden from view.

Even though the Kaliai recognize complete death by the various physical signs, the emphasis in any discussion of mate is on the process rather than the event. This process may begin with the social disaffiliation of an aged person, as for example with Koroi, may be reversible, and may continue after the body is buried. Death is processual, reversible, and has boundaries other than the ones we recognize because the separation of a person's spiritual component from his body is not necessarily permanent. The spirit leaves the body during dreams and visions, during serious illness, and in death, and it may return under all these circumstances. We know of a number of people of all ages who have been defined as 'completely dead' only to return to life. Three of these people were men for whom mourning ceremonies had already begun and who reported having 'near-death experiences' (see Counts 1983 for discussion and analysis of these experiences). It is sufficient to note here that no one related having experiences identical to those reported by Moody (1975), such as hearing one's self pronounced dead; feelings of peace and quiet; findings one's self out of one's own body; being able to see and hear but not communicate with others; having unusual and often unpleasant auditory sensations; being pulled through a dark tunnel; and encountering a 'being of light'. Kaliai did report meeting friends, kin, and supernatural beings; finding a boundary they could

not cross; and being required to return to life--
experiences that Moody reports are common among
North Americans who are near death but return to
life.   It is also noteworthy that although return
of the spirit to the dead body is not uncommon, no
one expressed any fear of being buried alive, nor
do our consultants report the occurrence of live
burial in the past.

If a person's spiritual component permanently
separates from the body and burial takes place, the
ghost may remain near its home village and appear
to its living kin and friends.   These appearances
usually occur at dusk and are most likely to take
place if the death has not been avenged or no
compensation has been paid. The disembodied spirit
(of a still-living person as well as of a dead one)
may also appear as a signal to the community that
a death is about to occur. Someone (people do not
yet know who) is dying, and villagers wait
anxiously until the identity of the dying person is
revealed.

The Kaliai do not ordinarily respond to death
with the passivity that Lofland suggests is
characteristic of people living in societies with
premodern technology. We know of no instance when
a terminally ill Kaliai committed suicide and of no
case when others hurried the process by killing the
dying person (but see Scaletta's discussion in
chapter 11 of a case in which the Kabana, who is in
Bariai to the west of Kaliai, argued that death
should be hastened for a woman who was dying in
great pain). Furthermore, the public acknowledgment that an individual has begun dying in no way
implies that his kin passively accept either his
fate or the inevitability of the process. Indeed,
relatives and friends will probably work frantical-
ly in an attempt to change the course of the
illness and promote the victim's recovery. This is

true even for the old if the individual has not been categorized as 'decrepit' and if the onset of the illness is sudden.

If, however, the dying person is <u>taurai</u> (decrepit), if he is physically dependent and mentally incapacitated and his dying is seen as the result of his gradual deterioration, then his kin are fatalistic about his death and passively accept it. On the rare occasions when a person dies of old age (<u>imate ngani i taurai</u>, 'he died of being old'), his kin do not attribute culpability or seek an external cause, nor does mourning go beyond the quiet grief of his immediate family. Informants who have witnessed death from old age say that the family gathers around to talk with the dying person and to hear his bones loosen and break one by one, beginning with the ribs. Finally the backbone breaks, the dying person crumples, and he is wrapped in pandanus mats and soon buried.

Summing Up

There are three points emerging from this consideration of the Kaliai experience of aging and dying that we believe deserve emphasis.

First, some of the confusion that exists in the literature on aging and death derives from generalizations by scholars who have failed to take into account indigenous concepts or the sociocultural context. We are not original in recognizing this problem (for example see Watson and Maxwell 1977). However, it is important to call attention to the fallacy underlying the assumption that there is a necessary relationship between a people's technology and the way in which they define and respond to aging and death. A simple technology does not imply a simple cosmology.

Second, Kaliai provides a contrast to societies, such as those in the New Guinea Highlands, where sexual opposition and gender reversal are pronounced. The Kaliai say that sexual activity is debilitating and that sexual effluvia is contaminating, and their public norms clearly distinguish between the behavior and tasks that are appropriate to males and females. However, in Kaliai as elsewhere, individuals often depart from ideal standards. When the parenting years are over, sexual division of labor becomes flexible and sexual dimorphism fades. When we compare this situation with the Highlands we are tempted to speculate that societies characterized by strongly polarised gender distinctions during youth and the parenting years may balance that polarization by moving to pronounced gender-role change for the aged. Conversely, in societies where sexual opposition and role distinctions are more balanced or muted during the parenting years, gender roles are likely to undergo much less dramatic change in old age (Lepowsky, in chapter 8, also argues and presents data that document this point). Instead, people in these societies superficially resemble a more common pattern, one that Gutmann, Grunes, and Griffin call the 'normal androgyny of later life' (1980: 122). Our data and that of Lepowsky (chapter 8) suggest that the term 'androgyny' may be inappropriate for analysis of the processes of gender changes in old age in some Melanesian societies. Very old Lusi do not enter a third gender category. They are not without gender, nor are they at once both male and female. Women and men remain distinctive, but their separateness is muted in old age and, as in young children, may be of little practical consequence in everyday life.

Finally, if we are to develop hypotheses about

aging and dying that have cross-cultural validity we must treat aging and dying as dynamic and processual. Old age and death are not rigid, biologically determined categories with fixed, immutable boundaries within which people are frozen. Instead, old age and death are descriptions of social categories. The old and even the dead may have vital roles to play, roles that are defined in terms of relationships with others. If we would understand why old people in Kaliai, or any other community, behave as they do and why they are treated as they are, we must ask the same questions about them that we would ask about any other social group. How, for instance, is a person identified as an old person; or as a defunct one? What are the criteria by which one kind of old person is distinguished from another or from the dead, and what difference does this identification make to the individual and to his kin? Can a person negotiate his status? Does he have the option to define or redefine himself, as Nathan did, and can he refuse the category imposed upon him by others, as Sally did? If a person has choices and can decide how to present himself, what factors influence his decision? What strategies are available to the old?

So we end this study of aging and dying in Kaliai with questions. But this is appropriate, for if the old and even the dead are to be seen as involved in ongoing processes then we must ask of them the same questions about identity, activity, ideology, and relationships that we ask of the other members of human society.

Notes

We collected the data on which the study is based in northwest New Britain in 1966-67, 1971, 1975-76, and 1981. Our research was funded by predoctoral research grants from the U.S. National Science Foundation and by Southern Illinois University in 1966-67; by the Canada Council, Wenner-Gren Foundation Grant 1809, and the University of Waterloo in 1971; and by the Social Sciences and Humanities Research Council of Canada and by sabbatical leaves from the University of Waterloo and McMaster University in 1975-76 and 1981.

1. The term *sol* is a Tok Pisin term; there is no Lusi equivalent of the unitary concept that is glossed 'soul' in English.

2. In 1981 there were 360 people living in Kandoka: 186 infants and children born in 1965 or later; 53 unmarried people born before 1964 or who were married but childless; 81 'parents of dependent children'; 33 'seniors' or 'elders'; and 7 *taurai* (decrepit persons). Of the 'elders', 18 were women and 15 were men, while 6 of the 'decrepit persons' were women and one was a man.

3.   All personal names are fictitious.

4.   The *kina* is the unit of currency in Papua New Guinea.   In 1981 it was valued at about $1.60 (U.S.).

5.   Koroi died in 1984.

IV. SOCIAL SUPPORT NETWORK

A TIME TO LIVE, A TIME TO GRIEVE: PATTERNS AND PROCESSES OF MOURNING AMONG THE YOLNGU OF AUSTRALIA

Janice Reid

Abstract

Anthropological studies of mortuary ceremonies have focused primarily on their social and structural correlates and functions. Little attention has been given to their role in facilitating the expression and resolution of grief by the bereaved. The elaborate and extended mortuary rites of the people of northeastern Arnhem Land, Australia (the 'Murngin') have several characteristics which promote and structure the mourning process and facilitate the full reintegration of the bereaved into the social life of the community.

The Yolngu are Australian Aborigines who live in northeastern Arnhem Land, Northern Territory. 'Yolngu' is a general term by which the people of the clans of this area of Australia refer to themselves. The clan is a named patrilineal descent group the members of which acknowledge common ancestry, hold in common rights in land and share a common religious heritage. Each clan belongs to one of two moieties, Yirritja or Dhuwa. Clan and moiety exogamy are prescribed. The marriage of choice is that of a man to his mother's

Reprinted from <u>Culture, Medicine and Psychiatry</u> 3(1979): 319-346, permission of Kluwer Academic Publishers.

brother's daughter (MBD). The data presented here
were obtained during 12 months of field research at
Yirrkala during 1974 and 1975, during two short
return visits in 1978, and during a month spent in
the community in 1979. Much of this time was given
to a study of change in the indigenous medical
system, but data were also collected on such
related topics as Yolngu attitudes towards Western
medicine and the ways in which community members
cope with old age, dying and death.

While Yirrkala remains a major resource centre
for many of the people of this area, not all
members of the Aboriginal population are resident
at Yirrkala itself. Several extended family and
clan groups have since 1973, as their members
sometimes put it, "gone home." These groups have
voluntarily established small 'outstations' on
traditional clan lands. By 1978 twelve such
outstations affiliated with Yirrkala had been
established. A total of 930 Aborigines were living
either at Yirrkala or its outstations. A similar
decentralization movement (and associated cultural
revival) has occurred simultaneously and
spontaneously in other parts of Australia. It was
prompted primarily by the desire to return home,
but also inspired by the greater availability of
funds for Aboriginal initiatives with a change of
government in 1972, by perceived threat to
traditional estates presented by mining and
pastoral companies, by the breakdown of health and
social control in the large and heterogeneous
settlements and by the stresses of close contact
with European society (Coombs 1973).

The Yolngu were the only permanent inhabitants
of this remote area of Australia until the
Methodist Church established missions at
Milingimbi, Yirrkala and Galiwin'ku (Elcho Island)
in 1922, 1935, and 1942, respectively. Several

early observers (Chaseling 1957; Thomson in Peterson 1976; Warner 1937/58) described aspects of Yolngu society. A particular focus of their writings is the ceremonial complex, a complex of artistic wealth and ritual diversity which was and is informed by a highly elaborated and pervasive religious doctrine. They also wrote of individuals and groups linked to each other by an intricate mesh of kinship ties (the 'Murngin' kinship system) which maps in general terms, the rights, obligations, emotional bonds and interactions of daily and ritual life.

Now, as then, when an individual dies, the tenets of Yolngu religion and the affective and formal links between people are manifest in the extended and highly patterned mortuary ceremonies. Much has been written of the form, content, meaning, symbolism and social functions of these ceremonies (Berndt and Berndt 1964; Berndt 1974; Chaseling 1975; Keen 1977; Morphy 1977; Munn 1969; Peterson 1976; Warner 1937/58). Little attention has been paid, however, to the psychological effects of the mortuary ceremonies, to their impact on the individual and, in particular, to their role in facilitating the expression and resolution of emotion by the bereaved.

This paper addresses these issues. It is based on the premises that grief is an inevitable response to a death among those for whom the deceased was a valued and loved person, that social continuity and stability can only be assured if grief is resolved and bereaved individuals become reconciled to the reality of a death, and that mortuary ceremonies are, for Yolngu, the primary vehicle for mourning and the resolution of grief following a death. It is argued, by extension, that if the opportunity to mourn is denied an individual, he (or she) is likely to remain distressed for a period of time which is socially unacceptable and to be impaired in his[1] ability to fulfil his social roles.

Grief and Mourning

Grief, bereavement and mourning have been variously defined (Averill 1968; Brandt 1971; Raphael 1976a; Kastenbaum and Costa 1977). For the purposes of this paper, I define grief as the affective response to a loss (in this case a death), a response which may be an amalgam of such emotions as sorrow, anger, anxiety, despair and hopelessness. Bereavement is a term indicative of the status of a survivor of a death. Mourning is the culturally patterned behavioral response to a death.   In this paper I am concerned with the bereaved individual in Yolngu society and the way in which he demonstrates, copes with, and eventually works through his grief (the process of mourning).

While few studies of individual grief and mourning in non-Western societies have been undertaken, research on the processes of mourning and the outcomes of grief among Europeans has enabled psychiatrists and others to delineate the characteristics in Western society of both 'normal' and 'pathological' grief and to define the steps which lead to a healthy or adaptive resolution of grief. Lindemann, for instance, concludes (1944) that the symptoms associated with normal acute grief include somatic distress, alterations of the senses and preoccupation with the image of the deceased (both of which may lead to a fear of approaching insanity), feelings of guilt, a disconcerting loss of warmth (and even hostility) in relationships to others, and an inability to initiate and maintain organized patterns of activity.   The duration of the grief reaction depends on the success with which a person 'does the grief work' (Lindemann 1944:   143), that is, accepts the pain of bereavement, expresses his sorrow, formulates his future relationship to the deceased and acquires new and appropriate patterns of conduct.

An adaptive pattern or sequence of mourning (Raphael 1977) which effects a transition from the period of anguished grief to that of resolution and reintegration into the social environment consists of several stages. Following an initial reaction (which can include stunned disbelief, sudden and immense pain or a sense of numbness) is an intense emotional experience of separation from the person who has died.   The sense of separation is accompanied by intense anxiety, sadness, helplessness and anger, with a yearning for the loss not to have occurred and perhaps a misperception that the dead person renews his interest in life and his emotional investment in the continuing relationships of this world, and the former relationship with the deceased becomes a residual relationship in memory.

By contrast, a morbid or pathological grief reaction may ensue if grief is not resolved. Lindemann (1944) and Raphael (1977) are among those who have documented non-adaptive responses to a death. These are marked by absent or suppressed grief, distorted or chronic grief, decompensation into recognizable medical disease, conspicuous or deleterious alteration in relationships to others, furious hostility against others, lasting loss of patterns of social-interaction behavior detrimental to the individual's (or to his dependents') social and economic existence, agitated depression and suicidal feelings.

The patterns of normal and pathological grief and of successful resolution of grief summarized are drawn from case studies of European 'survivors.' They are, therefore, affected by the cultural prescriptions and prohibitions surrounding mourning in European societies. In the absence of detailed case studies of individual emotional reactions to death in non-Western societies it is necessary to assume that, at least in broad outline, similar patterns can be distinguished cross-culturally. It is certainly reasonable to assume that all people feel deep sorrow when a person with whom they have a close personal relationship dies (Averill 1968). I am also assuming that, to have mourned successfully, a bereaved individual must minimally be able to assume his usual duties and obligations, to reformulate and continue personal relationships and to show no signs of behavior which his society considers abnormal (and related to his loss).

One of the few studies which deals analytically with individual grief and mourning across cultures, and which lends some support to these assumptions is a review of the ethnographic literature by Rosenblatt et al. (1976). The authors found that people (predominantly women) almost everywhere cry or keen following a death. They also found that expressed anger and aggression, fear of the corpse and fear of the ghost are common. In the case of women anger is often self-directed. In the case of men it is frequently directed towards others. The authors conclude that, "It seems basically human for emotions to be expressed in bereavement" and that "[a]t least in dim outline, the emotional responses of people in almost any culture resemble those of people in almost any other" (1976: 21). Within the limitations of the ethnographic data available to them, the authors also found that societies which perform final ceremonies some time after death lack prolonged expressions of grief, whereas grief is prolonged (and often disturbed: disrupted work and sleep, suicidal behavior, illness, unbridled expression) in societies which lack final (post-burial) ceremonies.   They suggest such ceremonies serve both to provide an adequate length of time for mourning and to mark clearly its conclusion.

Averill's (1968) analysis of the nature and significance of grief also draws on existing anthropological studies of mourning customs.   He concludes that these "serve two functions: they help reinforce the religious and social structure of the group, and, when no conflict is involved, they help assuage the emotions of the bereaved" (1968:   727).   The principal focus of the paper, however, is the adaptive value of grief.   Averill argues that the stereotyped set of psychological and physiological reactions commonly called 'grief' is universal among humans and, perhaps, higher primates and that these reactions are biological in origin.   Their evolutionary function is to ensure group cohesiveness in species for which the maintenance of social bonds is necessary for survival.   This is accomplished by making separation from the group or individuals an extremely stressful event.   Where separation cannot be avoided (as a result, for example, of death) the grief reaction must run its biological course.   This course is tempered by the circumstances and past history of the bereaved and by the customs and mores of his society.

In this paper it is argued that Yolngu culture provides members of the society with highly adaptive means of mourning the dead.   The various mechanisms and opportunities for the expression of grief ensure rapid and positive adjustment to loss in Yolngu society and minimize the possibility of pathological grief reactions. Specifically it will be shown first that mourning is ritually structured, and confined in place and time; second, that it is expected, and collectively and publicly expressed; third, that it is interwoven with the demands and activities of daily life; fourth, that those aspects of mourning facilitate the resolution of grief and contribute to the ongoing integrity and functioning of Yolngu society when its members are confronted with the threatening and potentially disruptive presence of death.

Before the mortuary ceremonies and expression of grief in Yolngu society are described, this analysis is placed in context by a selective review of the principal and recurrent themes in anthropological studies of mortuary institutions.

Mortuary Institutions Across Cultures

Hertz (1907/60) and van Gennep (1908/60) viewed death as a transition both for the deceased and for his survivors. In his analysis of the double disposal of the dead, Hertz postulates that the double funeral transfers the soul of the dead person from the visible society of the living to the invisible society of the dead, frees the bereaved from the obligations of mourning and reintegrates them into their community. Van Gennep characterizes death as one of several 'rites of passage' or changes of status which are an integral part of every person's life cycle. All such rites consist of three phases: separation, transition, and incorporation. It is in the funeral ceremonies that the dead and the living pass through each of these phases to attain new statuses and to be incorporated into their respective societies.

Durkheim (1915/65) analyzes death primarily in terms of its significance for the society as an entity. Durkheim draws heavily on the available ethnographies of Australian Aboriginal society to argue that when someone dies, the family group feels itself lessened and reacts against this loss by assembling. The 'peculiar rites' which follow produce a 'state of effervescence' among participants and provide the opportunity for a renewal of 'collective sentiments.' In coming together the group begins to live and hope again and to regain its social vitality.

In Durkheim's writings and, to a lesser extent, in those of Hertz and van Gennep, the individual is, for the purposes of analysis, lost within the collectivity. Malinowski gives greater weight to the needs and emotions of the bereaved. The emotional response to death, he writes, is complex and contradictory, the dominant elements being the love and attachment felt for the dead person and the disgust and fear of the transformation wrought by death. A death "shakes the moral foundations of society" (1954: 52) and "threatens the very cohesion and solidarity of the group, and upon this depends the organization of that society..." (1954: 53). In the ceremonies of death and in the belief in a spirit, "religion counteracts the centrifugal forces of fear, dismay, demoralization, and provides the most powerful means of reintegration of the group's shaken solidarity and of the re-establishment of its morale" (1954: 53).

A structural-functional perspective dominates these and later anthropological studies of mortuary institutions. Mandelbaum (1959), writing of the Kota of South India, views funeral rites as having positive latent social and psychological functions (such as reaffirmation of the social order, social cohesion and the sequences of precedence and rank in society, and the reorientation of the shocked and grieved survivors). Goody (1962) and others focus on the tensions and conflicts which are highlighted in mourning ceremonies. The mortuary customs of the LoDagaa of West Africa, he writes, "map out the patterns of social relations." Further, Goody describes differences in the ritual surrounding a dead man's estate, funeral ceremonies and contributions, beliefs concerning witchcraft and the worship and propitiation of the ancestors in two different communities. The ritual and religious differences between them, he maintains, can be explained in terms of variations in the ownership and mode of inheritance of property in each. Associations between aspects of the social structure and the form and content of mortuary rites have also been hypothesized by Opler (1945, 1946). He suggests that the dread of ghosts and the extremely strict requirements for a bereaved spouse are causally linked to the tensions of matrilocal residence among the Lipan and Mescalero Apache and to the control which the family of the deceased exerts over the widow or widower (particularly with respect to remarriage).

The attenuated mortuary rituals of Western society and their structural correlates have increasingly become subjects of study over the past decade. Blauner (1966) maintains that the individualization and deritualization of bereavement in Western society is the result of low mortality rates, of the irrelevance of a death to the larger society, and of the youthful orientation of the West. The loss of social significance of the old and dead, he argues, itself reacts on and weakens the religious structure, for the need to maintain symbolic interpersonal relations with the dead (in the form of their spirits) no longer exists. Goody (1975) suggests that funerals have diminished in significance in Western industrial society simply because they "have so much less work to do" than those of earlier times and other cultures. The absence of a need to reallocate resources and roles after a death, the lack of gemeinschaft, smaller households and lowered mortality mean that "only the bare bones of death are seen today in Western societies" (1975:   7). Aries (1975), in a historical review of attitudes to death in Western society, delineates the attitudes to death and dying which have accompanied the rise of individualism in the West and associated socio-structural change.   Modern society, he writes, deprives man of his death and allows him the privilege of dying only if he does not use it to upset the living. In a reciprocal way, the relatives of the dead are expected in public to feign indifference; society demands from them a self-control corresponding to the propriety it imposes on the dying (1975:   151).

Mourning Among Australian Aborigines

In Australia the literature on mourning in Aboriginal societies is replete with descriptions of the expression of grief (keening, self-mutilation, marking of the mourners, taboos on speech), and of the mortuary rites, disposal of the corpse, conceptions of the soul and afterlife, inquest and talk of sorcery, and retribution (for instance, Beckett 1957; Berndy and Berndt 1964; Berndt 1974; Elkin 1975; Kaberry 1935, 1939; Meggitt 1974; Spencer and Gillen 1899). Much of the ethnography of death and mortuary ritual in Australia has been descriptive. To some extent it reflects the "parochialization of inquiry and the folklorization of culture" which Fabian (1972) has criticized as being obstacles to a nontrivial anthropology of death (1972:   560). The systematic

analyses which have been made of mortuary rites
have generally adopted such approaches as those
discussed above.   The Australian authors discuss
the implication of a death for the society: the
shattering of the family, the ambivalence of
relatives towards the corpse (the desire to hold
on, the desire to let go), the desire to sever
connections with the spirit and to ensure its
passage to the Land of the Dead, and the
reaffirmation of the status and priority of the
living through the elaborate and extended mortuary
rites.

Warner (1937/58) distinguishes several primary
motives in the 'Murngin death rituals' of
northeastern Arnhem Land.   ('Murngin' is the term
Warner used to describe the group of clans, or
'tribes,' which includes the Yolngu.) The rituals,
he writes, are designed symbolically to translate
the soul of the dead out of all profane and worldly
contacts, to spiritualize the soul and place it in
the sacred totemic realm.   The rituals also remove
all contact between the dead and the living and
reintegrate the society, close its ranks and assert
its solidarity.   The long mourning rituals, he
maintains, allow the bereaved relatives to adjust
to this major crisis.   He further suggests that the
period of mourning corresponds to the period
necessary for readjustment of the social structure
to the loss of a member of the social group.

The most recent discussion of mortuary rites
in northeastern Arnhem Land is that of Morphy
(1977), who examines the manner in which art
objects are used in the context of burial and other
ceremonies.   His analysis includes a description of
the ceremonies, a discussion of their iconography,
an elucidation of their major themes, and a
consideration of the function, integration and
sociological aspects of the sacred clan paintings.

Of relevance is his discussion of the themes of the
mortuary ceremonies. Recurrent themes are the
journey of the soul of the dead person from the
land of the living to the land of the dead, the
driving away of the dangerous aspect of the spirit
of the dead person, the expression of grief and
anger at the death, and the desire for vengeance.
These themes and the form and content of Yolngu
mortuary ceremonies are also captured in the
excellent ethnographic film "Madarrpa Funeral at
Gurka'wuy" (Dunlop 1978).   This film, which was
made on an outstation in northeastern Arnhem Land
affiliated with Yirrkala, illustrates many of the
observable features of Yolngu mortuary rites
discussed in this paper.[2]

   The majority of the ethnographies both of
Australian Aboriginal and of other societies have
been concerned primarily not with the individual
actor but with the social system, its response to
death and its reintegration through mortuary
ceremonies. In a major and detailed recent study
of bereavement among the Tiwi, Brandl (1971)
specifically excludes consideration of individual
grief. She focuses on "the public social dimension
of behavior--not the private" (1971: 522). Brandl
analyses the mortuary rituals in their social
context and concludes that they "affirm, in
dramatic form, the structural and organizational
aspects of Tiwi social order...[and]...illustrate
the values and beliefs which underpin that order"
(1971: 2). Her thesis is, in part, that

     through their beliefs about death and their
     socio-culturally patterned bereavement
     behavior, the Tiwi have a perspective on
     their social existence, as this includes
     and relates them to their fellows and the
     empirical and non-empirical settings of
     their   world   [author's   emphasis]...

> bereavement behavior is not only a reaction
> to death; it is a set of ritual statements
> about life.(1971: 2-3)

Although anthropological studies of mortuary ceremonies have elucidated the relationship between the ceremonial (collective) response to death and such variables as social structure, social cohesion, conflict, beliefs and values, their analytical focus on the social system has meant that the individual, its basic unit, has largely been ignored. Clearly it is the individual, not the society, who is bereaved following a death. If there is social disarray when someone dies, it is because there is individual emotional disarray. If mortuary ceremonies collectively affirm the vitality and primacy of the group, it is because the individual makes a personal affirmation. The threat to social cohesion after a loss which has been widely posited is posed largely by the individuals who are anguished and isolated in their loss. The locus of the emotion is the individual and it is his feelings which must be expressed and resolved if the society is to remain viable.

One of the few studies of Aboriginal mortuary rites which is addressed directly to the grief and needs of the bereaved is that of Hiatt (1961). Hiatt writes of the mortuary ceremonies of central Arnhem Land which are, in many respects, very similar to those of the northeast. In a re-examination of Hertz's analysis of the double disposal of the dead, Hiatt disputes Hertz's contention that the primary purpose of temporary burial is to bring about the transition of the soul from the land of the living to the society of the dead, and to free the living from their duty to mourn. Hiatt argues that this custom arises from the desire of the bereaved to prolong physical relations with the deceased, not to secure the deliverance of his soul. "In short, we may suppose that beliefs about the fate of the soul in this culture arise largely as projections of the emotions and interests of the bereaved" (1961: 6).

Hiatt extends his argument to take issue with Warner's assertion that the length and elaborations of the mortuary rites correspond to the period of readjustment of the social structure and to the structural importance of the deceased. Hiatt suggests that apart from the fact that such hypotheses are virtually untestable, mourners attend a funeral not out of a sense of formal obligation but because the death was a personal loss for them. A baby's funeral is short because his death does not cause a widespread sense of loss. Hiatt concludes that, "death arouses in people emotions and desires of the very strongest kind, and...it is these, rather than a disinterested quest for truth, which determine what they believe and how they behave" (1961: 10). In the following section the modes and contexts of expression of these emotions in the mortuary ceremonies of the Yolngu of northeastern Arnhem Land are described.

The Conventions and Context of Mourning Among the Yolngu

The most sustained, acute and widespread expressions of grief occur in Yolngu, as in other societies, immediately after a death and during the mortuary ceremonies of the ensuing weeks. The earliest recorded observations of Yolngu mortuary ceremonies were made in northeastern Arnhem Land in the late 1920s and 1930s by Chaseling (1957), Thomson (Peterson 1976) and Warner (1937/58). At that time the ritual disposition of the corpse took place in three stages.

In the first stage the body (whether male or female) was removed from the view of women and children and painted by senior men with the sacred clan designs (miny'tji) of the deceased's clan (or, occasionally, of his mother's mother's brother's [MMB] clan). At the same time women and men danced to the accompaniment of the sacred clan songs (manikay) sung by the initiated men of the deceased's clan and of other clans of the same moiety. At the conclusion of this stage the body was either buried or was placed on an above-ground platform where it was left until the flesh had substantially decayed and fallen away from the bones.

In the second stage of the mortuary ceremonies the remains were exhumed or taken from the platform. The bones were then ritually retrieved and cleaned, placed in a bark coffin or container and given into the custody of close relatives of the deceased. In the third stage (weeks, months or years later), the bones were ceremonially placed in a hollow log coffin which, like the body, was painted by senior men with the totemic clan designs. This log was placed upright and left exposed to the elements, eventually to decay and disappear.

While the recovery of the bones and secondary disposal are no longer widely practiced in northeastern Arnhem Land,[3] the general structure and ritual content of contemporary mortuary ceremonies held at Yirrkala remains similar to that described by the earlier authors. The description of the ceremonies and associated activities given here is based on funerals of infants and adults which I observed at Yirrkala in 1974, 1975, 1978, and 1979. In contemporary funerals, the ritual leaders at the settlement are often constrained in planning a funeral by the demands of the secular (and particularly the European) sector. Accordingly they have found it necessary to make several organizational modifications to funerals held at Yirrkala. These are also discussed here.

Anticipation of Death

Unless a person dies suddenly and unexpectedly, close and distant relatives of the seriously ill individual will have begun to gather at his bedside days or even weeks before his death. While female kin care for him, senior men of his moiety sing the sacred songs of his clan or of his mother's clan. These songs are variously said to 'make him happy [to comfort him],' to 'keep his mind alive [alert],' and to ensure that 'the person will die in the right manikay [sacred song cycle] and land.' One of the main functions of these songs, as Warner has stated (1937/58: 414), is to draw the attention of his ancestors to his imminent death and to orient his spirit towards its home after death, that is, to ensure that it makes the transition to the spirit world and does not linger to harm the living. The decision to commence the song cycles may be taken by clan leaders after assessment of the sick person's condition. Frequently the ritual is begun at the request of the sufferer himself, who 'feels his power is going, feels soreness in his lungs or heart and feels he may be ready to die.' The manikay djama (literally, 'song work') is not a sign that death is inevitable, nor is it intended, as some European observers have critically and mistakenly observed, to hasten death. It is, as one man said, only "for guessing about the illness [its outcome]."[4] Individuals can and do recover after the singing has commenced and those who have gathered then

364 A Time to Live, A Time to Grieve

drift away from the sick person's camp and return home.

If there is a consensus that the sick person is dying, female relatives may weep or keen intermittently. The keening (or wailing) is described by the term _ngathi_ (as is crying or weeping without keening). A person may _ngathi_ for many reasons, such as the departure or absence of family members, the suffering of a son during circumcision, the disability or misfortune of another. It is, though, most usual to hear a woman _ngathi_ as "the singing of appropriate clan songs in a slow tempo and a minor key, with a special wailing rhythm, interspersed with heavy sighs and ... with relatively spontaneous expressions of anger or grief" (1950: 307). The keening often matches in tone and timing the sacred songs being sung by men to the accompaniment of clapsticks and didgeridoo (a hollowed-out pipe approximately 1-2 meters long which, when blown, emits long, low and vibrant notes).

In sombre tones broken by sobbing and permeated with emotion, the women lament the sick person's illness and his imminent death. Sometimes a daughter, wife, sister or other female relative keens alone while others continue to tend the patient, prepare food, attend to the children and talk to each other. Sometimes she is joined by others of the sick person's female kin, both real and classificatory. Although the women remain seated in the midst of an often large group of people as they keen, their demeanours, their cries, their tears and their postures during these expressions of sorrow signal to all that, though physically present, they are emotionally and functionally absent. Only a very small child would disturb a woman at such a time. After a period of lamentation, however, a woman returns with apparent

ease to the conversations and activities of the
group gathered around the sick person and may joke
and talk animatedly with others.

Death and the Initial Phase of the Mortuary Rites

With death, there is a sudden and dramatic
change in the emotional tenor of the assembled
group. The widow (assuming the deceased is a man)
and other first-order kin may throw themselves on
the body, screaming and crying uncontrollably in
their grief. Others are quiet. As Warner says of
this time, "a stillness comes over the camp which
is very noticeable to anyone accustomed to the
general noisiness of all the Murngin camps"
(1937/58: 415). The senior men, if not already
present, are apprised of the death and prepare for
the ritual announcement of death to the people of
this and other areas of the settlement. The death
is not openly acknowledged until the announcement
occurs.

The announcement of death is signalled by the
slow, ringing beat of ceremonial clapsticks and the
singing of part of a chosen manikay, usually that
of the deceased. After community members have
gathered, the speaker publicly indicates, without
mentioning the dead person's name, his identity.[5]
In response to this revelation the women keen
loudly, throw themselves on the ground and strike
their heads with sharp objects (such as stones,
knives and the sharp lids of open cans) in displays
of grief. Although the women throw themselves
heavily from a raised kneeling position sideways to
the ground, the force of the fall is taken on the
thigh and shoulder and does not usually cause
permanent or serious injury. Similarly, the self-
inflicted scalp wounds from which blood flows down
the face, or mats the hair, are inflicted with

blows which usually are not hard enough to cause serious injury. Nevertheless, relatives who are standing or sitting nearby, especially the men, are expected to restrain the women, to pull the weapons from their hands and throw the weapons out of reach. Although relatives normally offer only token restraint the women almost always submit to their efforts and heed their entreaties to desist. The actions of relatives at these times are intended both to protect the bereaved and to signify the support and concern of those who intervene.

At these collective displays of grief, men who are closely related to the dead person (sons, fathers, husbands and others) may cry and occasionally keen, but the most dramatic and audible evidence of grief comes from the women. The men are more likely to express the group's feelings of anger at a death. These feelings were eloquently described by a clan leader in the following terms:

> Before the body has been laid to rest in the coffin, you are very angry. You feel wild, you break down, you are against the songs, against the body, everything. If you just use your feelings then you are against the box or against the people--you must...hold yourself, make yourself still and you'll be settled down. (Morphy 1977: 121)

Sentiments of aggression may be directed towards those who, it is asserted, neglected the deceased during his lifetime and last days, thus contributing to his death. They may be evidenced indirectly, as in the public airing of old or unrelated disputes. They may be channelled into energetic and even violent dancing which signifies hostility. They may occasionally be directed at a group in the community in an accusation that one of its members performed sorcery on the deceased.

Feelings of anger are also channelled throughout the community into speculations and suspicions that 'stranger Yolngu' from distantly related (or unrelated) groups in other townships travelled secretly to the area and ensorcelled the person now deceased. These attacks by sorcery may be attributed to an ongoing dispute between the sorcerer's group and that of the dead person, to a past social or ritual offence committed by the deceased, or simply to the malice of the sorcerer. Community members are particularly fearful of the individuals who come from other, distant settlements to drink at the hotel in the nearby European mining town of Nhulunbuy (23 kilometers by road from Yirrkala). In the decade since Nhulunbuy was established, some men of Yirrkala have frequented the hotel regularly and there have come in contact with 'stranger Yolngu' from other settlements. The deaths of three middle-aged men of Yirrkala in 1974 and 1975 were attributed by many people to sorcery worked on the men by unknown Aborigines who were drinking at the hotel (Reid and Mununggurr 1977).

Shortly before or after a death, the traditional healer (marrnggitj) may be called in to divine the identity of the sorcerer. The acknowledged abilities of the only practicing marrnggitj presently living at Yirrkala include being able to see the faces of killers with the aid of powerful stones which he possesses, and to enlist the help of his spirit familiars in identifying them. It is stated (though I do not know whether the technique is actually used) that if a hot wire is inserted into the body of the deceased the murderer will suffer intense pain,

serious illness and that he will eventually die.
If the identity of the sorcerer can be established
(and normally suspicion falls on individuals or
groups who relatives of the deceased believe had
cause to attack the deceased), the brothers or
fathers of the deceased will ask the sisters' sons
to exact revenge. Vengeance may take the form of
an overt attack on the supposed murderer (rare in
contemporary times) or, it is asserted, a covert
attack by a sorcerer from elsewhere who has been
retained by relatives of the deceased.

Relatives of the deceased may not be at
Yirrkala when a death occurs. Some may be living
elsewhere. Accordingly messages are sent through
the outpost radio network to outstations, to
Galiwin'ku and to Milingimbi where clan leaders
also make a ritual announcement of death to
relatives of the deceased. Family members who
happen to be in more distant parts, such as Darwin
or a southern city, are contacted and asked to come
home. While these absent family members may
suspect the identity of the deceased, they are not
told until they arrive and another ritual
announcement of death is made.

Individuals living or visiting elsewhere
expect that they may sometimes be visited in their
dreams or while awake by the spirit of the person
who has died and thus know that something is wrong
at home. A disturbed night, a dream, the
implacable distress of a young child, the
appearance of the face of a relative are all clues
that a death has occurred. Nor are such
apparitions expected to be confined to Yolngu.
When a young man from a northeastern Arnhem Land
settlement visited Sydney to attend land-rights
meetings, he asked me if I knew that my waku
(classificatory son) had died suddenly at Yirrkala.
I had already received a telephone call to this

effect and simply nodded in the affirmative. He paused and asked, "<u>Nhe nhama mokuy</u>? [Did you see the ghost?]."

Within days of the death of an adult, groups begin to arrive by commercial aircraft from Galiwin'ku and Milingimbi and by four-wheel drive vehicle or single-engine mission plane from the outstations. Each is ushered in ritual procession from the periphery of the ceremonial area to the main assembly. If the incoming group contains close relatives of the dead man, their close female relatives (such as mothers and wives) will cling to them and keen. They will cry for the loss the newly arrived have suffered, commiserate with them in their grief, and lament that they were away and thus unable to see the dead person before he died. Prior to the opening of a hospital in Nhulunbuy in 1971, the funeral organizers were forced to balance the time it was felt wise to keep a body in the camp against the time needed to notify all relevant kin and wait for them to reach Yirrkala. Since 1971 bodies have been taken to the morgue whether the deceased died in hospital or at home and kept there until all participants have arrived and until a decision is taken to hold the ceremonies.

The presence of a hospital nearby has also alleviated another logistical problem, that of purchasing a coffin and raising the money necessary to have the body flown home if the deceased died in a distant hospital. There are no sealed all-weather roads into northeastern Arnhem Land from other parts of the Northern Territory and the Department of Health does not take responsibility for returning the bodies of patients who have died after being evacuated to hospital for medical care. A period of four months recently elapsed between the death of an infant in Darwin Hospital and his burial at Yirrkala because, according to the child's paternal grandmother, it took the family that long to raise the necessary $200 to bring the body home. When recalling the first time someone (a prominent clan head) had died at Darwin Hospital, and the protracted negotiations with the authorities which finally led to the return of the body to Yirrkala, a clan and community leader commented,

> It's hard, but you have to do it that way ...These days if a man dies in hospital with no <u>manikay</u>, we will sing very hard over his coffin to make his spirit go back to his father's and grandfather's land and not come back to his family. They may sing for a long time. Women will also scream and cry and sing.

Principal Phase of Mortuary Ceremonies

Following the initial phases of the mortuary ceremonies, the clan elders decide upon the location, structure and ceremonial content of the remainder of the ceremonies. Several leaders and categories of kin have rights to contribute to the discussions about the organization of the ceremonies and to have their opinions taken into account. Proposed plans cannot be implemented until a consensus of all those who have a legitimate interest in the decision is obtained. The processes of decision-making have been analyzed in depth by Williams (1978) with respect to a set of negotiations concerning the ceremonial and burial site following the death of a middle-aged man at Yirrkala.

Once general agreement about the plans for the ceremonies is secured, the body is ceremonially recovered from the morgue at the hospital.

Participants travel to town and take part in the slow, emotional and ritualized transport of the coffin and body back to Yirrkala. As the convoy of cars enters the camp the horns are sounded and the coffin is conveyed with dancing and singing to a shelter in which it will lie until the day of burial. Even the cars become integral elements of the procession; they are stopped, started, and reversed in keeping with the ritualized movements of the dancers. Within the shelter the coffin is placed in a large commercial refrigerator which is connected to the electricity supply by extension cord. Two such refrigerators, one for deceased of the Dhuwa moiety and one for deceased of the Yirritja moiety, are available for use during funerals. Each is mounted on a base with wheels such that it can be towed behind a vehicle.

The social life of a considerable segment of the community becomes oriented around the shelter (normally a tent or rough-hewn wood framework covered with tarpaulins) which holds the body, coffin and ritual objects. Family groups camp, often sleeping where they sit, at varying distances from the shelter. The shelter itself is often placed near the house in which the deceased lived and therefore in the vicinity of houses occupied by close kin (such as brothers, father and affinal kin). Close relatives of the dead person are readily identified by the pipeclay which they have smeared over their bodies. Mothers (real and classificatory) of the deceased have a V-shaped band of red or yellow ochre painted from their shoulders to a midpoint between their breasts. sisters have their legs below the knee painted in bands of white clay and yellow ochre. Throughout the following days and nights senior men lead the singing of the deceased's clan songs in shifts. Groups of women and young girls stand as each song begins and dance in a rapid, repetitive step to the beat of the music, patterning the subject of each song (the flight of a bird, the making of bark string, paddling a canoe or other) with a stylized movement of their hands. At certain times during the ceremonies the men--predominantly but not always those who are young and fit--enact in dance specific segments of the myths recounted in song, their miming more realistic (less stylized) and more vigorous than that of the women.

The song cycles chosen by the senior men on these occasions follow in content the travels of mythical creator beings (either of human or animal form) who traversed the land in the 'Dreaming' or wangarr time creating human beings and becoming or animating animals, rocks, trees, and other features of the country which can now be seen. During their journeys these spirit beings vested in different clan groups certain areas of land and the sacred, totemic objects linked and constituting title to that land.

The song cycles and dances performed during the course of a mortuary ceremony commemorate segments of the travels of the wangarr beings. They are, at the same time, providing the path along which the spirit (birrimbirr) of the dead person travels to its spiritual resting place. As a senior man explained:

> The manikay is so the person will die in the right manikay and land. When the man dies we continue to sing a song for the spirit. We can't bring the spirit back to the community again. We send him to the spirit land community. All the Dhuwa moiety will go to Burralku area. We can't see it but we know it's the place for spirit Yolngu. If you are Yirritja moiety your spirit will go to Yumaynga area.

These are just two of the spirit areas
after death. There are others as well.

Ritual objects, such as the hand-made ropes of
bark string bearing clumps of white feathers which
represent the Morning Star of the Dhawa moiety, and
ceremonial woven dilly bags decorated with strings
interwoven with the bright red feathers of native
parrots are hung around the inside of the shelter.

Inside the shelter senior men paint the lid of
the coffin with a sacred and restricted clan design
which may not be seen by women or children. Morphy
(1977) interprets the miny'tji as a mechanism for
transferring the soul from the human to the
ancestral plane; the painting is held to be a
manifestation of the wangarr ancestors and thus a
way of mediating between the soul of the dead and
the ancestors of his clan. A senior man explained
it to me thus:

> When he dies we paint the lid of the
> coffin. We give these sacred paintings to
> him so he'll take them with him when he
> becomes a spirit, when his old dead
> relatives [usually said to be F, FF and
> MMB][6] come close to him and take him to his
> sacred land. In days before the mission we
> smeared red ochre all over his body and
> painted that instead.

Throughout the days and nights of the mortuary
ceremonies, grief continues to be openly expressed.
Individual women in particular will keen for a
time. The sentiments which Berndt (1950) found to
predominate in these songs include a wish for the
dead to return, a desire for revenge, recollection
of events which took place during the lifetime of
the deceased, reference to the future of the
deceased's spirit and body and, in the anger of

grief, to the associations of a husband (if still living) with other women. After keening the women return to the demands of children and families, to the task of preparing food for the male singers, to dancing or to other activities expected at this time. There are clearly defined jobs to be done and a considerable expenditure of effort is required during a funeral. The men frequently sing throughout the days and nights, sleeping only briefly in shifts. At the end of long ceremonies they are often tired and hoarse. The women also work hard. When a European friend commented to the wife of a senior man how diligently and tirelessly the men had been singing over a period of days, she, mildly offended, protested that the women work too hard 'crying and dancing'. On another occasion her husband remarked appreciatively upon the effort which the women expend, saying that "some women are good at singing [keening] and staying".

Burial and Purification Rites

After an appropriate period of time a decision will be taken by the ceremonial leaders to conclude the ceremonies with the burial. A burial is often held on a Saturday to ensure that as many people as possible can be present. While some of those who are working may have taken time from their jobs to attend the funeral, others will have been attending only after work and on the weekends. Before the coffin is finally sealed and removed from the shelter, the women crowd around the coffin and, in a concerted voice, cry and protest the final journey of the remains to the grave. They then join the singing and dancing procession of men, women and children to the graveside. The senior men normally inform the Christian minister (a member of the mission staff) of the approximate time of burial. He meets the group and waits for the final ceremonies and lowering of the coffin into the grave. At this point some of those present drift away, but others remain and stand or sit silently while the minister reads the burial service. The minister's words are usually the only oration at the graveside. On rare occasions senior men or women present may take the opportunity to reproach those who have been derelict in observing their duties to the deceased while he was alive. At the burial of an infant, for instance, the most senior man present admonished the young people for drinking, gambling and ignoring the needs of their young ('letting them cry and cry') and, by implication, contributing to the sicknesses and deaths of their children.

The mourners usually return to the ceremonial site after the burial to participate in the man'tjarr ceremony in which the living are switched with the leaves of burning branches to remove the lingering effects of the spirit and to drive it permanently away. At a later ceremony certain possessions of the dead person may be burned.

In the words of a clan leader these purification ceremonies

> ...make the spirit of the dead person go away back to the grave and not follow his wife. The woman has always been alongside her husband, eating, gathering food and hunting. In these ceremonies she gets rid of his spirit. The children and wife might get sick if his mokuy birrimbirr [the spirit of the dead man] still hangs around and gets into their hearts or bodies.

Close relatives of the deceased are not the only ones endangered by the lingering presence of the spirit. Those who have handled the body, who were close relatives and thus conceptualized as 'having the sweat of the dead person on them', and others who were closely associated with the deceased before or after his death are in a state of ritual pollution. They may not give food or cigarettes to others or interact with them freely. Similarly the car (and even the plane) which carried the coffin and body is considered polluted and may not be used until freed of the restrictions placed upon it. These categories of individuals may be painted with <u>meku</u> (red ochre) to cleanse them and to ensure that 'no one will get sick' and that they can safely 'take and give food to others again'. Immediately after the burial or some weeks later a <u>liyalupthun</u> or ritual washing ceremony is held in which people, car and other objects belonging to or used by the deceased which were not burned are 'freed'.

Several months or even years later further ceremonies are held, for instance, to free the house of the deceased for habitation and to cleanse his belongings for use by the survivors. These later ceremonies are sometimes combined with others. In one case an elderly woman who had been ill was 'washed' (ritually cleansed) in a sand sculpture representing the sacred well of her clan (a <u>liyalupthun</u> ceremony) to remove the polluting effect of the blood which she had shed and of the illness itself. With no discernible break in the ceremony, some of the effects of her classificatory son, who had died six months before were brought out by relatives who had been 'looking after them' and washed. (Some criticisms were forthcoming from community members after this collapsed ceremony because the washing of the clothes and blankets of a Yirritja man had taken place in Dhuwa water and well.)

At all rituals which are continuations, however much later, of the mortuary ceremonies, the women again keen and cry as they remember their dead relative. Women may also keen on occasions not directly related to the death. One man died several years before his son's circumcision, a highly significant religious occasion in the boy's life and the first stage in the rites of revelation which continue well into his adult years. His mother who, because of a structurally important position in several clans, had taken a major hand in the execution of the ceremony and had been extremely busy all day, suddenly stopped, sat in an open patch of ground, and sobbed and keened sorrowfully. It is usual for the mothers and sisters of young boys to cry for them at the moment of circumcision, but she later said that she was crying, not for her son, but for the boy's father. He by rights should have been present and taking a leading role in the ceremony and the occasion reminded her of him. Women, and very occasionally men, may also cry alone at night when others are asleep or talking quietly around the camp fires for a husband, child or other kinsperson who has died months or years before. The cues or reminders for such expressions vary, but they almost always occur when the day's activities have ended and the camp is quiet. When someone keens late at night the mournful singing can be heard over a large area of the settlement, reminding others of the death and of the sorrow which the mourner still feels.

The Characteristics of Mourning and Resolution of Grief

During the period of more than a year which I spent in research on, among other things, the indigenous theory of disease causation, grief or a preoccupation with a dead relative were rarely mentioned as causes of either physical or psychological illness or of death. Any such sequellae of a death would be most noticeable at Yirrkala where relationships are highly interdependent and individuals live in close proximity. I heard grief mentioned as a possible etiological factor only once. In this instance a young woman said she thought that the death of her ailing grandfather may have been hastened by the deaths of three of his elderly wives within the preceding two months. My own observations suggest that, given the opportunity to mourn fully and expressively, an individual who has lost a mother, father, spouse, child or other loved relative, can and will resume family and social life unreservedly.

Only one person with whom I was personally acquainted had been deprived of the opportunity to participate and mourn in the mortuary ceremonies of very close kin. (To the best of my knowledge others whom I knew relatively well had always been in attendance at the funerals of kin, even if their presence necessitated a long and expensive trip home.) Her recollections and reactions to the deaths suggest a pathological grief reaction having some of the characteristics defined earlier in this paper (chronic grief, depression and suicidal feelings).

The woman's husband died in 1960 in Darwin Hospital. She recalls, "I sent his money and a suitcase of his belongings to Darwin and it went into the grave with him. His other things were all burned. Only a photograph of him is left". Ten years later, her father underwent surgery. She said she had serious misgivings about the advisability of surgery but that the doctor had convinced her that, although it would make him ill for a while, he would quickly recover. But, in her words:

>   After my father came home from
> hospital I had a dream and a real person
> talked to me and said, "Your Dad won't be
> with you for long. You'll lose him".   I
> didn't tell my father about the dream.
> After he had been back at Yirrkala for two
> or three weeks he got sick again.   I left
> him in the care of his brother's family
> because I had to go to Darwin with my
> daughter who was attending a course there.
> After we were there one week that dream
> came to me again and the man--maybe Christ-
> said, "Your father is in my hands. Don't
> worry because he's with me".

>   We were staying at the mission house
> in Darwin. I was a cleaner there. In the
> morning I went to prayers.   I was still
> crying from that dream and I was scared.
> I cleaned and mopped the offices till
> morning tea time but I couldn't concentrate
> on my work because I was thinking about
> that dream. As I walked back to my room at
> 10 a.m. I could hear the minister and some
> of the other staff talking loudly. They
> said my father's name. Then the minister
> said, "Tell [name] her father passed away
> on Saturday".

>   I ran back to my house. For two
> weeks I didn't go to work. I wanted to go
> back for the funeral but it was too late
> and that was sad for me. And I wanted to
> stay with my daughter until her course
> finished. Then a week later someone rang
> from Yirrkala again to say that my uncle
> [mother's brother] had died. I couldn't
> think that I'd stay alive. I felt mad.

Like I'd throw myself under a car. But
they were holding me and saying, "You can't
kill yourself".   I stayed in Darwin for
four weeks without working. Then the next
week I heard that my [classificatory]
father had died. I felt quite mad when I
heard that these three people had died.
The minister in charge didn't want me to go
back to Yirrkala because I had a job to do
in Darwin--house-cleaning and cleaning
offices. But I couldn't work anyway. And
I couldn't leave my daughter behind.   I
cried day and night. I couldn't eat. The
doctor came to see me and said there was
nothing wrong with me--that I was just
worried about my father. They gave me a
special tablet to stop the worrying which
helped me.

This woman was subsequently diagnosed as
apathetically depressed and hypochondriacal and was
prescribed tranquilizing medication by the visiting
psychiatrist.[7] When I first met her she had only
recently stopped taking tranquilizers but, although
considerable pressure was brought to bear on her
to take various positions, she declined all offers
of employment. During the times she spent talking
with and teaching me she spoke often of her father
and of the religious knowledge which he had passed
on to her. Her mood remained variable and, when I
enquired after her health six months after our
initial conversations, she replied:

My head--sometimes I can think
properly and sometimes I can't. I forget
where I've put things. I used to cry a lot
for my father and hit my head--that's why
it's bad. I can't talk properly. My
children laugh at me. I told [a classificatory father's sister] how I feel but she

can't understand what's wrong.

> I was wondering if I'm not alive
> because I have no feeling. I see food
> anywhere and go up and take it. I feel as
> though something has bitten me inside--a
> stinging. I think I'll get some bush
> medicine for myself. I don't take pills
> now but they used to help me sleep. I saw
> [the female traditional healer] last year.
> She pulled a broken needle from the back of
> my head [a sign of sorcery]. I felt good
> for a little while after that.[8]

This woman's preoccupation with her father's
memory and with the deaths of other relatives whose
funerals she had been unable to attend suggests
that the opportunity to grieve in private or, if in
public, entirely alone, is not adequate for the
successful resolution of grief in Yolngu society.
For this woman the ritual, the structure, the
social support, the presence of the body and the
social permission (or compulsion) to keen were
missing. She was deprived further of the different
kinds of work which a funeral necessitates
(keening, dancing, cooking, organizing), work which
carries the bereaved, makes death a reality and
demands a reorientation towards life. In addition,
she may have harbored the guilt of having placed
her daughter's welfare and the minister's
exhortations above her duty to honor her
obligations as a survivor. She did not attempt to
explain why she might have been the victim of
sorcery; however, a failure to fulfil ritual
obligations is often cited as reasonable
provocation for an assault by a sorcerer. Thus her
guilt and grief may have been compounded by anxiety
concerning her own safety which all those who have
neglected their responsibilities to the living or
the dead can be expected to feel.

By demonstrating the emotional disorganization
and suffering which can ensue if a bereaved person
is unable to mourn in the accustomed way, this
woman's   case   poignantly   highlights   several
characteristics of the mourning process in Yolngu
society which promote the resolution of the grief
of   the   bereaved.   These   are   discussed   with
reference to the mortuary ceremonies and modes of
expressing sorrow which have been described.

The Structuring of Expressions of Grief

Mourning   is   ritually   structured   and   takes
place within clearly delineated periods of time and
social contexts.   Individuals may cry out in pain
and grief immediately after a death, but subsequent
visible expressions of grief are expected to take
conventionalized   forms   (such   as   keening)   and   to
occur in predictable contexts (prior to a death,
during all stages of the mortuary ceremonies and at
other   times   only   when   they   do   not   disrupt   daily
life).   The   opportunity   to   express   anticipatory
grief by keening for the ill or dying person is
particularly significant in enabling a surviving
relative to adjust to the death when it does occur
and in attenuating the normal reactions of shock
and anguish.

The   channelling   of   emotion   in   these   ways
enables bereaved individuals who have obligations
and duties to the living to mourn deeply for finite
periods of time and then return voluntarily and
unambiguously to the demands and interests of their
families.   It is thus very unusual for a person to
present   a   consistently   depressed   and   sad   visage
following a death.   The sudden changes in affect
which I frequently observed during funerals (from
anger to warmth, from sorrow to laughter) were also

noted in central Australia by Spencer and Gillen (1899) and later taken up by Durkheim in his analysis of mortuary behavior. They explained these rapid emotional shifts by asserting that the "self-inflicted pain and loud lamentings" (1899: 510) were tribal customs, rather than a measure of grief actually felt. While it is impossible to assess accurately the subjective state of another person, I would maintain that for many people at Yirrkala mourning behavior is an accurate reflection of the mourner's emotional state and a realistic response to a social situation which simultaneously contains a painful loss and the compensations of relationships with those still living.

As time goes by, grief is assuaged and the memory of the deceased becomes less vivid, episodes of keening become less and less frequent. But even in the years after a death mourning is guided, directed and limited by ritual and convention. The 'unlimited' mourning and the inability of a person to get over his grief, which Gorer (1965) associates in part with the absence of ritual (individual or social, lay or religious) in Western society, are very rare in Yolngu society.

Social Expectations and Public Mourning

The second characteristic of mourning in Yolngu society relevant here is that it is expected and collectively and publicly expressed. Not only do members of the immediate family bewail their loss; classificatory relatives also gather to grieve and to express their empathy and solidarity with the bereaved in open expressions of grief. These visible displays of sorrow are expected and their absence would deeply offend. At a funeral ceremony in 1979, for instance, a classificatory sister of a woman who had died walked away from the group of keening women gathered round the coffin and loudly deplored the fact that she and members of this small group had been carrying the burden of the public mourning while other women simply sat or danced.

The dense and interconnected social networks of Yolngu society and the close face-to-face contact which many people have for long periods of their lives ensure that a death will leave many bereft and upset. The emotions expressed are thus for many people felt and genuine. It is also true that distant relatives who may have had strained relations with the bereaved or his group will endeavour to convey their sorrow at his passing and thereby affirm publicly that they would not have wished (or done) him harm. The opportunity to mourn may also afford relatives, whatever their relationship to the deceased, a guise under which old losses which deeply affected them may be relived and reworked. Further, they may provide a context in which individuals, faced with the visible evidence of the inevitability of death, can mourn their own mortality and express indirectly the anxieties which confrontation with death generates. Whatever the motivations of individuals, the collective expression of grief provides visible social support for the bereaved.

The importance of manifest social support is indicated by studies among Europeans. It has been shown that, for bereaved European women, the variable most strongly associated with poor resolution of grief (as reflected in substantially increased incidence of a wide range of symptoms, psychological and psychosomatic) is the subject's perception of her social network as failing to support her and to encourage her to express her feelings during her time of crisis (Raphael 1976b).

Schwab et al. (1976) have also concluded that the
absence of a social support system may be the
single most important factor in the etiology of
unresolved grief. At present the social isolation
and lack of support during bereavement which
characterize Western society (Aries 1975; Gorer
1965) are rare in Yirrkala, for few people have
left the community permanently and those who are
away can and do (in contrast to the woman whose
solitary mourning is described above) almost always
return for a funeral.   Were significant out-
migration to towns and cities to occur, however, it
is likely that more people would have to weather
their loss away from home and so be at risk of not
resolving their grief.

The Demands of Living

Mourning is interwoven with the demands and
rewards of daily life.   The structuring or
compartmentalization of grief enables the
individual to give vent to his emotions and at the
same time to carry on with living. The mortuary
ceremonies not only provide a vehicle to carry the
bereaved through the shock of death, but also a
series of necessary tasks which direct the energies
of all constructively and predictably. The men are
expected to take their place in the organization
and execution of the rituals.   The women are
expected to keep the assembled company fed, to
participate in the ceremonies and to look after the
children and other dependents.

The Expression of Anger and Aggression

The ambivalence which can mark an individual's
response to the death of a relative (Averill 1968;
Freud 1913/52) and the attendant risk of a

pathological grief reaction is minimized by certain
ritual conventions which enable those who were
close to the deceased to express not only sorrow,
grief and remembered affection, but anger, anxiety
and guilt.   The mortuary ceremonies provide a
culturally   sanctioned   opportunity   to   vent
potentially maladaptive emotions in a socially and
personally non-disruptive manner.   These emotions
are channelled either into ceremonial displays,
into speculation and accusations (usually directed
at people living in other communities) of sorcery,
or (though this is rarely discussed) into plans to
avenge the death. Morphy (1977) vividly describes
the ritual attack with spears on the tent in which
the body of a child lay during a funeral at an
outstation.   At one level this was said to be
driving away the hostile aspect of the child's
spirit (the mokuy).   At another level it
represented an attack on those believed to have
caused the death.   It is possible that, at yet
another level, it constituted an expression of
anger against the deceased for leaving his family
and causing pain for his kinfolk. The men danced
with ceremonial dilly bags clenched between their
teeth as they would were they engaged in an
avenging expedition. Morphy concludes that "biting
the dilly bag...enables aggression felt by those
mourning the death to be controlled...in the
context of a dance that enacts the spearing of the
ground and draining of blood." (1977:   122)

The presence and direction given by the senior
men, the ritual leaders, during the ceremonies
(which often resemble the actions of stage
managers, as instructions are given to
participants, dances rehearsed and groups assembled
and directed in ceremonial maneuvers) may reduce
the likelihood of overt aggression at these times.
Rosenblatt et al. (1972) have found an apparent
reduction in anger and aggression in societies

where ritual specialists are used up to and including body disposal. (By contrast, societies which have institutionalized patterns of anger and aggression seem to deal with the problem of keeping these emotions channelled by the customary marking and isolation of the bereaved.)

The Socially Prescribed Limits to Grief

Mourning is expected by community members to take a finite course; there is general social agreement on what constitutes 'normal' and 'pathological' grief. A person who wails and retreats from social duties excessively after a funeral has finished is gradually accorded less and less support. Private and restricted grief over the death of a relative is considered natural for many years after a death. But community members expect that this will not intrude into his daily life and impair his ability to interact productively with the living. Moreover, although a certain amount of self-mutilation is accepted when a woman is in the throes of grief, individuals speak reproachfully of women who have so severely and consistently hit their heads or thrown themselves on the ground that they have sustained presumed internal injuries. Of 43 people whom I questioned about the causes of bawa'mirri ('madness'), which is normally attributed to the actions of sorcerers and spirits or to severe interpersonal problems, four attributed it to the harm which women inflict on themselves when mourning. Three attributed the symptom 'coughing up blood' (which usually occurs in this area as a result of tuberculosis or pneumonia) to self-inflicted internal injury sustained during mourning. Thus, while women who are 'good at singing [keening] and staying' are praised for their contribution to ceremonies, they are expected not to mourn in excess and to submit to restraint when it is applied.

Conclusion

Each of the five characteristics of the mourning process described eases the mourning of the bereaved and facilitates their reintegration into the community.   While it is no doubt also true, as argued by those who are concerned with the social functions of mortuary rituals, that they "are a mnemonic of the structure of social relationships" and "occasions to symbolize and ratify social relations and social order" (Brandl 1971:529), it has been argued here that the primary determinant and beneficiary of the course and content of mortuary ceremonies is the individual. In northeastern Arnhem Land the mortuary ceremonies not only affirm, in dramatic form, the relations and beliefs of the living, but enable the bereaved to mourn in a culturally structured and contained context, to resolve grief and to resume social roles.   In short, mortuary ceremonies afford the bereaved "a time to live" and "a time to grieve".

Sydney University

Acknowledgements

This paper is based on research funded by the National Science Foundation (U.S.A.), the National Health and Medical Research Council (under the program 'Australian Transcultural Psychiatry'), and the Australian Institute of Aboriginal Studies. I am very grateful to Banguyarri Dhamarrandji, Jeremy Beckett, David Biernoff, Maria Brandl, Russ Hausfeld, Les Hiatt, Howard Morphy, Beverly Raphael, and Cherry Swain for their guidance and help. I owe a particular debt to Nancy Williams for many hours spent reading and discussing this manuscript. Thanks also go to the Dhanbul Council of Yirrkala for its permission to carry out this research and to all teachers and friends at Yirrkala who contributed to the study.

Notes

1. 'He', 'his', and 'him' are used to refer both to a man and a woman unless the sex of the individual is clear from the context.

2. A segment of mortuary ceremonies held at Galiwin'ku (Elcho Island) has also been recorded on film by Cawte et al.(1974)

3. Clunies Ross and Hiatt (1977) observed a larrakan ceremony (in which the bones are crushed and placed in a hollow log coffin) at an outstation in central Arnhem Land in 1975. The bones had been disinterred in 1958 and placed in the care of relatives (bokabod ceremony). The authors

390 A Time to Live, A Time to Grieve

attribute the abnormally long interval of 17 years between <u>larrakan</u> and <u>bokabod</u> to the difficulties of holding a <u>larrakan</u> at Maningrida settlement where many of the relevant individuals had been living for much of that time.

4. The <u>manikay</u> may have been mistakenly associated in the minds of Europeans with the technique of sorcery called <u>nyira</u> at Yirrkala but known by other names elsewhere in Aboriginal Australia and translated in English as 'singing' (a person to death). The <u>manikay</u> and <u>nyira</u> are completely unrelated.

5. After a death the name of the dead person is not again mentioned for at least a decade. He is identified in terms of his relationships to others or in other indirect ways which make his identity clear. Others who have been named after him use different names from then on. Words in the language which are likely to remind people of his name are changed. Photographs of the dead person are hidden, burned or taken away from his closest kin. Everyone is conscientious in avoiding saying his name at all. Mistakes, though, are sometimes made. An adult who inadvertently names a dead person in conversation is always, as I have observed, mortified by his breach of convention.

6. The mother's mother's brother (MMB) - sister's daughter's son (ZDS) or <u>mari-gutharra</u> relationship is the 'backbone' of Yolngu society. A man has an obligation to his mother's mother's (=MMB's) land-owning group to protect both them and their land. This obligation entails receprocal rights in persons, land and the ritual property which symbolizes these rights. A man has a right to expect that his MMB (<u>mari</u>) will bestow one of

his (MMB's) daughters on him as a mother-in-law, and that he will therefore be able to claim her daughterrs as his wives. Men of the <u>mari</u> clan have major responsibility for organizing mortuary rites for a deceased member of the <u>gutharra</u> clan. This relationship and its implications are explained in detail by Morphy (1977) and Williams (1978).

7. Dr. H.D. Eastwell.

8. This account reflects this woman's involvement in church activities at the time of the deaths. On other occasions she spoke at length about traditional matters, about the reappearance of spirits of the dead and about the role of sorcery in deaths. Although she clearly linked her suffering to the deaths of close relatives, it should be noted that her ability to cope with these may have been impaired by difficulties she was experiencing concerning remarriage, by an unusual responsibility for religious knowledge passed on to her by her father, and by the intermittently wayward behavior of two of her four sons. It is also possible that the occurrence of a series of deaths in such a short period of time exacerbated her disturbed reaction. However, the observed ability of other individuals to adjust to multiple losses suggests that her response was unusual.

References

Aries, P. 1975. The Reversal of Death: Changes
   in Attitudes Toward Death in Western
   Societies. In D.E. Stannard, ed., _Death in_
   America. Pennsylvania: University of
   Pennsylvania Press.

Averill, J.R. 1968. Grief: Its Nature and
   Significance. _Psychological Bulletin_ 70:
   721-748.

Beckett, J. 1975. A Death in the Family: Some
   Torres Strait Ghost Stories. In L.R. Hiatt,
   ed., _Australian Aboriginal Mythology_.
   Canberra: Australian Institute of Aboriginal
   Studies.

Berndt, C.H. 1950. Expressions of Grief Among
   Aboriginal Women. _Oceania_ 20: 286-332.

Berndt, R.M. 1974. _Australian Aboriginal_
   Religion. Leiden: E.J. Brill.

Berndt, R.M. and C.H. Berndt. 1964. _The World of_
   the First Australians. London: Angus and
   Robertson.

Blauner, R. 1966. Death and Social Structure.
   Psychiatry 29: 378-394.

Brandl, M.M. 1971. Pukumani: The Social Context
   of Bereavement in a North Australian
   Aboriginal Tribe. Ph.D. Dissertation,
   University of Western Australia.

Cawte, J., D. Baglin, and T. Cawte. 1974.
    Aboriginal Death Rites, Arnhem Land, 1974.
    16mm film. Canberra: Australian Institute
    of Aboriginal Studies.

Chaseling, W. 1957. <u>Yulengor: Nomads of Arnhem
    Land</u>. London: The Epworth Press.

Clunies Ross, M., and L.R. Hiatt. 1977. Sand
    Sculptures at a Gidjingali Burial Rite.   In
    P.J. Ucko, ed., <u>Form in Indigenous Art:
    Schematisation in the Art of Aboriginal
    Australia and Prehistoric Europe</u>. Canberra:
    Australian Institute of Aboriginal Studies.

Coombs, H.C. 1973. Decentralisation Trends Among
    Aboriginal Communities. Paper presented at
    the 1973 Congress of the Australian and New
    Zealand Association for the Advancement of
    Science.

Dunlop, I. 1978. Madarrpa Funeral at Guika'wuy.
    A Way of Coping with Death in Northeast Arnhem
    Land Through Ties of Clan, Religion and Land.
    90 minute 16mm film. Sydney: Film Australia,
    and Los Angeles: Australian Film Commission.

Durkheim, E. 1965(1915). <u>The Elementary Form of
    Religious Life</u>. New York: The Free Press
    (First French Edition 1912).

Elkin, A.P. 1975. <u>The Australian Aborigines</u>.
    Sydney: Angus and Robertson.

Fabian, J. 1972. How Others Die--Reflections on
    the Anthropology of Death. <u>Social Research</u>
    39: 543-567.

Freud, S. 1952(1913). <u>Totem and Taboo</u>. New York:
    Norton.

Goody, J. 1962. Death, Property and the
    Ancestors: A Study of the Mortuary Customs
    of the LoDagaa of West Africa. London:
    Tavistock Publications.

_____. 1975. Death and the Interpretation of
    Culture: A Bibliographic Overview. In
    D. E. Stannard, ed., Death in America.
    Pennsylvania: University of Pennsylvania
    Press.

Gorer, G. 1965. Death, Grief, and Mourning in
    Contemporary Britain. London: Cresset Press.

Hertz, R. 1960(1907). A Contribution to the Study
    of the Collective Representation of Death. In
    Death and the Right Hand. Trans. by R. and
    C. Needham. Glencoe: Free Press.

Hiatt, L.R. 1961. Mortuary Rites and Practices
    in Central Arnhem Land. Paper presented at
    the Australian National University.

Kaberry, P.M. 1935. Death and Deferred Mourning
    Ceremonies in the Forrest River Tribes,
    Northwest Australia. Oceania 6: 33-47.

_____. 1939. Aboriginal Woman: Sacred and
    Profane. London: George Routledge and Sons.

Kastenbaum, R., and P.T. Costa. 1977.
    Psychological Perspectives on Death. Ann.
    Rev. Psychol. 28: 225-249.

Keen, I. 1977. Yolngu Sand Sculptures in Context.
    In P.J. Ucko, ed., Form in Indigenous Art:
    Schematisation in the Art of Aboriginal
    Australia and Prehistoric Europe. Canberra:
    Australian Institute of Aboriginal Studies.

Lindemann, E. 1944. Symptomatology and Management
    of Acute Grief. Amer. Journal of Psychiatry
    101: 141-148.

Malinowski, B. 1954. Magic, Science and Religion
    and Other Essays. New York: Doubleday and
    Company.

Mandelbaum, D.G. 1959. Social Uses of Funeral
    Rites. In H. Feifel, ed., The Meaning of
    Death. New York: McGraw-Hill.

Meggitt, M.J. 1974(1962). Desert People. Sydney:
    Angus and Robertson.

Morphy, H. 1977. Too Many Meanings: An Analysis
    of the Artistic System of the Yolngu of
    Northeast Arnhem Land. Ph.D. Dissertation.
    Canberra: Australian National University.

Munn, N.D. 1969. The Effectiveness Of Symbols in
    Murngin Rite and Myth. In V. Turner, ed.,
    Forms of Symbolic Action. Seattle:
    University of Washington Press.

Opler, M.E. 1945. The Lipan Apache Death Complex
    and Its Extensions. S. W. J. Anth. 1: 122-
    141.

_____. 1946. Reaction to Death Among the
    Mescalero Apache. S. W. J. Anth. 2: 454-
    467.

Peterson, N. 1967. Mortuary Customs of Northeast
    Arnhem Land: An Account Compiled from Donald
    Thomson's Fieldnotes. Mem. Nat. Mus. Vic. 37:
    97-108.

Raphael, B.   1967a.   The Management of Bereavement.
    In G. Burrows, ed., Handbook on Studies of
    Depression.   Amsterdam: ASP Biological
    Press.

_____.   1967b.   Adaptation Patterns of Women in
    Crisis.   Paper presented at the 47th ANZAAS
    Conference, Hobart.

_____.   1977.   Bereavement and Prevention.   New
    Doctor 4:   41-45.

Reid, J., and D. Mununggurr.   1977.   We Are Losing
    Our Brothers: Sorcery and Alcohol in an
    Aboriginal Community.   Med. J. Aust. Spec.
    Supp. 2:   1-5.

Rosenblatt, P.C., D.A. Jackson, and R.P. Walsh.
    1972.   Coping with Anger and Aggression in
    Mourning.   Omega 3:   271-284.

Rosenblatt, P.C., D.A. Jackson, and R.P. Walsh.
    1976.   Grief and Mourning in Cross-Cultural
    Perspective.   H. R. A. F. Press.

Schwab, J.J., et al.   1976.   Funeral Behavior and
    Unresolved Grief.   In V. R. Pine et al.,
    eds., Acute Grief and the Funeral.
    Springfield: Charles C. Thomas Publishers.

Spencer, B., and F.J. Gillen.   1899.   The Native
    Tribes of Central Australia.   London:
    Macmillan and Company.   (Republished by Dover
    Publications, New York 1968).

van Gennep, A.   1980(1960).   The Rites of Passage.
    London: Routledge and Kegan Paul.   (First
    French edition 1909).

Warner, W.L.   1958(1937).   <u>A Black Civilization:
    A Social Study of an Australian Tribe</u>.   New
    York: Harper and Brothers.

Williams, N.M.   1978.   On Aboriginal Decision
    Making.   D.   Barwick, J. Beckett, and M. Reay,
    eds., In <u>Festschrift for Emeritus Professor
    W.E.H. Stanner</u>. Forthcoming.

DYING, DEATH, AND BEREAVEMENT
AMONG THE MAYA INDIANS OF MESOAMERICA:
A STUDY IN ANTHROPOLOGICAL PSYCHOLOGY

Richard L. Steele

Abstract

Death, dying, and bereavement are complex psychological and biosocial problems of 20th-century Western civilization. Some earlier cultures and societies responded successfully to the phenomena of dying and death and the intense emotions attendant upon them. For us today, possible solutions to these problems exist in rediscovering the effective adjustive methods of the ancients. In light of this, the civilization of the pre-Columbian Maya of Mesoamerica is discussed, with particular emphasis on the Maya's death-related beliefs and rituals, treatment of the fatally ill, burial practices, and family and social attitudes toward death. In the classical Maya civilization, the primary cultural controls over death, dying, and bereavement were myths and rituals that were accepted as truth. These rituals specified how victims and their families were to respond; social pressures ensured the continuation of time-honored ritual practices. Parallels are drawn with the societies of the ancient Hebrews, early Christians, Buddhists, Hindus, and Navajos.

399

Death, dying, and bereavement are complex psychological and biosocial problems in 20th-century Western civilization, a fact dramatically illustrated by the burgeoning number of books and articles on death and dying (Cohen, 1976). Feifel's (1959) observation almost two decades ago addressed with acute poignancy what might be considered the core of the problem:

> In the presence of death western culture by and large has tended to run, hide and seek refuge in group norms and actuarial statistics. The individual face of death becomes blurred by embarrassed curiosity and institutionalization. (p. xii)

Modern man, in effect, endeavors to hide the dead and the fact of death by various means, means that function to provide psychological distance between the deceased and the survivors. We live in an age in which society attempts to repress and negate the fact of death (Ammon & Hamlister, 1975). New terminology reflects this attitude of maintaining impersonal distance (a form of negation) from death--for example, Herman Kahn's (1960) coinage of the term 'megadeath' for mass death resulting from nuclear warfare.

In attempts to understand this problem, psychologists, psychiatrists, mental health professionals, and social scientists might recognize that several cultures have experienced substantial success in preparing individuals to deal with the highly phenomenological and social fact of death and the intense emotions attendant upon it.[1]   But solutions concerning death,even among the several ancient cultures relatively successful in resolving it, were not easily derived, for "even among the most primitive peoples, the attitude towards death is infinitely more complex and...more akin to our own, than is usually assumed" (Malinowski, 1954). Modern man may or may not accept death as a personal reality, but many of the primitive, ritualistic, and symbolic ways of coping with the experience of dying remain in our society. A knowledge of the ancient ways of dealing with death provides a means of evaluating the efficiency of modern coping methods.[2] The process of dying and death need not be catastrophic for the respective individual, for his or her family (the "survivor-victim" in Shneidman's [1973] terminology), or for society. Solutions to this problem may lie in rediscovering the effective adjustive methods of the ancients, methods that sufficed within some specific cultures for over a millennium.

The 'ancients' under discussion in this article are the Maya, whose civilization reached its highest peak (classic age) between the 3rd and 9th centuries. These people continue to live today, but time and the encroachment of alien cultures have forced them to alter many of their pre-Columbian ways. Native Maya literary sources provide the most direct, uncluttered pathway to gathering knowledge of their ancient civilization. The Popol Vuh and Title of the Lords of Totonicopan, written anonymously by people of the Quiche Maya, relate the life of that Maya notion (Goetz, 1953; Goetz & Morley, 1950). The Annals of the Cakchiquels, written in the Cakchiquel language, describes the life of the highland Maya (Recinos & Goetz, 1953). And Books of the Jaguar Priest (of Chumayel, of Mani, and of Tizimin), written in European characters because the Spanish conquerors forbade writing with the ancient hieroglyphs, tell of the ancient native ceremonies and prophecies of the Maya (Makemson, 1951). Several other informative sources exist: Spanish chroniclers recorded oral traditions; witnesses of the Spanish conquest provided ethnographic data; and, more recently, archeological expeditions have discovered information relating to the ancient Maya (Gann & Thompson, 1931; Morley, 1956; Nash, 1970; Redfield, 1941, 1950; Thompson, 1930, 1966; Tozzer, 1941). A discussion of death in the Maya world can be better appreciated after a brief review of that civilization's ecology, formal organization, economic endeavors, and beliefs and mythologies. That the psychology of a culture cannot be understood without knowledge of the culture itself should go without saying.

Background

Ecological Setting

The ancient Maya largely occupied the areas in which they may still be found today: the states of Yucatan, Campeche, Tabasco, the eastern half of Chiapas, and the territory of Quintana Roo in the Republic of Mexico; in Guatemala, the Department of Peten and the mountain highlands lying to the south; and the western area of Honduras and all of Belize--a total of approximately 125,000 square miles (Morley, 1956).

Yucatan, Campeche, and the territory of Quintana Roo are drier than the other areas, receiving at times only 18 inches of rain a year. Vegetation in this region is short, stunted, and scrublike. In places, the limestone has collapsed, forming natural wells.   Jaguars, opossums, iguanas, turkey, deer, and the smaller animal life are found here.

The   Maya   developed   their   greatest civilization in the lowlands of present-day Guatemala.   These   lowlands   housed   the   great temple-cities of the Maya--Tikal, Yaxchilan, Uaxactun, Calakmul. Forests surrounding these cities yielded cedar for building canoes; <u>copal</u>, an odiferous resin used in religious ceremonies; brazilwood for red dye; the sapodilla tree, from which chicle was bled; and the broadnut tree, whose fruit was beneficial to both humans and animals. Jaguars, red deer, tapirs, peccary, agoute, sloths, spider and howler monkeys, pheasants, parrots, toucans, and the curassow inhabit this region.

In the mountains of present-day Guatemala and Mexico's state of Chiapas, the Maya found volcanic stones for grinding corn; obsidian and volcanic glass for making knives, sharp-edged clubs, mirrors, and scrapers; and jade, which was considered life-giving, for use in sacred ornaments. The volcanic soil provided the civilized Maya with crops of beans, maize, squash, sweet potatoes, and the cacao bean, which was used as a standard of trade. High cloud forests supported the quetzal bird, greatly prized by the Maya for its four, long, iridescent, blue-green tail feathers.

Maya Culture

Direct evidence concerning Maya social organization is lacking. Pictorial art found on murals, vases, and sculptures from the age of the classic Maya supplies what little knowledge we have of their society. We know that Maya society was based upon a temple-city organization, and it is strongly suspected that religion was of supreme importance in government, with the priest forming a highly organized and dogmatic, rigid, religious cult ruling over the temple-cities (Morley, 1956).

The social organization of the pre-Columbian Maya consisted of four classes: the nobility, the priesthood, the common man, and the multitudes of slaves. At the time of the conquest, the Maya ruler was called <u>halach uinic</u>, or 'true man.' The mass of people supported the <u>halach uinic</u>, the local lesser lords, the local priesthood, and their own families by farming small plots of corn. Occasionally they were conscripted to labor on the great stone highways. Most of the common people lived near a temple-city, the distance of their house from the central plaza being dependent upon the family's social position (Morley, 1956).

The economic endeavors of the Maya depended totally upon the labors and skills of the common people. Traditionally, every man worked in the <u>milpa</u>, or cornfield, and every woman made pottery, except in the highlands where they wove cotton and woolen materials primarily. To the Maya, corn growing was of great religious importance and was symbolized in the form of, Yum Kaax, the corn god. In the <u>milpa</u>, besides corn, there could be found beans that grew up the corn stalks, squash, pumpkins, chili peppers, and sweet potatoes. Papayas and avocados were planted nearer the laborer's house. Hemp, grown for its fiber, was made into ropes, bowstrings, sandals, fishing cord, and other items. On market days, many varieties of vegetable produce were brought from or taken to distant villages and traded.

The trade routes of the Maya were extensive; the highlands were connected to both coasts by trails, then by a system of stone highways. The Usumacinta River, a popular trade route, passed close to the highly populated temple-cities. Traders from the mountains exchanged obsidian, jade, sacred quetzal feathers, the incense <u>copal</u>, flint, alum, and cochineal for the cotton, salt, honey, wax, balche, cacao, dried fish, and deer meat of the lowland Maya. Commerce between lowland and highland peoples brought new styles of weaving, improvements in weapons, and a taste for different foods and goods.

Maya life was ruled by gods of the sky, earth, and underworld. Maya cosmology held that the sky had 13 heavens with a god dwelling in each. The sky was supported by four gods, the <u>Bacabs</u>, who stood on each of the four cardinal directions, represented by four different colors: red, east; white, north; black, west; and yellow, south. At each of the four sides of the heavens stood a sacred ceiba tree. Nine underworlds were presided over by the nine gods of the lower world, the <u>Bolontiku</u>. Ah Puch, the Lord of Death and a malevolent deity, ruled over the lowest underworld, <u>Mitnal</u>. In illustrations, Ah Puch has a skull for a head, bare ribs, and protruding talon-like vertebrae. When clothed with flesh, his body is bloated and covered by black circles, suggesting decomposition. The head of the Maya sky pantheon was Itzamna, the word for lizard. Itzamna, provider of food, patron of healing, and inventor of writing, was titled Lord of the Heavens and Lord of Day and of Night. Chac, another sky god and the god of rain in sculptures, is depicted with a long nose and two fangs that curl downward from his mouth. There is a <u>chac</u> as well as an <u>itzamna</u> for each of the four cardinal points. Chac, benevolent like Itzamna, symbolized creation and life. The most important earth god was Yum Kaax, god of corn and Lord of the Forests. Yum Kaax was always depicted as youthful and either wearing an ear of corn as a headdress or holding a plant of corn.

Important ceremonies were held to invoke each of the gods, beginning with fasts, abstinences, purification rituals, and sacrificial offerings of food, and, in times of severe turmoil, human victims.   There were many ceremonial rites, according to the needs of the individual or the villages, but similarities occur in all of them: (a)   preliminary   fasting   and   abstinences symbolizing   spiritual   purification;   (b)   the choosing of an auspicious day for the event by the priests; (c) the expulsion of evil spirits from the worshippers; (d) the spreading of incense before idols; (e) prayers; and (f) a sacrifice of a living animal or a human (Morley, 1956).

One ancient and most important ceremony dating back to the classic age accompanied the erection of the Katun stone at the end of each katun, or 7,200-day period.   The dominant feature of this ceremony was the erection of a limestone monument that bore hieroglyphical inscriptions giving the Mayan   chronological   date   plus   astronomical, chronological, and ritualistic data. On one side, a priest or a ruler was often sculpted. New Year ceremonies began in the closing 5 days of the preceding year. These were the Uayeb, or unlucky days, when everyone remained in their villages in order to avoid misfortune.   Celebrations occurred for each of the 19 Maya months, each represented by a different patron deity.   The objectives of and the participants in the ceremonies varied with the   month: New Year rites included general participation; physicians and sorcerers attended during Uo, the second month, held for the gods of medicine;   owners   of   bee   hives   attended   the ceremony for the god of bees; when Moc came, old men attended the ceremony to secure rains for the corn; warriors, in order to gain victory, attended the ceremony held in the month of Pax.

The Maya may have believed, as did the Aztec, that the world had been created five times and destroyed four times. The <u>Chilam Balam of Chumayed</u> expresses the tone of the creation in these words:

> Where there was neither heaven nor earth sounded the first word of God. And He unloosed Himself from His stone, and declared His divinity. And all the vastness of eternity shuddered. And His word was a measure of grace, and He broke and pierced the backbone of the mountains. Who was born there? Who? Father, thou knowest; He who was tender in Heaven came into Being. (Nicholson, 1970, p. 148)

At the beginning, water was everywhere. When the gods of creation cried "Earth," land was created. The land was covered with trees, rivers, and animals. Since the animals could neither speak nor propitiate their creators, a superior species was needed. Mud was first used, but these beings could not speak, think, or move about; worse yet, they dissolved in water. The gods destroyed them. Next, wood was tried. These beings spoke, ate, and reproduced but were dry, bloodless creatures. Rains were called to destroy them. A few escaped and became the ancestors of the monkeys. Next, four beings were made from a gruel of yellow and white maize. These four men were too gifted, and the gods felt threatened. So, with a light mist the gods dulled the eyes of these men and then created wives for them. Then came the dawn, the morning star, and the sun. The men began to worship their creators (Thompson, 1966).

Dying, Death, Burial and the Hereafter

Mythology and Religion

Disease brings on death and evil winds bring on disease, according to Maya folklore. Evil winds arose in ancient times when a sorcerer became angered at the inhabitants of a village and decided to destroy them, according to the Maya of Socotz, who inhabit Belize (Thompson, 1930):

> The sorcerer made nine dolls of black wax which he buried near each of the streams which ran through the village. Luckily another sorcerer foresaw the intended wickedness and searched for the nine dolls, but he was able to find only seven. They searched all night, knowing that at dawn, if the two dolls were not found and destroyed, they would begin their evil tricks upon the village. The dolls were not found. The villagers, angered, dragged the evil sorcerer and his family into the woods and murdered them. But the evil was done. To this day the village of Socotz suffers sickness from two evil winds caused by the two hidden wax dolls. (pp. 166-167)

Of course, variations of this tale exist in different villages. Today, in Uaxactun, the following prayer may be offered:

> I stand to beg your aid for [so and so's] pulse, veins, and flesh. You evil winds that cause him to tremble, whence do you come? Are you the wind that blows over the water? Or are you the wind that comes across the earth? I have found you out.

You lie hid in his foot, in his heart but
I will drag you out, you evil winds of
sickness. (Thompson, 1930, p. 73)

Winds, associated with movements of the air,
were considered malevolent, supernatural, and as
forms of disease themselves. Usually they were
connected with caves, wells, streams, and with
water in general. The winds entered into the body
of the affected person; treatment consisted of
forcing the winds out by ritual and symbolism.

Sickness could also be brought about by certain
magic persons born with the power to cause sickness
simply by looking at someone. These individuals
bore a special mark near their eyes or nose
(Redfield, 1941). Illness could also be the result
of past misdeeds, but confession of these misdeeds
to a family member was thought to prevent one's
becoming ill. In Quintana Roo, the belief existed
that inattention to the souls of the dead caused
sickness.

When a man was ill, a priest, shaman, or
sorcerer was called. This curer, using prayers,
ceremonies, and herbs, either killed or cured his
patients. According to Landa (in Tozzer, 1941):

The sorcerers and physicians performed
their cures by bleedings of the parts,
which gave pain to the sick man (p. 112)
...the Maya believed that death, illness
and disease resulted from doing wrong; they
confessed themselves when already sick.
(p. 106)

Certain dreams and omens presaged death. A
dream of floating on air or of having a tooth
pulled and feeling intense pain foretold an
immediate family member's death. To dream of red

tomatoes meant a baby would die. Dreaming that a
black bull pushed its way into one's home or that
a water jug broke also indicated that a member of
the family would die.

When the time came to die, the Maya did not
fight it. Old ones might at any time announce that
their time had come and retreat to their mat or
hammock, where they would lie quietly, awaiting
death.

Immortality and an afterlife existed in Maya
beliefs. Those who committed suicide, or were
killed in battle, or died as sacrificial victims,
women who died in childbirth, and priests went to
the Maya's conception of paradise, a delightful
place overflowing with food and drink, where the
shade of the ceiba tree sheltered one forever.
Those who voyaged after death to the lower region
of Mitnal were tormented by hunger, cold, fatigue,
and sadness. The soul (spirit) itself did not die
and went on forever in one of these regions.

In the Chiapas highlands, folklore has it that
when death occurs, the soul leaves through the
tongue (Nash, 1970). The family then finds a
suitable resting place for the soul. If death is
caused by a 'good' illness (one not caused by
witchcraft), the soul lingers for 8 days before
going to paradise. In the case of a violent death,
the soul remains in the village for 20 days because
"the gods did not choose the hour of death, and the
soul doesn't know where to go." This waiting
period allows the dead person to "finish his
heart," that is, to end his emotional ties with
family and friends.

The screech owl and the dog symbolized death
and burial; occasionally, among the Lacandon Maya,
a dog figurine would be buried on the grave of the

deceased.   Even today, many Indians of Central
America and Mexico believe that when an owl
screeches, someone will die (Nicholson, 1970).

The naguales, guardian spirits taking an animal
or bird form, presided over man's fate from birth
to death.   Man acquired a nagual by journeying into
the forest and sleeping among birds and beasts.
There he would be confronted by his guardian
spirit, who remained with him for life.   Birth and
death were linked to the nagual, and when a man
died, his nagual died, and vice versa.

Treatment of the Fatally Ill

Treatment of the dying involved sorcery and the
use of medicinal herbs.   An enemy, the 'evil
winds,' or forgetting to offer necessary sacrifices
and prayers may have brought the sickness, and it
was the sorcerer's duty to overcome these forces
with his strength and special knowledge.   The
sorcerer first made divinations, scattering piles
of pito beans on the ground and placing them in
piles of four or, as in the land of the Mam,
rubbing the patient's legs and observing the
twitching of his muscles.   If the leg twitched,
death would come.   In the territories of the Maya,
'medicinal' herbs and plants were plentiful--a
fungus, a euphorbia, or the sap of a rubber tree
might be used: just as probably, the patient might
be bled or given the testicles of a cockerel, the
blood of a bat, dog excrement, etc.   But in any
case, if the diviner forecast death, the patient
usually accepted the forecast and died.

Once an elderly man made up his mind to die, he
would consult with the village sorcerer to divine
on which day it would be best to die.   Then he
would suddenly take to his hammock or sleeping mat,

saying to his relatives and friends, "I am going to
die" (Gann & Thompson, 1931). Wrapping himself in
his woven coverlet, he would refuse food, drink,
and further intercourse with men until he died.
Not unexpectedly, a man would frequently die on the
day forecast by the diviner.

Burial Practices

Burial of the dead varied according to the
status of the deceased and the local customs.
After death, the body of the deceased was washed
and then wrapped in his <u>manta</u>, or shroud. A jade
bead or a bite of maize was placed in the
deceased's mouth so that food would be available
during the journey toward his destination. The
dead man's dog was sacrificed and placed near him
so that he might be guided on his journey to the
next world. His possessions were buried close at
hand to ensure that if he were a fisherman he could
continue to fish, or if a hunter, continue to hunt.
If a woman died, her household possessions such as
the corn grinder and weaving materials were buried
with her. In a tomb beneath a pyramid at
Kaminaljuyu, near present-day Guatemala City, a
nobleman was found buried with two male attendants,
many pieces of jade, shell beads, obsidian points,
an alabaster vase and other fine pottery vessels
(probably originally containing various foods), a
dog, the jaws of a jaguar, the skull of a coyote,
corn-grinding stones, and a wooden litter to make
his journey easier. The common man was buried
beneath the hard mud floor of his house. After
several such burials by a family in their house,
the house was abandoned and became a family shrine.

In northern Yucatan, the bodies of deceased
nobility were cremated, with the ashes of the dead
enclosed in hollow statues of pottery or wood. The

statues were carved to depict a likeness of the deceased noble. These statues and crematory urns were worshiped along with other family idols. At Mayapan, the Cocom practiced a different burial custom. Cocom nobles, after death, were boiled until all flesh fell from their bones. The posterior part of the head was sawed off, but the front was left intact. Where the flesh had been originally wax or bitumen was used to reconstruct the lord's face. Completion of these death faces provided occasions for important feasts.

Today, in the Chiapas highlands among descendants of the ancient Maya, a wake, "watching over the dead," is held by relatives of the father, mother, and spouse of the deceased (Nash, 1970). When midnight arrives, the closest female kin begins a stylized crying for the dead. During this time, the mourner presents the way the dead man passed his life. If a widow, she mourns for herself, saying,

How can I eat now with my children?
You will not see how I shall live.
You are of one heart in the ground.
But you do not see how I shall eat with the children.

If it was a violent death, the widow sings of the blamelessness of her husband. The burial is a replica of that which has been practiced for centuries. The man's food, drink, and special possessions are buried with him. During the burial, the female closest of kin continues to wail her mourning cry. When dirt begins to be thrown over the body, certain persons who are expected to show signs of mourning before a select audience begin their wails. Nash (1970) suggests that this ritual is important as a means of controlled communication.

Family and Social Attitudes

Family and social attitudes were concerned first with outward appearances. Burial of the deceased was required to meet the expectations of the community and of the relatives of the deceased. Thus, there were different rituals for lords, for common men, and for slaves. Today in the Maya community of Amatenango del Valle near San Cristobal Las Casas, the adult children of one who dies are expected by the deceased's fellow villagers to provide a funeral appropriate to the deceased's former station in life and to his wealth (Nash, 1970). In Chan Kom, rituals for the deceased served the important purpose of providing a safe separation of the spirit from the earth and the speeding of it on its journey to the other world, where the soul or spirit would be of no danger to the living. According to Redfield (1941), the Maya man struck with a severe illness asks at once, "Have I made my prayers for my dead father and mother?"

Death did not necessarily break the ties with the living. The spirit, even though released from the body, did not speed directly to the other world. It took the correct behavior of the living and their attention to ritual details to conduce the soul or spirit through successive stages to its eventual destination. Chants were sung over the dying to ease the separation of the spirit from the body. In some regions, an opening in the roof of the house was required so that the spirit could pass through. Sometimes to ensure that a spirit did not become lost, a dog was killed so that the dog's spirit could guide the deceased, or a path was laid with grains of corn. And finally, the soul might be directed to its destination by the speech of the living.

The survivors were faced with certain taboos. They were to keep the rituals or the deceased would return to claim something from them (von Hagen, 1960). A widow became 'unclean' at her husband's death. The uncleanliness continued as long as a tie to the deceased remained. Social pressure, in this instance, undoubtedly served to shorten the mourning period for the widow and to motivate her to turn her thoughts and activities elsewhere.

The mourning period, although a matter of days rather than months, was a time for the display of community-sanctioned intense feelings of loss and despair. Centuries ago, Landa observed the excessive grief of the Maya:

> But when, in time, they came to die, it was indeed a thing to see the sorrow and the cries which they made for their dead, and the great grief it caused them. During the day they wept for them in silence; and at night with loud and very sad cries, so that it was pitiful to hear them. And they passed many days in deep sorrow. (Tozzer, 1941, p. 129)

Summary and Interpretations

The Maya during the classic age in pre-Columbian history were a highly civilized people. Their achievements were substantial in the areas of commerce, agriculture, and architecture—more than that, the Maya were unified spiritually. As a people they seem to have possessed an adaptive wisdom that enabled them to live more productive and creative lives than did those peoples with whom they came in contact. Certainly the Maya were less tied to a day-by-day existence.

Mythological beliefs pervaded their lives and existence. Sometimes profound and totally compatible with the nature of their environment, these beliefs provided a major source of spiritual sustenance, even in the face of death. In few societies was the approach of death faced with the fearlessness and equanimity shown by the old ones of the Maya, who, when they felt death approaching, retreated calmly to their mats to await it. The Navajo culture, before the penetration of European thought, showed a similar resignation and gentle acceptance of death.[3]

If they were fortunate enough to foresee death approaching, the old ones of both the Navajo and Maya peoples were required to perform certain duties for their families in the form of rituals that attempted to assuage or fend off the designs of evil spirits and enemies, prior to their deaths. Relatives, in turn, were also duty-bound to follow prescribed mourning procedures subsequent to a death in the family or clan. For the Maya, mythological and practical aspects of death were concentrated into one widely adopted process of ritual, allowing for family and social responses to death to be integrated within an expected, even socially demanded, attitudinal and mourning response. This feature removed the aspect of uncertainty and doubt concerning natural and supernatural consequences, a potentially overwhelming and frequent source of emotional upheaval. As evidence of this, Redfield (1950) reported the general impression upon his revisit after 17 years to the Maya village of Chan Kom that the people were "less easily resigned to die while [they] were more troubled about how to live." Sickness in the community once had a more determined, less varied course when the h-men, or curer, was called. One did what he was told by the h-men full of conviction and the certainty that his way was the only way; one got well or one died. Redfield observed during his second visit that there were now several alternatives, or several remedies, from which to choose. One could no longer be assured that he had done all that he could do, and there was no guidance as to when, finally, to leave it up to the supernatural.

In today's Western society, in an age of emphasis upon reality, upon the observable 'real/mechanical world,' we as individuals and as a cultural entity lack a common and specific source of spiritual sustenance. We have disdained to follow a process of mythical ritual and are left with little more than science to provide the support and guidance on matters of death that ritual and belief once provided. But science, in practice, is amoral and offers little spiritual consolation. Social and cultural controls have disintegrated, and adequate substitutes for facing death, one's own or another's, are failing to develop within our culture. We are living in an age in which society represses and negates the fact of death. As we lose cultural ties and ties with traditional beliefs and values, we lose our convictions of what death is and how we are to meet it. Salzberger (1975) astutely pointed out that the hazards of death and bereavement in our society are attributed partly to the lack of mourning ritual, partly to the social consequences of bereavement, and partly to the lack of ideological content. In pre-Columbian Mayan culture, myths relating to death and dying were strongly integrated and accepted as truths and realities. These myths were effective in promoting continued cultural growth. They were the primary cultural control over death, dying, and bereavement and specified how the victim and his or her relatives were to respond.

Several early cultures responded to the needs of individuals by guiding them in their dealings with death and dying.   In classical Judaism, according to the Old Testament, both the beginning and the end of life occur within the social framework of the sacred community, with death conceptualized as a "reception into the bosom of Abraham."   The living honored their deceased ancestors and incorporated them into a community of permanence having the widest framework regarding time and generations (Parsons, Rox, & Lidz, 1973). Death in Judaism is an accepted fact, and the dead are honored in memory.   At variance with this feature, but still a source of guidance and consolation, is man's relationship to death as formulated in the New Testament.   There the relationship between a man and God is one of human temporality and divine eternity (Parsons et al., 1973).   Through Mary, the divine eternal becomes the human temporal, and humanity as a whole is upgraded past the Judaic conception of it: "But as many as received him, to them he gave the power to become the sons of God" (John 1:12).   Thus was born the idea of redemption, the idea that the temporal life of man may be exchanged for the divine, eternal life of God.   Death, then, loses its sting for the authentic believer.

Outside Western traditions, Hindu and Buddhist doctrines also face the issue of death.   With some exceptions, the life of each individual as he lives it is conceptualized as only one of a stream of lives extending into the past and toward the future.   Death does not stop life.[4]   The important place of religion in the cultural response to death was directly addressed by Malinowski (1954) when he wrote,

The   ceremonial   of   death   which   ties   the

> survivors to the body and rivets them to
> the place of death, the beliefs in the
> existence of the spirit, in its beneficent
> influences or malevolent intention, in the
> duties of a series of commemorative or
> sacrificial ceremonies--in all this
> religion counteracts the centrifugal forces
> of fear, dismay, demoralization, and
> provides the most powerful means of
> reintegration of the group's shaken
> solidarity and of the re-establishment of
> its morale. (p. 53)

Among the still somewhat primitive Mayan and, to a
lesser extent, Navajo cultures of today, the
elderly accept old age as a realistic prelude to
death. Life is viewed as a drama with protagonists
of evil spirits and good powers that are brought
forth through manipulations specific to the
respective culture (Gutmann, 1973).

In the classical Maya culture, individual and
social responses to death and dying were dealt with
through a common acceptance of specific
supernatural myths and rituals. These myths and
rituals served as a form of social control. The
nature of death and fatal disease took on qualities
beyond the reach of common man, and myths gave to
death a sacred, untouchable aspect. If death could
not be prevented by the sorcerer, there were at
least specific steps a family could take in order
to speed their departed relative's spirit toward
paradise. This ritual, demanded by society, served
as a form of social control. It gave to 'survivor-
victims' an important task during the time of
mourning. The ritual, because it involved
continued worship of statues and crematory urns
representing the deceased, also served to inhibit
the family's achieving full psychological
separation from the deceased. Maya mythology, with

its <u>Milnal</u> and paradise, filled a void and gave
purpose and meaning to death.

As anthropological psychologists, we lack a
<u>reliable</u> means of assessing the success of these
myths and rituals of the Maya as a form of social
control for this potentially devastating problem.
But the fact that the aged in Maya society
possessed an equanimity that allowed them to
retreat to their hammocks to tranquilly await death
suggests some successful resolution of the problem.
For the family, intense periods of bereavement were
expected so that successful separation of the
deceased's spirit from this life could occur.   The
community's grief and sense of loss were expressed
openly, largely at night, in pitiful cries and
wails.   Today we know that open and spontaneous
expression of grief promotes psychological health.

Death, May (1973) writes, "exposes a man, his
culture, and the helping professions in the sense
that it reveals them in all their glaring
inadequacies."   Anthropological psychologists,
among others, are most aware of these deficiencies.
Their understanding of death, or any other human
phenomenon, through the study of past cultures is
often indirect and lacking in pertinent
information, particularly regarding the older
cultures. For data concerning ancient cultures we
may search through museums, visit out-of-the-way
archeological sites, or (as in the case of the
Maya) obtain copies of rare, faded, illegible
eyewitness reports by men autocratically Christian
and probably biased in their observations.
Authenticating evidence is at times unavailable.
But man's early history is filled with instances of
men and cultures facing problems that we face
today.   Death, dying, and bereavement are such
problems. A study of 'prehistoric' peoples, as are

the Maya in the New World, may offer some light concerning ontogenetic cultural development and may possibly provide effective ways of responding psychologically to specific problems within our own contemporary cultures.

Notes

1. Aguilar and Wood's (1976) approach is a notable example of utilizing cross-cultural knowledge to facilitate cathartic emotional responses in the face of death.

2. Salzberger (1975), studying the devastating effects of death upon survivors, examined the mortuary customs of a number of primitive tribes and made several productive observations.

3. The dynamics of psychogenic death, as these behaviors might represent, are well presented by Stumpfe (1975).

4. Exceptions to this point of view may be found in the Vedic literature, the sacred writings of hinduism, wherein death does follow life and one's life is not repeated. But this belief is not found in Hindu practice.

422 Dying, Death and Bereavement

References

Ammon, G., & Hamlister, H. 1975. "Ego-Psychological and Group-Dynamic Aspects of Death and Dying." <u>Dynamische Psychiatrie</u> 8, 129-142.

Anguilar, I., & Wood, V. 1976. "Therapy Through Death Ritual." <u>Social Work</u>, 21, 49-54.

Cohen, R.J. 1976. "Is Dying Being Worked to Death?" <u>American Journal of Psychiatry</u> 133, 575-577.

Feifel, H. 1959. <u>The Meaning of Death</u>. New York: McGraw-Hill.

Gann, T., & Thompson, J. 1931. <u>The History of the Maya</u>. New York: Scribner's.

Goetz, D. 1953. <u>Title of the Lords of Totonicapan</u>. Norman: University of Oklahoma Press.

Goetz, E., & Morley, S. (eds.). 1950. <u>Popol Vuh: The Sacred Book of the Ancient Quiche Maya</u>. Norman: University of Oklahoma Press.

Gutmann, D. 1973. "The Premature Gerontocracy: Themes of Aging and Death in the Youth Culture." In <u>Death in American Experience</u>, A. Mack, ed. New York: Schocken Books.

Kahn, H. 1960. <u>On Thermonuclear War</u>. Princeton, N.J.: Princeton University Press.

Makemson, M. 1951. <u>The Book of the Jaguar Priest: A Translation of the Book of Chilam Balam of Tisimin</u>. New York: Henry Schuman.

Malinowski, B. 1954. Magic, Science and Religion. New York: Garden City Books.

May, W. 1973. "The Social Power of Death in Contemporary Experience." In Death in American Experience, A. Mack, ed. New York: Schocken Books.

Morley, S. 1956. The Ancient Maya, 3rd ed., rev. by G. Brainerd. Stanford, California: Stanford University Press.

Nash, J. 1970. In the Eyes of the Ancestors. New Haven, Conn.: Yale University Press.

Nicholson, I. 1970. "Mexican and Central American Mythology." In Mythology of the Americas, ed., C. Burland, I. Nicholson, & H. Osborne. London, England: Hamlyn Publishing Group.

Parsons, T., Fox, R., & Lidz, V. 1973. "The Gift of Life' and Its Reciprocation." In Death in American Experience, ed., A. Mack. New York: Schocken Books.

Recinos, A., & Goetz, D. 1953. The Annals of the Cakchiquels. Norman: University of Oklahoma Press.

Redfield, R. 1941. The Folk Culture of Yucatan. Chicago: University of Chicago Press.

_____. 1950. A Village that Chose Progress: Chan Kom Revisited. Chicago: University of Chicago Press.

Salzberger, R. 1975. "Death: Beliefs, Activities and Reactions of the Bereaved: Some Psychological and Anthropological Observations." Human Context, 7, 103-116.

Shneidman, E. 1973. Deaths of Man. New York: Quadrangle/The New York Times Book Co.

Stumple, D. 1975. "The Dynamics of Psychogenic Death." Dynamische Psychiarie, 8, 100-105.

Thompson, J. 1930. Ethnology of the Mayas of Southern and Central British Honduras. Chicago: Field Museum of Natural History.

_____. 1966. The Rise and Fall of Maya Civilization. Norman: University of Oklahoma Press.

Tozzer, A. 1941. Landa's Relacion de las cosas de Yucatan, Vol. 18. Cambridge, Mass.: Peabody Museum of Archaeology and Ethnology, Harvard University.

von Hagen, V. 1960. World of the Maya. New York: New American Library.